Hand Knits by Machine

The Ultimate Guide for Hand and Machine Knitters

Susan Guagliumi

Hand Knits by Machine

Susan Guagliumi

Third Edition ISBN 978-1-7333121-4-1

(Previous ISBN Numbers)

ISBN-13: 978-1503065758

ISBN-10: 1503065758

Library of Congress Control Number: 2014919820s

© 2014 Susan Fletcher Guagliumi

All rights reserved

All photographs and illustrations by the author except as noted.

www.guagliumi.com

Other books by Susan Guagliumi:

Handmade for the Garden

More Hand-Manipulated Stitches for Machine Knitters

Hand-Manipulated Stitches for Machine Knitters

Twelve Sweaters One Way: Knitting Cuff-to-Cuff

Twelve Sweaters One Way: Knitting Saddle Style

GUAGLIUMIDOTCOM

This book is dedicated to...

Helen Deckelman who took a chance back in 1983 and gave me a job selling knitting machines – just days after I had learned to cast on. It was the start of a wonderful, rewarding career and a beautiful friendship.

Contents

Part One

1   Machines, Yarn and Basic Stitches

23   Casting On

33   Increasing and Decreasing

47   Binding Off

57   Picking Up Stitches

65   Loose Ends

Part Two

99 Lace

123 Mosaic Knitting

135 Entrelac

151 Modular Knitting

183 Acknowledgments

184 Supplies and Sources

185 Index

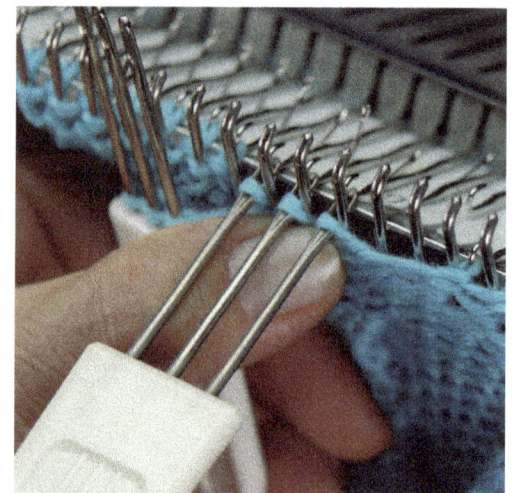

PART ONE

Machines, Yarn and Basic Stitches

Casting On

Increasing and Decreasing

Binding Off

Picking Up Stitches

Loose Ends

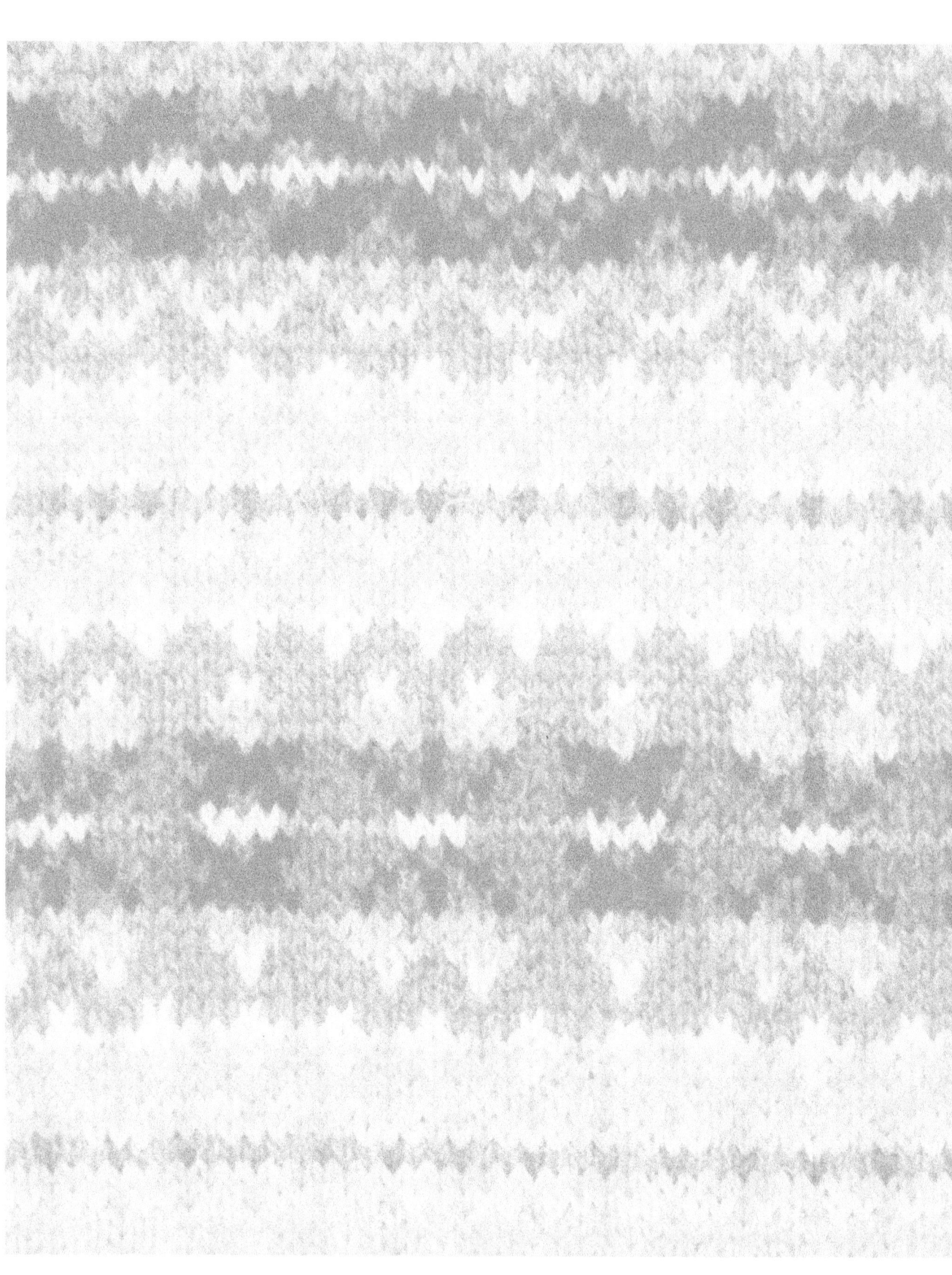

Machines, Stitches and Yarn

Hand knits by machine is a topic that appeals to two very different groups of knitters: Machine knitters who do not knit by hand or do so in a very limited way and hand knitters who want to produce specific hand knit designs or techniques on the machine. They are both looking for very different information and guidance and, although I am a little intimidated by the challenge, I hope to satisfy both groups in the pages that follow.

In order for this book to stand on its own (as every good book should) and to address both of these groups of knitters at the same time, I need to provide information that might seem very basic to one group or the other and I apologize for that in advance. I have included some information that was covered in my first book, *Hand-Manipulated Stitches for Machine Knitters* and bridging is a topic I covered in extensive detail in my second book, *More Hand-Manipulated Stitches for Machine Knitters*. However, If you are a machine knitter who owns either of those books and are familiar with those techniques, I hope I have included this information in a fresh way that will add to your knowledge; if you are a hand knitter making the jump to a machine, you may want to consult these books when you are ready to expand your machine knitting skills.

Manuals are notorious for telling you *what* to do, but they seldom explain *why*. Although I know that the information in the first part of this book will add to and clarify the information contained in your machine's manuals, this book is not a replacement for the manual or for your own experience.

Hand knitters sometimes turn to machines to speed up their production or to "knit the boring parts" of sweaters and are often surprised that they can't just sit down at a machine and knit a sweater right away. Like any skill worth having, competence and success come from practice and, in the case of a knitting machine, it requires a basic level of comfort with the equipment itself. There are techniques and tools that are unique to machines and, although being a hand knitter may make them easier to understand, understanding and executing are two very different things.

Simple machines (the plastic, hobby models) are the fastest to learn, but will always require input from the user. Patterning is hand selected and the yarn may or may not require hand tensioning. On the other hand, punch card and electronic machines are somewhat more involved and have a steeper learning curve, but once you master the mechanics, these machines automatically produce endless patterns, as the carriage glides across the bed.

First, Lets Talk About Machines

Knitting, by hand or by machine, is just a matter of repeating rows of stitches. Whether they are formed with a bed of latch hooks or a pair of size 8 needles, the stitches still look and function the same way. There are, however, some very real differences in how the stitches are worked and how easily they can be produced by each method.

Just as no single pair of hand knitting needles is suitable for every yarn, neither is one knitting machine. When choosing a machine, two of the most important things to consider are the range of yarns that each machine can knit and its patterning capabilities. Also, keep in mind that what may not seem important to you at the outset may be very important later on and may or *may not* be an add-on option.

Gauge

Most hand knitters own dozens of needles in various sizes, lengths and configurations to accommodate any and all of the yarns they want to work with and to 'tweak' their gauges as needed. Because a knitting machine is considerably more expensive than a pair of knitting needles and requires much more physical space, machines knitters are somewhat more limited in the choices they can make. And, although some machine knitters do own more than a few knitting machines, *most* of us only own one or two so it is important to choose a machine(s) that will fill most of your needs.

Every machine has an ideal range of stitch sizes/gauges that can be achieved using a specific range of yarns. Rather than changing needles, machine knitters tweak the stitch gauge by changing the stitch size dial and adjusting the tension on the yarn.

Keep in mind that each carriage is individually calibrated and stitch sizes can vary slightly from one machine to the next. So, even though a yarn knits at a certain stitch size on one machine, it does not mean that you will achieve the same gauge on a different machine. You still have to do a gauge swatch.

Differing stitch sizes are even more pronounced when lace or intarsia carriages are used in combination with the main carriage on your machine. You must gauge for each carriage or risk seeing a dividing row where you change from one to the other.

Lots of yarns and patterns can be knitted equally well by hand or machine, but when machine knitters specifically try to achieve a "hand knit look", they usually rely on mid-gauge and chunky-gauge machines, which can accommodate the majority of the yarns used by hand knitters. Granted, there are still plenty of super bulky or novelty yarns that are just too heavy for any knitting machine and those still need to be knitted by hand.

While mid-gauge and chunky machines are especially useful for duplicating many hand knits, lace and traditional Fair Isle or Scandinavian designs are generally worked with finer weight yarns and involve lots more patterning. These patterns can often be duplicated – or well approximated – on a standard gauge machine with automatic patterning capabilities.

	Fine	Standard	Mid–Gauge	Bulky/Chunky
# of ndls	250	180 European 200 Japanese	100–150 by brand	100–120 by brand
ndl spacing	3.6 mm	4.5 mm Japanese 5 mm European	6–7 mm by brand	8–9 by brand
Typical gauge sts/inch	8–12	6–10	4–6	3–5
Relative (U.S.) hand knitting ndl sizes	–3	1–5	4–10	7+
Range of suitable yarns	Industrials lace weight fingering	Industrials fingering sport	Sport DK worsted	Worsted Aran bulkies and novelties
Extended range working on EON	sport	worsted	Aran bulkies novelties	Heavier bulkies and novelties

The table on the previous page offers an overview of the yarns you can expect to readily knit on various machines. In the past, some machines were available in extended length beds (i.e. more needles) and some had bed extensions available, but I have not included those options here as their availability now or in the future is uncertain.

Combining Methods

If you want to combine hand and machine knitting in the same garment, chances are you will be able to match the stitch gauge spot-on, but you may have to make some adjustments for the row gauge because machine-knit row gauges tend to be a bit more compressed. That said, if you want to combine methods, plan on knitting gauge swatches by both hand and machine and buy an extra ball of yarn to do this. Some machine knitters enjoy knitting the bodies of (yoked) sweaters, for example, on the machine and then they pick up the live stitches to work the yokes by hand. Many use the machine to knit plain sleeves and concentrate their efforts on the patterned body of the garment. Either of these examples requires working two sets of gauge swatches. Me, I usually knit complete garments by machine, but every once in a while I opt for a combo.

Working EON

The chart on the previous page also lists a range of yarns that might knit on each machine when worked on every-other-needle (EON). Working EON extends the range by creating more space between stitches. When the finished fabric is tugged lengthwise to redistribute this extra length into the adjacent stitches, it usually narrows considerably.

Working EON isn't difficult, but there are a couple of caveats. First of all, it cuts in half the number of needles you have available for knitting your garment. In many instances it limits you to either very small sizes or working garments in pieces, incorporating extra seams.

Second, it limits the patterning capabilities of punch card and electronic machines because you must refigure designs for the missing needles.

Finally, the yarn still needs to fit comfortably into the hooks of the needles so that stitches are not split or needles jammed. You need to use more weight and knit more slowly. I always recommend casting on with waste yarn and hanging weights first. It goes without saying that working EON is not for rank beginners and I would never recommend buying a machine based on the EON possibilities. You should aim for a machine that easily knits the yarns you will use most of the time.

Yarn Tensioning

The auto-tension that most (but not all) machines employ to tension and feed the yarn can also affect stitch size and be used to tweak gauges. There are usually numbers on the dials that regulate the tension wires, but it is more important to recognize when the unit is working correctly.

The wires that hold the yarn should bob up and down as you work, pulling up any slack at the beginning of every row and dropping down as the carriage advances across the bed. If the tension is too tight, the wires will pull the yarn and cause jamming or dropped stitches at the edges. If the tension is too loose, there are bound to be loops at the edges, which can wrap around the carriage brushes or cause dropped stitches. Pay more attention to the bobbing motion than to the numbers on the dial and you will be fine.

There are some simple, inexpensive machines that do not have tension units and operate in intarsia mode (see page 10) all the time. A tension unit streamlines the work because you don't need to bother handling the yarn and laying it into the hooks of the needles before each row. More importantly, it assures that stitch after stitch, row after row, the tension is constant so that your gauge never changes.

Weights

Most knitting machines function best when claw weights are used to hold down the edge stitches at each end of the bed. The claws should be moved up every 10–15 rows and should be positioned so that one tooth hangs off the edge of the fabric to make sure the weight is pulling in the right direction.

Ribber beds are supplied with combs and weights for double bed knitting and extra weights are sometimes advisable when knitting highly textured fabrics on a single bed machine. Too little/much weight can cause problems so I usually recommend starting with just the requisite edge claws and then adding more weight if you find the knitting is lifting off the needles or stitches are splitting.

Yarn Choices

Because all machines are calibrated to work their very best with a certain size yarn, I usually find that the ideal yarn is one that knits right in the middle of the stitch dial for mid-gauge and chunky machines (4–6) and just a bit higher on most standard gauge machines (stitch sizes 6–8). That is the range where you don't have to make any special concessions to ensure smooth knitting. Also, whenever I try out a new idea or technique, it eliminates the possibility for yarn problems if I work within the ranges I listed on the chart on page 3.

Let me be clear about the yarns. I have listed the yarns that each machine was designed to handle - *easily and without various concessions from the user*. With experience, you can extend those ranges (and stitch gauges) considerably. Those "concessions" include, but are not limited to:

- using more or fewer weights
- knitting more slowly
- hand-feeding certain yarns, rather than passing them through the auto-tension unit
- bringing needles to HP before knitting each row so the carriage knits them back more easily
- utilizing "drop stitch" to increase stitch size
- starting with weighted waste knitting

Cotton and linen have little elasticity, which makes them peskier to knit by hand *and* by machine. Yarns that have some natural stretch, like wool and wool blends, are much easier to use - especially for hand-manipulated stitches like cables and twisted stitches. Chenille, mohair and many novelty yarns will knit better with extra weights and reduced speed.

Make sure textured yarns are stable by sliding your pinched fore-finger and thumb along a length of the yarn. If the texture slides along the core and ends up in a lump, it probably won't pass through the tension unit without doing the same. Save those yarns for hand knitting projects.

I don't recommend that rank beginners start with linen or a fuzzy mohair sweater though, with experience and practice, neither will be much of a challenge later on. I definitely recommend avoiding yarns like rayon because dropped stitches tend to run faster than you can catch them and, with most beginners, there are bound to be some dropped stitches. Why invite frustration?

Once you are adept at using your machine, these stitch size guidelines will be less important and you will find yourself working all over the dial and with all kinds of yarns. Initially, however, you can make things much easier on yourself if you work within the ranges I have suggested. To be more specific, I prefer DK weight on mid-gauge machines, worsted on bulkies and fingering on standard gauge and I think that wool or a good blend is the easiest, most forgiving fiber to work with.

Waste Yarn (Scrap Yarn)

Waste yarn is (ideally) the same size as the yarn you use for your project, but is usually a less expensive yarn or a left-over from a previous project. I often purchase cones or balls of deeply discounted yarns in really awful colors to use for waste because, like most machine knitters, I use a lot of waste yarn and the purchase of waste yarn is the one time that "cheaping out" on the yarn is acceptable!

Cones or Balls?

Many machine knitters prefer using yarn on cones because they do not need to concern themselves with balls ending mid-row. For standard gauge machines, I prefer working from cones because it can be difficult to prevent finer yarns from tangling when wound in balls.

For mid-gauge and bulky knitting, however, I usually work from skeins and balls because very few hand knitting yarns are available on cones. That said, just make sure that the yarn pulls smoothly from the center of the ball or skein as any interruption in the yarn can cause uneven tension or even jam the carriage.

Ball winders are fairly inexpensive and widely available. Even when skeins *seem* to be pulling smoothly from the center, I often re-wind them to be sure. If there is *any* interruption in the flow of the yarn, whether it is caused by incorrectly threading the tension unit or a badly wound ball, it *will* show in the fabric.

First and foremost, if you cast on with waste yarn, you have a heading where you can hang weights before you start working with the main yarn. This is especially helpful with textured or very fragile yarns that require special attention to make sure they knit cleanly or don't break.

Sometimes, after having cast on with waste yarn, I just start knitting with the main yarn, retaining live stitches on the lower edge so that I can deal with them later. Other times, I work a cast on across the *same* needles so that I have a closed edge when I eventually remove the waste.

There are lots of times when I just "scrap off", rather than binding off an edge. That is, I knit about 10 rows with waste yarn and then just drop the work from the machine. The stitches are not bound off, but this allows me to go back later to deal with the live stitches. Perhaps I will rehang them for ribbing or a special trim or to join two pieces together on the machine. Scrap also makes it easy to pick up the live stitches on hand knitting needles.

If I find myself unable to finish a project in a single sitting and don't expect to get back to the machine for some time, I might remove the piece on scrap knitting and re-hang it at a later date. This prevents the stitches from stretching while they hang on the needles waiting for me to return. Waste knitting can be a wonderful, flexible stitch holder, capable of holding all the stitches on your bed.

Ravel Cord

Most machines come with ravel cord, a tightly braided, brightly colored nylon cord that is intended as a dividing row between the main knitting and the waste knitting. It usually comes in 2-3 yard lengths and needs to be hand fed through the carriage to knit one row. I always hang a clothespin on the end of the ravel cord to help weight it down at the beginning and I keep mine wound on bobbins to prevent tangling.

Ravel cord serves a couple of purposes. First of all, it prevents any fuzz from that cheap orange acrylic waste yarn from contaminating your white wool. It makes it easier to pick up stitches later because it is fairly crisp and forces the stitches to stand up more clearly. Finally, it makes it easier to separate the main knitting from the waste because you can just pull the ravel cord right through the stitches – once you have secured them if they were live.

Stitch Patterning

Knitting machines are capable of making three kinds of stitches: stockinet, tuck and slip. The differences between machines are most clearly defined by how easily or automatically each machine executes these stitches or can combine them for patterning.

Also, machines are able to knit these patterned stitches by three means: manual needle selection, punch cards and electronics. All machines are operated by pushing a carriage back and forth across the bed unless you add the option of an electric motor drive.

All knitting machine manuals include directions for knitting stockinet, slip, tuck and Fair Isle stitches as well as a variety of basic techniques and other stitches. Before we go any further, let me say that you should rely on your manual for basic information and that you should also know how your machine operates - this book is not a guide to specific machine operation.

Also, please make sure that your machine is clean, well oiled and in good repair to maximize your chances for success. Bent or damaged needles should be replaced and disposed of; they are never worth trying to straighten or repair and will usually result in distorted or mis-knitted stitches throughout the fabric.

The sponge bar that provides tension on the needles (so that they do not slop around in their slots) needs to be changed when it has flattened out – as they all do after a while. A bad sponge bar can cause all kinds of problems when trying to place needles in holding position or just knitting plain stockinet fabric.

You can usually count on replacing the sponge bar right away when you purchase a used machine that has been in storage for a while.

Manual Machines
Manual selection is accomplished by the user manipulating carriage levers or knobs and pushing specific needles to HP, prior to knitting every row. You can easily follow hand knitting charts for many patterns and it is easy - if slow - to do. Manual machines are the least expensive and are usually fast and easy to learn because there are fewer knobs and dials to reckon with. However, even with increased experience and skill, needle selection will always be by hand.

Punch Card Machines
Punch card machines have more knobs and controls built into them because these machines can select needles to knit two different kinds of stitches or colors in the same row by reading a series of holes punched in cards. The cards rotate through the machine as you knit and can pattern endlessly, repeating each row on the card across the width of the bed. Every machine manual provides instruction on its patterning system, which can differ from brand to brand. Mechanical systems like this have been in use for years and are reliable and reasonably priced. Punch card machines have been produced in both standard and bulky gauges.

All machines come with a standard set of punch cards and you can buy blank cards and a punch to make your own. Be aware that all punch card machines have a definite limit on the size of the designs that can repeat across the bed and that all designs must be multiples of that number. Typically, punch cards patterns must be 12, 24 or 40 stitches wide (or smaller multiples that will repeat within that limit). Also, when punching your own cards, you must punch enough lengthwise repeats of

---

Hand knitters see the right side of the fabric and refer to right and wrong side rows
BUT
machine knitters always see the back/purl side of the fabric and are more apt to refer to odd and even numbered rows.

Hand Knitters can measure length (inches or centimeters) while they work
BUT
machine knitters must rely on an accurate row gauge and a row counter.

Hand knitters often place markers and recount stitches as they work
BUT
machine knitters can rely on the numbered strip on the front of the bed.

Hand knitters can use longer needles to accommodate more stitches
BUT
machines can only handle a finite number of stitches.

Hand Knitters can easily work garter stitch and knit/purl patterning
BUT
these are slow and/or involved on most machines. By contrast, machine knitters can more easily work fair isle, intarsia, short rows and ribs.

Hand knitters can use a wide variety of yarns by inexpensively changing needle sizes
BUT
machine knitters can only work a specific range of yarns on each machine.

Cables and twisted stitches and increasing and decreasing are hand manipulated by both hand and machine knitters.

---

a pattern for the two ends of the card to overlap and clip together so that it rotates continuously through the machine. (see page 124)

Electronic Machines
Some electronic machines have pattern selection built right into the machine, while others rely on an external controller or a computer connection. These systems allow you to decide how large your design repeats will be, unrestricted by any format, and can even accommodate a single motif that extends the full width of the machine. They have various controls built in that allow you to reverse a design's direction or colors with the press of a button. Electronic machines tend to be the most expensive and they have a slightly steeper learning curve; which is offset by greater pattern flexibility and capability.

Stitch Specifics

Hand knitting patterns that include charted stitch designs are the easiest to translate for the machine because the symbols are universal and make it easy to visualize what is happening to the stitches relative to each other. See page 22 for some of the most common symbols used by both hand and machine knitters.

With lengthy verbal directions, you need to remember that hand knitters work with the knit and purl sides alternately facing them. Machine knitters always face the purl side of the work so references to right and wrong side may not be as helpful as specifying odd and even rows. A good schematic and clear stitch symbols, however, are totally unambiguous .

When patterning directions are verbal, I convert them to a chart, using the standard symbols. This is helpful whether I am hand selecting needles or converting to a punch card or electronic design card.

All knitting machine manuals cover the basic operation of the machine and provide introductory information for knitting garments. For years, experienced machine knitters in the U.S. and abroad have published patterns and books chock full of slick tricks and short cut methods and although some of the garments may be out of fashion, the information is always useful.

Stockinet

Hand knitters work stockinet by alternating knit and purl rows because they need to turn the work over after every row to continue working right to left and when they turn the work, the face of the fabric alternates knit and

"Sanpoku" by Norah Gaughan is an easy stockinet sweater to knit by machine. The pattern is available as a free PDF from Berroco.com. Photo courtesy of Berroco.

This Drape Front Sweater by Roberta Rosenfeld is design #12 from the Winter 2011/12 issue of Vogue Knitting Magazine. Knitted in stockinet with a construction twist, this is a snap to kit on any machine. Photo courtesy of *Vogue Knitting Magazine*.

purl sides. A machine eliminates the need for turning the knitting over as the carriage works the same in both directions.

Garter Stitch and Knit/Purl Combinations

Garter stitch is probably the easiest stitch for hand knitters to work because every row is a knit row and they do not need to purl. Not so on a knitting machine, which forms the stitches the same way row after row. By machine, garter stitch is time consuming and cumbersome because the fabric has to be turned over and then rehung after each row by removing all of the stitches on a garter bar or scrap knitting.

Sometimes you can approximate the look of garter stitch by working narrow bands (2-4 rows) of reverse stockinet, which will cut the number of turns in half. Turning the work for blocks or bands of color is also a less time-consuming option, but still not very fast.

That said, I recommend purchasing a garter bar for every machine you own because it is a valuable and useful accessory. (see Page 66) Mastering a garter bar requires patience and practice, but it is not really difficult and the tool can be used for much more than just turning the work over. For example, it is essential for making evenly spaced decreases or increases across a row, for removing work in progress to check the knit side and as a tool for vertical weaving.

I also use the garter bar when I need to pre-knit multiple pieces that will be rehung later on – like the Rowan sweater at right. When I knitted this sweater, I knitted each strip and removed it on the garter bar, stacking subsequent strips on top of previous ones until I had knitted them all. Then I just knotted and re-hung the strips across the width of the machine, overlapping them by one needle to avoid any gaps. The purl stitch zig-zag border above the knotted edge needs to be worked by re-forming specific stitches with a latch tool after each row, which is easy to do because the pattern includes a stitch chart that shows their exact placement.

Because *all the needles on a machine face in one direction and form stitches that all face the same way,* knit/purl combination stitches are only possible by reforming stitches with a latch tool or transferring stitches back and forth between two beds. Even with a ribber, no machines are capable of doing this automatically.

Brother standard gauge machines had an accessory garter carriage that chugged along and reversed and knit the stitches at the same time, row after row, and produced beautiful knit/purl fabrics. Garter carriages are no longer being manufactured and while there may still be used carriages available, they were only manufactured for standard gauge Brother machines (no bulkies or mid-gauge). These are motorized carriages that operate independently, and quite slowly, but they do make easy work of knit/purl combination stitches. As with all used equipment, buyer beware. If you find a used garter carriage, try to see it in use before you part with any money and make sure it is suitable for your make and model.

Designed by Amanda Griffiths, this raglan pullover begins with pre-knitted strips, knotted at the lower edge and features cabled, purled and ribbed details. The pattern is #26 from Rowan Book Number Eight. Photo courtesy of Rowan Yarns.

Working stripes may require cutting the yarn if the stripes are very wide or you can opt to carry the yarn up the side for narrow stripes. When working an odd number of rows per color, it might also be necessary to free-pass the empty carriage to the opposite end of the bed to continue working (without registering a row on the row counter), which all manuals explain. When carrying the yarn up the side of the knitting, it is usually a good idea to bind it to the edge stitch every so many rows with a separate strand of yarn or by wrapping it around the edge needle. If you need to cut the yarn after each color change, weaving in the ends as you work avoids lots of tedious finishing later on.

Intarsia

Intarsia is much easier to manage by machine than it is by hand and even complex designs are easy to keep track of as you work. The bobbins are less likely to tangle and all of the colors can be placed in the needle hooks *before* knitting each row - which leaves you plenty of time to correct misplacements. While most knitting machines require the use of an accessory carriage to knit intarsia, some machines do have an intarsia setting on the main carriage and some very basic machines always operate in intarsia mode. In any case, the carriage, which carries no yarn, always returns the needles to Upper Working Position (UWP) with the previous row's stitches behind the latches and the latches open, ready for the next row. You lay the yarn across the open hooks according to the pattern chart and then move the carriage across the bed to knit each row.

Intarsia is a single bed technique and can be worked on a flat mounted machine or one that has been elevated on ribber clamps, with the ribber itself removed for ease of working.

Whether intarsia is built into your main carriage or your machine requires an accessory carriage, it is worked exactly the same way.

As I stated earlier, you must do separate gauge swatches for each carriage if you want to use the main carriage to knit large, plain areas in combination with an intarsia carriage. Apart from carriages being calibrated differently, when you knit intarsia the yarn is tensioned manually, rather than passing through the tension unit and that affects the gauge.

Most hand knit intarsia charts are drawn to show the knit side, but you will be looking at the purl side as you work intarsia on a machine. So, whether you work from a hand knitting chart or design your own from scratch, *you need to draw intarsia designs in reverse* in order for them to read correctly from

Every time you change color, the yarns must twist around each, just as they would in hand knitting.

the right (knit) side. This is especially important if you use any letters, numbers or words in your design. A children's alphabet sweater, for example could read like backwards nonsense if you don't!

A B C D E F G vs. ꓨꓞꓱꓓꓛꓐꓯ

The simplest way to reverse any design is to scan it into a computer program that allows you to rotate or flip images. Graphics programs like Illustrator do this with a single key stroke and textile–specific programs like DesignaAKnit and Stitch Painter offer even more features. If you don't have a computer program with these capabilities, your local copy or office supply store can do it for you.

Sometimes, with very small blocks of color, I carry two yarns as though stranding Fair Isle. In that case, to prevent a hole at the edges, you need to catch one of the yarns around an adjacent needle (behind the open latch) and then alternate the two yarns as necessary. As one yarn lies in the needle hook(s), the other floats below. This will cause tension problems for large areas of color that should each have their own bobbin, but when there are just a couple of stitches of each color it creates less bulk than starting and ending new bobbins.

Whenever I start a new yarn, I always manually knit the first stitch of that color back to working position and leave it there. Then I lay the yarn across the open hooks of the appropriate needles and complete the row. With the next pass of the carriage, the needle I knitted manually returns to UWP with all of the others. Knitting that stitch manually ensures that the beginning end doesn't slip out of the needle and gives the remaining stitches something to tension against. I also hang a clothespin on the beginning end of every yarn to provide tension and prevent it slipping away from the needles for the first few rows.

Finishing off the ends on the back of an intarsia garment can sometimes take as much time and effort as knitting the sweater and bad finishing often shows on the knit side of the fabric. Instead, I weave in my ends while I work (see page 63), taking care to weave them

The Map of the World, designed by Kay Niederlitz, originally appeared in *Vogue Knitting Magazine* in 1991. The updated version is from the Fall, 2007 issue (garment #24). This is an excellent example of an intarsia design that simply *must* be reversed for knitting by machine! Photo courtesy of *Vogue Knitting Magazine*.

behind the open latches so that they do not get caught up in the stitches.

After a row or two, I use a latch tool to pull the beginning tails through the fabric to the knit side. It really doesn't matter where I pull them through because I just want to get rid of all the dangling ends that can tangle or confuse me while I work and it makes it much easier to see what I am doing. When the piece is off the machine, I just pull the ends back through to the purl side, check that they have been woven in securely and clip them close.

To carry the same yarn across (stranded like Fair Isle) you need to manually wrap an edge needle to prevent a hole. Notice that the light blue yarn (at right) has looped around the shaft of the last ndl holding a dark blue stitch. The latch remains open so that the dark blue yarn can be laid in for the next row. The two yarns alternate across the section.

Back view of stranded intarsia.

Front view of stranded intarsia. Wrapping alternately at each edge of the stranded area, prevented any gaps from opening between sections.

This Brandon Mably sweater, garment #1 in the Winter 2009/10 issue of *Vogue Knitting Magazine*, is a simple, sideways knitted intarsia. Photo courtesy of *Vogue Knitting Magazine*.

Ends that have not been woven in are easiest to conceal along the edges of blocks of color where the two colors cross, just as they would be in hand knit intarsia.

The yarns you use for intarsia should be wound on bobbins so that they have enough weight to hang down from the machine and tension the yarn. If you have lots and lots of colors working at the same time, you might prefer to wind finger "butterflies" for small bits of color. You should weight each one with a clothespin to provide some tension, which will prevent the yarn from lifting out of the needles and dropping stitches.

You can add cables, latched up purls and other texture stitches to intarsia if you remember to always return the needles to UWP with the stitches *behind* the open latches, ready for the next row.

To wind a butterfly, wrap the yarn in figure-8's around your thumb and fore-finger. Then use the end of the yarn to tie the bundle together. The other end will pull out length as needed.

Geometrics like this Missoni sweater from *Vogue Knitting Magazine*, Fall 2007, are easy designs to follow. This one also includes a few rows of vertically striped Fair Isle between the bands of intarsia patterning. Photo courtesy of *Vogue Knitting Magazine*.

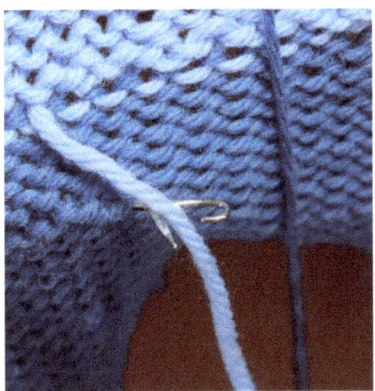

Pull ends through to the knit side with a latch tool to prevent them from tangling while you work

Ribbing

In order to automatically knit ribbed fabrics on a machine, there must be a second bed of needles mounted opposite the main bed. The reason is this: All of the needles on the main bed of the machine face the same direction and form stitches that all face in one direction. Having a second, opposing bed of needles means that those stitches will be formed in the opposite direction. Alternating needles from one bed to the other knits ribs and depending on how you space the needles (1 x 1 or 2 x 2, for example) you can vary the ribbing at will.

Some European machines were supplied as double bed machines, where the front bed was permanently attached but could be lowered out of the way for single bed knitting and most metal Japanese machines had ribber beds available as an add–on option.

None of the plastic knitting machines have ever had ribbers available so you need to reform stitches with a latch tool, knit the ribs by hand and transfer them to the machine or begin garment pieces on waste knitting so you can go back later and pick up the stitches to knit the ribs down. Most machine knitters who own these simple machines also become quite adept at finding interesting, functional alternatives to ribbing.

Ribbing can be knitted on single bed machines by latching up every-other stitch for 1 x 1 rib or every two stitches for 2 x 2 rib. You can also latch up in tuck for Fisherman ribs. Latching up is very doable for bands or along side cables, but it is unlikely you would want to reform too many rib stitches for the length of an entire sweater unless they are very widely spaced, like the example on the next page.

You can begin a garment piece by hanging hand knit ribbing on the needles, skipping an empty needle every so often to increase if called for in the pattern. Once the ribbing has been hung and before you start knitting, make sure you fill the empty needles with the purl bar from an adjacent stitch so that there are no holes.

Its all a matter of personal preference, but I like to start my garment pieces on waste knitting and then back later to pick up the live stitches on hand knitting needles, decreasing as necessary before beginning the rib band. Because I always use the hand–sewn bind off described on page 51, this ensures that all of my ribbed edges (hem, cuffs and neckline) match.

Even if you have a ribber for your machine, you can begin garment pieces with rib or start on waste knitting and knit the ribs later. For me, working the ribs last means that I can evaluate what the sweater really needs and sometimes it just isn't a ribbed band.

By hand, two-color ribs (vertically striped) are knitted with slip stitch, but when knitted on a machine with a ribber, some of the slipped floats show between the knitted stitches. So I prefer knitting striped Fair Isle and then reforming all the stitches in one of the colors. It can be a little awkward because you need to work behind the floats of the first color, but it isn't difficult. You can also work single bed tuck or slip as Mosaic to emulate striped ribbing (page 129). None of these options are very elastic, but neither is the hand knit version and striped ribs are generally used for their looks, rather than ribbed structure, when knitting traditional Fair Isle designs.

Transfer the last latched–up stitch to the machine by hooking the tool onto the needle, with the stitch behind the latch. Then just tip the tool upwards until the last stitch slides over the latch and onto the needle. Because the tool faces the opposite direction to the needles on the machine, the stitch will be formed in reverse, i.e. as a knit stitch, rather than a purl.

Machines, Stitches and Yarn 15

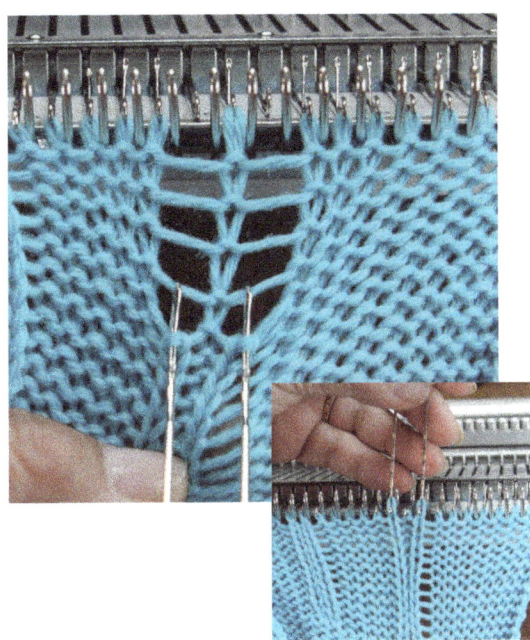

You can latch up one stitch at a time or use specialized latch tools that do two stitches at once. When latching up stitches with either a double latch tool (like the one below) or one spaced for EON (as above), you need to tug a little harder on the tool than you would when re-forming a single stitch. At the top of the column, transfer the stitches from the tool to the needles by holding the tool above the needles and poking the needles through the stitches. Then remove the tool.

Yvette Silverman's Venezia Worsted Flared Bottom V–Neck Cardigan is a pattern that would be very practical to knit by reforming every 6th stitch. This pattern is available as a free PDF on the Cascade web site. Photograph courtesy of Cascade Yarns.

You *can* latch up a column of stitches as garter stitch but it is slow and tedious. You need to work alternately from both sides of the fabric, using either two latch tools (one on each side of the fabric) or a double ended latch tool. These are available in standard gauge as replacement needles for the Brother garter carriage.

Re-form stitches as tuck by passing the latch tool under two bars of the dropped stitch-ladder. Then catch just the top bar in the hook of the tool and pull it through the old stitch. The lower bar will form the tuck.

Tuck Stitch

Hand knitters refer to tuck stitch in terms of knitting into the stitch below. Directions usually say something like "insert the right hand needle into the stitch below the first stitch on the left hand needle", which knits that stitch and deposits the stitch above it as a tuck or loop lying across it.

All knitting machines, both single and double bed, can produce tuck stitch. On manual machines, tuck stitches are formed by placing needles in HP for a specific number of rows and then returning the needles to work so that the accumulated loops are knitted with the stitch that was originally on the needle.

Machines with automatic patterning are able to form both knit and tuck stitches at the same time, according to either a punch card or an electronic impulse. When the cam lever on the carriage is set to "tuck", the carriage will tuck every needle on the bed *unless instructed not to* by a design card. So, the punched holes in the card represent knit stitches, not tucks.

This is important to understand so that you can evaluate the suitability of individual designs for knitting as tuck. Although you can sometimes tuck two adjacent needles, tuck is usually knitted on individual needles, separated by knit stitches to make sure that each stitch knits correctly. Tucking adjacent needles will usually jam the carriage.

The purl side is most often considered the right side of a single bed tuck fabric because the texture is much more visible. There are some small tuck stitch pattern repeats that also often stand in for knit/purl combination stitches. Double bed tuck stitches, on the other hand, can be quite 3-dimensional and interesting on both sides.

If you plan to combine tuck stitch and stockinet in a single garment, it is important to know that tuck gauges tend to be shorter and wider than the same yarn knitted at the same stitch size in stockinet. For a column of tuck stitches along side a cable, for example, this usually doesn't present any problems that can't be blocked out.

However, alternating bands of stockinet and tuck throughout a garment, would necessitate separate gauge swatches. While you may not mind the tuck bands being wider than the stockinet bands (and can probably hide them in the seams), if you knit an entire sweater based on the stockinet gauge, it will end up being too short; If you use the tuck gauge for the whole sweater, it would be too long.

When working cables on a single bed machine, I often latch up a stitch at each side of the cables as tuck stitch. It creates a more open, lacy effect along side the cables and, more importantly, does not pull in the way that a plain ribbed stitch would. So, in addition to helping the cables stand out against a stockinet ground, the tuck stitches prevent the fabric from pulling in and narrowing. Because cables tend to pull the work in to begin with, many cables across the width of a garment can cost you width. Using tuck stitches along side those cables actually helps prevent this.

The most common double bed tuck stitches are Full and Half English rib, sometimes called Fisherman's Rib. All ribber manuals give directions for knitting these stitches, which are identical to the hand knit versions.

Slip Stitch

Hand knitters work slip stitch patterns by passing a stitch, un-knitted, from the left to the right needle, knit–wise or purl–wise. When the directions specify wyf or wyb this is an indication that the yarn should be held in front or back of the work while making the slips.

Knitting machines produce slip stitches by preventing specific needles from moving in their slots when the carriage moves across the bed. The yarn always passes behind the slipped stitches (purl side) and the stitches always look as if slipped purl–wise. On all machines, passing the yarn on the front (knit side) of slipped stitches requires manual intervention. That is, removing a stitch from its needle with a transfer tool and replacing it behind the slip/float. To a very limited extent, this can be useful for patterning and is never done automatically on any machine.

Slip stitch fabrics tend to be longer and narrower than the same yarn knitted on the same stitch size in stockinet. So, combining stitch patterns may require several gauge swatches to ensure a garment that knits to size.

Slip can be worked on both single and double bed machines. On machines with automatic needle selection, the cam lever is set to "slip" and (like tuck), the design card indicates which needles override that command and knit instead. Unlike tuck, you can easily slip many adjacent stitches. Slip stitch fabrics vary greatly, with either side considered the right side.

Fair Isle

Hand knitters work Fair Isle patterns by carrying two yarns in their hands, knitting one color while the other slips behind - which is pretty much what a machine does. Punch card and electronic machines carry two yarns in the carriage at the same time and knit or slip each needle in the row according to the pattern on the design card.

As I said earlier, all machines have varying requirements for you to meet when designing your own patterns. Most punch cards, for example, typically require you to satisfy a 12, 24 or 40 stitch repeat in order for patterns to connect perfectly across the width of the fabric. You may need to adapt a hand knit motif by adding stitches or removing them from the repeats to conform to these requirements. Most electronic machines, however, will accommodate patterns up to at least 60 stitches wide, with no requirements about the size of various repeats. Instead, you are able to dictate the width of individual patterns. This is true with all electronic patterning, not just Fair Isle, and is one of the many things about electronic knitting that is so liberating.

Kathy Merrick's Banded Turtleneck from the Fall, 2010 issue of *Vogue Knitting Magazine* is a large scale Fair Isle that would be easy to knit on mid–gauge or chunky machines. Photo courtesy of *Vogue Knitting Magazine*.

Manual machines *without* selection devices generally only carry one color per row so Fair Isle needs to be knitted with two passes of the carriage per row of pattern. The colors need to be knitted (and the pattern manually selected) as color A, B and then B, A so you can knit two rows per color before having to re-thread the carriage. It takes steady concentration to maintain the pattern's needle selections and this color order.

If your manual machine has two yarn feeders and a cam lever with a Fair Isle setting, you may be able to knit one pass of the carriage per row of pattern by hand selecting the patterning (or contrast color) needles to UWP prior to knitting each row.

The Silver Reed LK-150 had a Fair Isle carriage available at one time, and although it is no longer manufactured you can occasionally find them used on the internet. It was the only inexpensive, plastic machine that had this option and the carriage will only fit the Silver Reed bed. The last time I checked, used FC-6 carriages were selling for almost as much as a machine.

Hand knitters can easily add a third color to a row of pattern by carrying the color along or picking it up from a bobbin as needed. For machine knitters, a third color means either hand-manipulation (un-knitting a stitch and re-knitting with the third color) after passing the carriage, placing a needle(s) in holding position to manually knit it after the carriage knits the row or knitting the entire fabric as 3-color slip stitch with one color knitting per row. It takes 3 passes of the carriage to knit one row of pattern when done this way, which creates a much thicker fabric and is not a method I recommend for beginners. In double bed work, multi-color jacquard designs are based on slip and pretty much require either a punch card or an electronic machine.

Whether knitted by hand or machine, the length of the floats between areas of color should not be long enough to catch fingers and should be bound to the back of the fabric. Hand knitters usually do this by twisting the two colors around each other where they intersect, but this is not possible on a machine.

By machine, the floats can be bound by individually lifting them onto a needle above so that they knit into the back of another stitch; by latching up a column of floats and then lifting the last stitch onto a needle above; or by using a separate, thinner strand of yarn (or, better yet, thread) to bind them to the back of the fabric. This separate strand method is similar to vertical weaving, a decorative

This fabric features several small, repeating Fair Isle motifs that all have short, controlled floats (see page 1 for right side view).

These floats have been bound to the back of the fabric by catching them with a separate strand every two rows. Normally I would use a matching strand of yarn or thread to do this. Eight rows down, you can see where individual floats were lifted onto needles to secure them.

Machines, Stitches and Yarn   19

With COR, the contrast yarn has been caught on the right edge by looping the yellow yarn over the first adjacent blue needle. It will knit behind the blue stitch, like the one at the left edge has done and will bind the edge of the isolated motif so that there are no gaps. At the center of the rectangle, the floats were latched up for 6 or 7 rows and then the last float was lifted onto a needle above. With the next pass of the carriage, that lifted float will be bound to the back of the fabric.

method worked on the purl side of fabrics. In this case, however, it is done for structural, rather than decorative, purposes and should be as invisible as possible.

Many traditional hand knit designs include "lice" or dots of the contrast color to ensure that the yarn is always on the correct side when working odd numbers of rows. By machine, it means not having to free-pass the carriage to the opposite end of the bed to continue working without breaking the yarn. Otherwise, you might need to frequently cut the yarn and restart it from the opposite end of the bed. Needless to say, that would increase the number of ends to weave in as you work or to deal with later.

Some traditional Fair Isle patterns that are knitted in the round call for the creation of a steek. Steeks are sections knitted in plain stockinet that is later stitched and cut to create armholes or the front opening of a cardigan. Because domestic machines cannot knit Fair Isle in the round, these patterns need to be re-interpreted with separately knitted fronts and backs.

Machines can easily knit two identical fronts and match patterns at the side seams so working a patterned garment in the round isn't of any advantage. Directional patterns need to be knitted in reverse for each front of a cardigan so that two reindeer, for example, both face away from each other if that is how the original pattern was drawn.

In spite of the fact that I used bright yellow to wrap the edges of this rectangle and to bind some of the floats, nothing shows on the right side. In practice, I would use a matching thread or yarn.

All of the floats are short and manageable in this sweater. The odd numbers of rows in the top stripes include "lice" that take care of keeping the carriage on the correct side at all times.

Plaiting

Be aware that some carriages look like they have two yarn feeders, but are actually just capable of carrying two yarns that plait as they knit. That is, both yarns knit every stitch, but one of the yarns is always held in front of the other. Plaiting is useful for doubling thinner yarns and for creating consistent salt and pepper effects. Some knitters use it to run absorbent cotton behind the wool when knitting ski-hat bands and to make metallic yarns more wearable. The plaiting feeder has its own uses, but it has nothing to do with Fair Isle.

Computer Aided Knitting

In addition to the paper and pencil method of converting stitch charts from hand to machine, you can also use computer programs like Stitch Painter and Design-A-Knit (DAK).

Being able to compose Fair Isle, tuck or slip designs on a computer screen is a lot of fun and it makes it so easy to move things around, flip them upside down, alter the size of repeats and experiment with color. DAK offers an optional lace module that can expand the basic, hand knit chart to account for all of the transfer rows on the machine.

Stitch Painter has a huge symbol library and allows you to create your own symbols as well. You can create "brushes" and stamps to repeat motifs and save them in the library for future use.

These programs are huge time savers and, if you knit on an electronic machine, connected to your computer, DAK also controls the needle selection. On Brother machines, the pattern is actually downloaded to the machine's electronics; on Silver Reed machines, the computer communicates interactively with the carriage as you knit.

While you cannot use a computer driven program to control the needle selection on a punch card (or manual) machine, you can use DAK for interactive knitting with a special cable and magnet fitting that will advance the design through the computer as you knit. It will allow you to see the pattern rows on the computer screen and replace the need for keeping notes next to you while you work.

Symbols and Abbreviations

Both hand and machine knitting patterns and instructions can get very lengthy so abbreviations and charted symbols are often used to make them more concise and manageable. The following charts show some of the most common symbols and abbreviations.

Abbreviations

[....	brackets identify a group of stitches or directions to be treated as a single unit.		inc	increase(ing)
			K/M	knitting machine
*....**	repeat stitches or directions between asterisks		KWK	knit, wrap, knit back
			MC	main color
A/R	alternate row(s)		ndl(s)	needle(s)
Adj	adjacent		NWP	non-working position
B/O	bind off		P/U	pick up
C/O	cast on		RC	row count(er)
CC	contrast color		S/O	scrap off
dec	decrease(ing)		S/R	short row
E/R	every row		st(s)	stitch(es)
EON	every other needle		Tog	together
EOR	every other row		UWP	upper working position
GB	garter bar		WP	working position
HK	hand knit			
HP	holding position			

Symbols

	Knit stitch
∣	Knit stitch
—	Purl stitch
∩	Tuck stitch
ʏ	Lifted increase at right
ʏ	Lifted increase at left
○	Yarn Over
ȣ	Twisted stitch
ʎ	Right decrease
ʎ	Left decrease
╱	Stitch slanting to the right
╲	Stitch slanting to the left
⅄	Two stitches decreased towards a center stitch
⅄	Two stitches decreased to the right
⅄	Two stitches decreased to the left
⋈	Right cross cable
⋈	Left cross cable

~~~~~~~~~~
e-wrapped edge

vvvvvvvvvvvvvvvvvv
Picked up edge

Casting On

The information in this chapter should augment the casting on instructions in your knitting machine manual and clarify their relevance to hand knitting. There are machine knit equivalents (or at least satisfactory stand-ins) for most hand knit techniques, though not *everything* you can knit by hand is possible on a machine.

Casting On

When a pattern calls for a very specific cast on, it might be to satisfy a structural requirement or it could simply be the designer's favorite method. Read through the pattern to see if there is a specific reason to use the suggested cast on. Otherwise, use whatever method you are comfortable with, with an eye towards the function and appearance of the edge it will create.

However, if you plan to knit part of a garment by hand and part by machine, you'll want the cast on edges to match as closely as possible and the methods that follow should fill most of your needs. For very unusual cast on methods, you can always cast on by hand, knit 1 row and then transfer the piece to the machine or you can start all pieces on waste yarn and bind off or finish all the edges later.

If you are determined to figure out the *exact* machine knit equivalent of any cast on or special stitch, try doing what I do: I work the cast on (for example) by hand and then immediately transfer it to the needles of the machine, where I slowly and methodically rip it out stitch by stitch, making notes as I go. This is much easier than trying to visualize what crosses or loops through where and it usually reveals the method for the most mysterious looking stitches.

The automatic, every-other-needle cast on is the one that many machine manuals teach first. It is a closed edge, but not a very attractive one and it has no hand knit equivalent. The EON cast on can be worked in two steps by bringing every other needle to WP, knitting one row and then bringing the remaining needles to WP. Some machines can do this in a single pass of the carriage by placing the alternate needles in WP and HP and laying the yarn across the HP needles.

Regardless, most machine knitters use this method just for swatching or casting on with waste yarn. After knitting some rows with the waste, they cast on again with the main yarn using one of the more attractive and functional methods.

In addition to the EON cast on, machine manuals usually explain e-wrap and latch tool (chain) cast on methods. Neither of those methods (by hand or machine) produces a particularly great edge, but the variations are endless so the following directions focus only on the variations that are useful in duplicating their hand knit counterparts.

Beginning machine knitters always question why they can't cast on to all the needles in WP with a single pass of the carriage. The answer is that there would be no loops formed to provide a base for the next row. In hand knitting terms, it would be like wrapping the yarn around one knitting needle and then trying to knit. By hand or machine, the individual cast on loops need to be defined somehow so that each one can be individually worked in the next row. This usually means twisting and crossing the yarn or pulling loops through

Some common hand knit cast on methods and their machine knit equivalents.

Hand Knit Cast On	Machine Knit Equivalent
simple looped cast on	e-wrap
knitted-on cast on	latch tool variation
picot cast on	latch tool variation
cable cast on	latch tool variation
open cast on	start with waste yarn
chain cast on	latch tool cast on
long tail cast on	e-wrap or knitted-back e-wrap variations
tubular cast on for ribs	most easily worked on double bed machine and described in all ribber manuals

each other after an initial loop is formed. The possibilities are endless and form the basis for the most common cast on methods.

The Open Cast On

Hand knit patterns sometimes call for an open cast on to preserve live stitches so they can be dealt with later. They might be picked up for a special trim or crocheted edge, joined to another piece or even knitted in the opposite direction.

When machine knitters need an open cast on, they begin with waste yarn, knit some rows and then just start knitting with the main yarn. This is so much easier to do than the hand knit method that I often begin hand knit projects on the machine, casting on with waste yarn and then transferring all the stitches to hand knitting needles after a few rows. Depending on the yarn and how I plan to remove the waste knitting later on, I may or may not use a row of ravel cord between the waste and the main knitting. (see page 6)

Crocheted (Chain) Cast On

The latch tool cast on is identical to the hand knitter's crocheted (chain) cast on and, like the hand knit version, doesn't have much elasticity. However, I have worked out a couple of variations on the latch tool method that are nearly identical to a knitted-on cast on and its first cousin, the cable cast on. With any of these hand-manipulated cast on methods, you should pay close attention to your tension so that you don't tighten the stitches and form a rigid, unforgiving edge.

Knitted-On Cast On

The knitted-on cast on is a common method for hand knitters, but generally not for machine knitters.

This knitted-on cast on edge was done on the machine, as described on the next page.

Because there can sometimes be several names assigned to the same technique, the three photographs below illustrate the common hand knit version of a knitted-on cast on that is comparable to the machine knit version described on the following page.

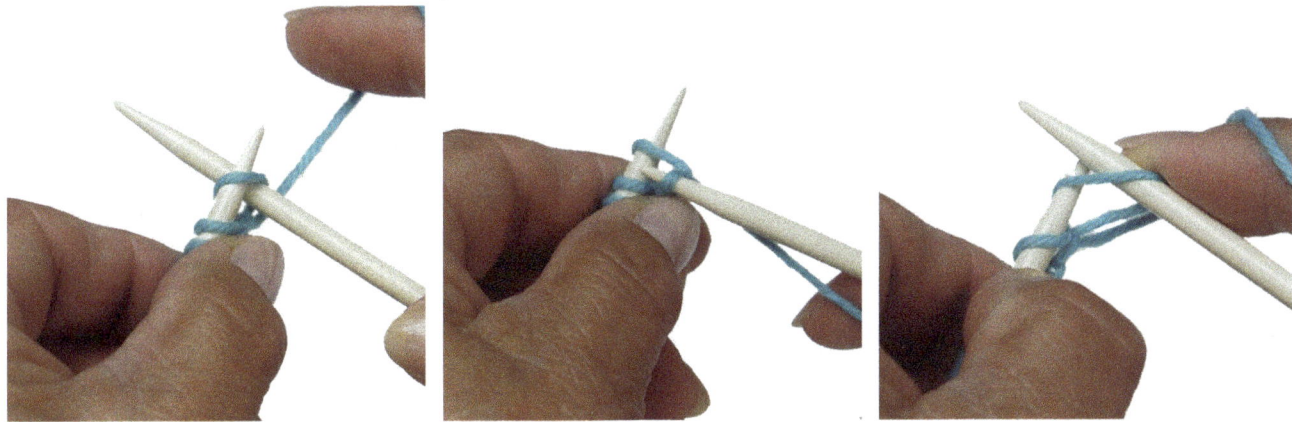

(1) Begin on the left end of the bed with COR. Make a loop and place it on the first needle. Then, (2) insert the latch tool from the back of this loop and pull a new loop of yarn through to form another stitch. Place this new stitch on the 2nd needle. *Poke the tool through from the back of the 2nd stitch, grab a loop of yarn with the tool and pull a new stitch through (3). (4) Deposit the new stitch on the 3rd needle.** Repeat * to ** across the bed (5) and then thread the carriage and begin knitting.

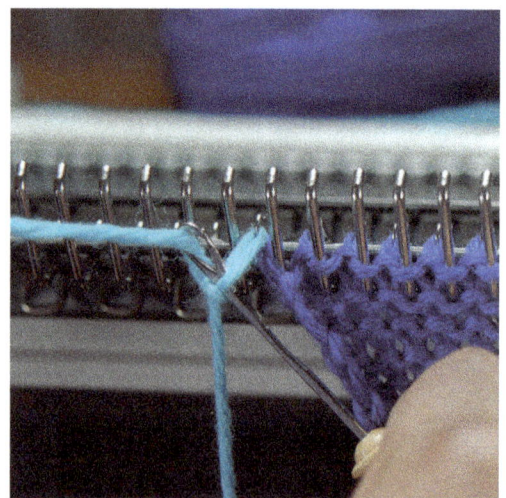

Casting On 27

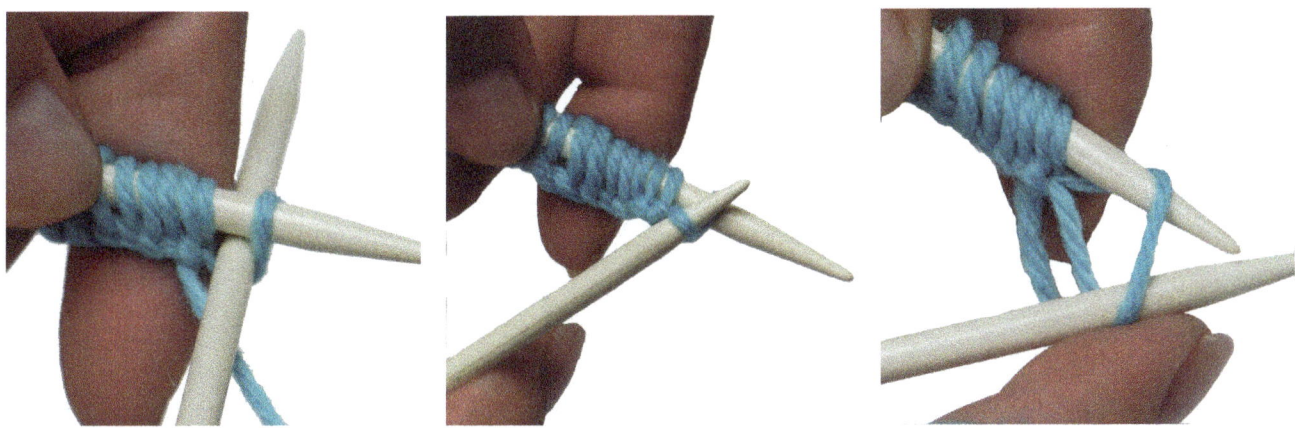

The hand knitted cable cast on is worked very much like the knitted-on cast on except that the right hand needle is inserted *between* stitches, rather than through them.

Cable Cast On Method

Begin on the left end of the bed with COR. Make a loop on the first needle, pull a loop through the first stitch and place it on the 2nd needle. Now, *(6) insert the latch tool between the 1st and 2nd stitches to hook a loop of yarn for the next stitch. (7) Place the new stitch on the 3rd needle. ** Continue (8) inserting the latch tool, from top to bottom, between the last 2 stitches formed to (9) take up a loop of yarn for a stitch and then place it on the next empty needle. Repeat * to ** across the bed and then thread the carriage and begin knitting.

The cable cast on above is a first cousin of the knitted-on cast on. The cable cast on, however, forms each new stitch *between* the previous two stitches, instead of through the last stitch. This is also the difference between the hand knit versions.

6

7

Picot Cast On Method

Begin on the left end of the bed with COR. You can work picots with either the knitted on or cable cast on method. *After working 4 stitches (for example), (10) chain 4 stitches with the latch tool. Then (11) insert the tool through the stitch at the top of the column and pull through a loop of yarn. (12) Place this loop on the next empty needle.** Repeat * to **.

Picot cast on edge

This picot edge was worked above a heading of (dark blue) waste yarn so that I could hang my weights before knitting the first row. With a cast on like this, I always bring all the needles to HP and allow the first pass of the carriage to kit them back into WP. This assures that none of the picots get tangled up in the stitches as they form.

Long Tail Cast On Method

There are several hand knit variations on this cast on and it is sometimes referred to as a double or left handed cast on. All of them involve looping the yarn around your thumb and forefinger as pictured at right.

Long tail cast on edge

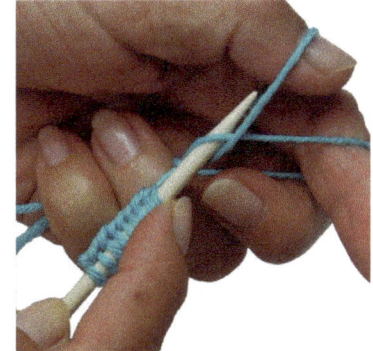 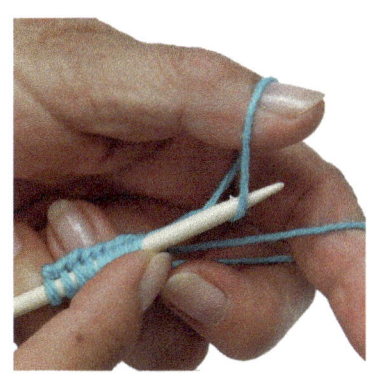

The hand knitted long tail cast on is quick to do once you master the mechanics of it.

Begin this cast on at the right end of the bed with COL. Pull out a double length of yarn about twice the width of the needles in WP. I'll refer to the end that is a continuation of the yarn coming from the ball or cone as the main yarn and the other end as the cut end.

Make a loop where the yarn folds in half and place this loop on the first needle at right. Then, *(13) using the cut end of the yarn, form a backwards e-wrap around your finger and (14) place it on the next empty needle to the left where it will (15) form a double twist. (16) Use the main yarn to knit this needle back to WP.** Repeat * to ** across the bed and then thread the carriage and begin knitting.

After each stitch is formed, make sure the cut end of the yarn is in front of the main yarn because this placement is critical to achieving the proper twist in the edge. Continue forming loops with the cut end and knitting them back with the main yarn.

13

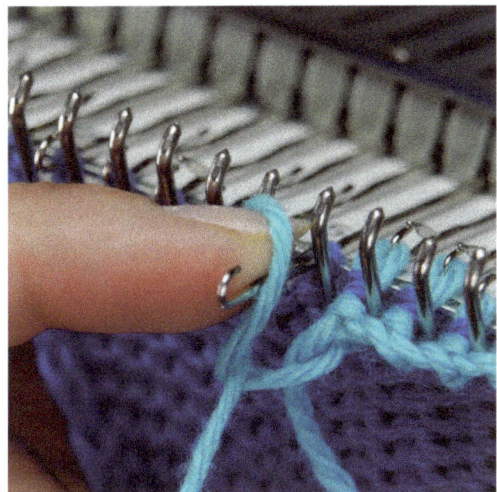

14

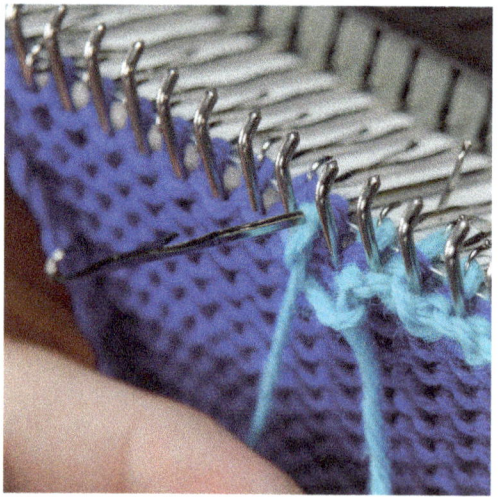
15

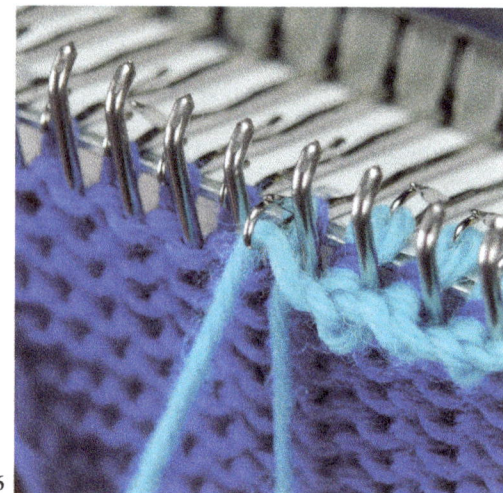
16

Figure-8 Cast On Method

Begin on the left end of the bed with COR. This is an interesting variation of an e-wrap that doesn't really have an *exact* equivalent in hand knitting, but I think it creates an edge that is decorative and well weighted.

Start with all needles in HP. (17) Make an e-wrap on the first needle at left. *(18) Then weave the yarn over the 2nd needle and under the 3rd. (19) Reverse direction and weave over the 3rd, under the 2nd needle and then knit the 1st needle back to WP.** (20 & 21) Repeat from * to ** across the bed (22) and then thread the carriage to begin knitting.

Figure–8 Cast On edge

You would normally begin working this cast on with all of the needles in HP, but in order to make the photographs easier to understand, I have only brought the needles to HP in the groups of 3 described in the text.

17

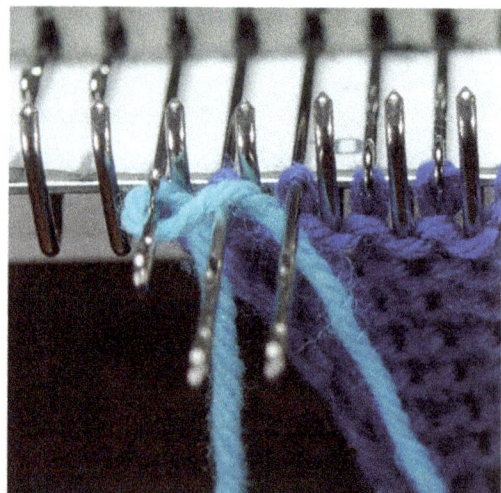
18

Casting On 31

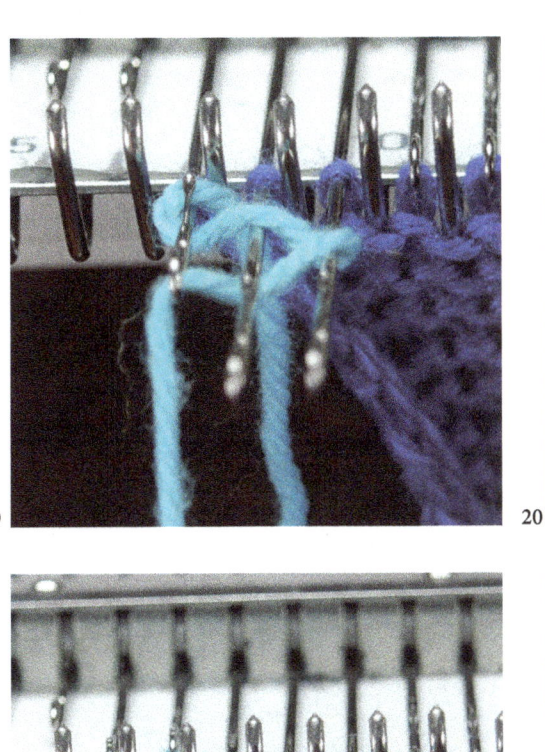
19

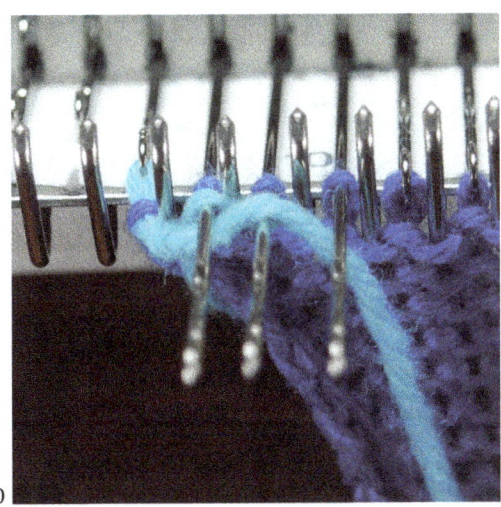
20

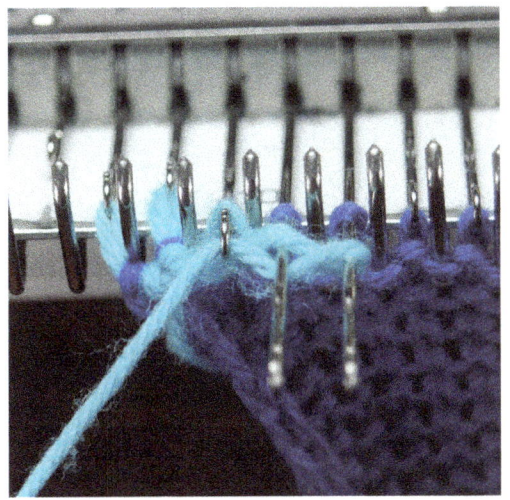
21

22

Rolled stockinet edging

It bears mentioning that machine knit stockinet tends to roll back on itself a little more enthusiastically than hand knit stockinet. However, for a plain stockinet shawl or scarf, where the lower edges will show, weightier cast on methods help to minimize this as does a narrow trim or ribbed edge.

Rolled stockinet can form interesting, soft edges on a garment and can be worked as part of a cast on (or bind off). I cast on (usually with a simple e-wrap), knit 8-10 rows and then work a garter stitch ridge (page 67) as

Rolled stockinet can prevent the lower edge of a garment from rolling, without pulling it in as ribbing would do.

a dividing row to discourage the edge from rolling any higher than I want it to and to add a small, decorative touch to the edge.

Double Bed Casting On

All ribber manuals provide detailed instructions for casting on for a variety of rib methods, including a tubular cast on so I won't address any of them here. I will, however, offer the following tip for better ribber cast ons, regardless of which method you use.

I always cast on with waste yarn so that I protect the edge of my garment from broken or stretched stitches.

With waste yarn, knit the initial "zig-zag" row with the same size stitch you plan to use for the body of your ribbing. Hang the comb and weights and knit 6-8 rows. With ravel cord, knit two circular rows, one on each bed.

Then change to the main yarn and re-set the carriage for the smallest size stitch you would normally use for the zig-zag row. Knit that row and then, adjusting stitch size as usual, follow it with two circular rows. From there, increase the stitch size by one dot on both carriages, every row until you reach the size you want to use for the body of the ribbing. Then knit the required number of rows.

Knitting those first few rows with waste only takes an extra minute or two, but it can save all kinds of aggravation and produce much more attractive ribs. First of all, because the comb and weights are already in place, the initial zig-zag row with the main yarn is protected from stretching or breaking. The weight, already in place, allows you to work with smaller stitch sizes without fear of snapping the yarn or jamming the carriage.

When you remove the work from the machine simply pull the ravel cord to separate the waste from the main knitting and you will have as perfect a rib edge as possible.

Increasing and Decreasing

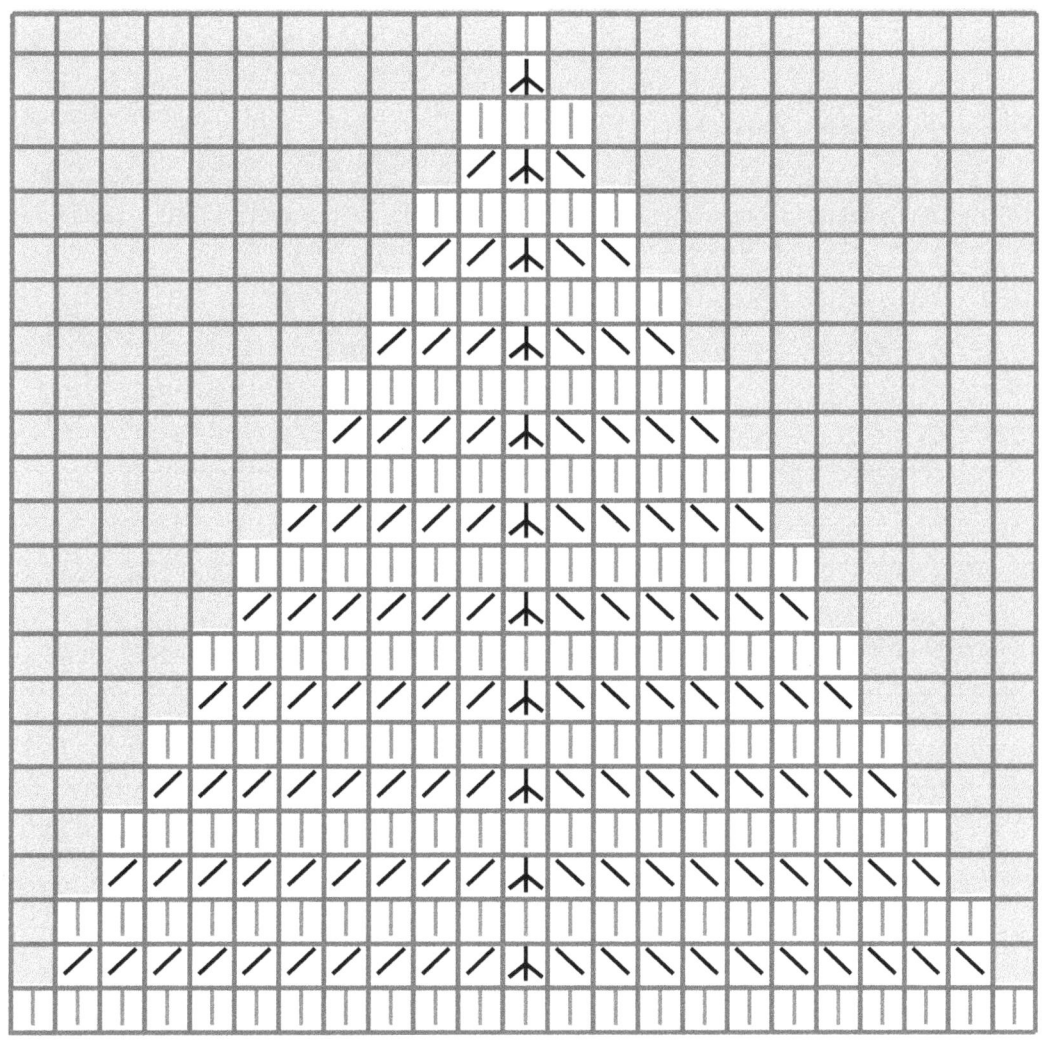

The majority of the time, though not always, hand knit increases and decreases are made on knit side rows. However, they are always worked with the purl side facing you on a machine. In order to replicate a hand knit increase or decrease on the machine, it is essential to know which way the stitches are supposed to slant and which stitch should show on the knit face of the fabric.

All knitting machine manuals give a basic, one-step method for decreasing and a couple of ways to increase, but the decreases in particular may not satisfy the requirements of some hand knit stitches or techniques.

The single most important thing to know about machine knit increases and decreases is this:

The first stitch that is placed on a needle will show on the knit side of the fabric.

Also, remember that the symbols that are used to designate hand knit increases and decreases always indicate the direction as seen from the knit side of the fabric. Therefore, they need to be worked in reverse for machine knitting and sometimes may require more than one step.

Increasing

Edge Increases

The chart at the bottom of this page lists the machine knit equivalents for some common hand knit increase methods. Just as you can only make an increase at the working end of a hand knitting needle, so too, there are some restrictions on a machine.

Simple Edge Increase
The problem with edge increases is that they disrupt the selvage of the fabric by constantly changing the edge stitch.

Hand Knit Increasing	Machine Knit Increasing
edge increase	Bring an empty ndl to WP on the carriage side.
lifted increase	Use a transfer tool to lift the purl bar of an adjacent stitch onto an empty ndl at left or right.
make 1	Leave an empty ndl in WP. Knit the next row and then, with a transfer tool, twist the yarn that caught in the empty ndl like an e-wrap.
yarn over, eyelet	Leave an empty ndl in WP and allow it to cast on without twisting the loop.
knit front and back of the same stitch	Twist a loop from the side of an adjacent stitch to fill the empty needle.
full fashion increase	Use a multi-prong transfer tool to move a group of stitches one ndl to the left or right and then pick up the purl bar of an adjacent stitch to fill empty ndl.
increase evenly across a row	Use scrap knitting or a garter bar to remove and rehang the knitting skipping empty ndl as required. Then fill the empty ndls by picking up the purl bars from stitches adjacent to the empty ndls.
increasing multiple stitches	On the carriage side e-wrap or chain cast on. Hang a "rag" to preserve open stitches.
short rows	Short rows increasing as described on page 45

The edge increase method that I call the "quick and sloppy" increase is done by bringing a single needle to WP on the carriage side prior to knitting a row. It creates a small loop at the edge of the fabric and isn't a pretty increase that adds anything to the look of a fabric. That said, it is quick and works quite well for pieces that will be trimmed in some way. Because the edge stitch of a sleeve, for example, would keep changing if increased this way, the edges would be difficult to seam evenly.

The "quick and sloppy" edge increase

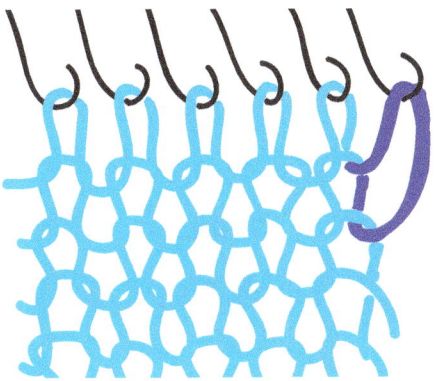

Full Fashioned Increasing

Instead of using a single prong transfer tool to move the edge stitch over by one needle, you can use a 2 or 3–pronged tool to move 2 or 3 stitches at the same time. The increase itself is several stitches from the edge so this method simplifies finishing because the edge stitch remains constant and provides a straight, unchanging column of stitches to seam.

2–stitch full fashioned increase

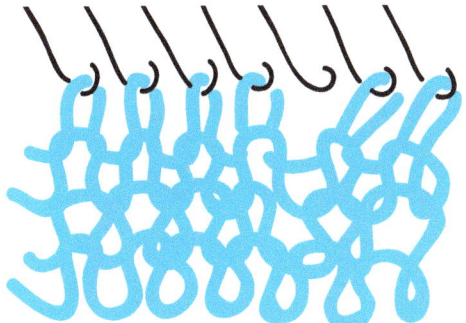

Eyelets vs. Closed Increases

With any full fashioned increasing, however, you are left with an empty needle that needs to be dealt with in some way. You can allow it to cast on and form an eyelet or prevent the eyelet from forming by making or lifting a stitch to fill the empty needle.

Yarn Overs/Eyelets

When you make a full fashioned increase, the needle that the (last) stitch was removed from remains in WP. It picks up the yarn with the next pass of the carriage and, after a second row, will form an eyelet. In lace knitting, this is intentional and creates the design itself. When shaping sleeves, however, the eyelets don't usually add anything to the appearance of the garment so there are ways to prevent them from forming.

Make 1

Rather than allowing the eyelets to form, you can work a "make 1" increase by removing the yarn from the needle after the first pass of the carriage and, using a transfer tool, twist the strand (like an e-wrap) and return it to the needle.

Hand Knit

The left side of this sample was increased with simple eyelets, two stitches from the edge. On the right edge, I chose to use Make 1 increases to close the eyelets. The Make 1 increases look about the same, but the eyelets are definitely larger on the machine knit swatch on the next page.

Machine knit eyelet and Make 1 increases.

Both of the swatches below were increased with lifted increases. The hand knit swatch is on the top and the machine knit swatch is below. It is nearly impossible to tell them apart.

Hand knit lifted increases

Lifted Increases

In addition to these two increases, you can work a (left or right) lifted increase by using the transfer tool to lift the purl bar from an adjacent stitch onto the empty needle. This method creates a much more invisible increase, especially if you consistently lift the stitch from the left or right. There is also an interesting twisted, lifted increase described on page 123 that I stumbled upon to create a sharper division between a leaf motif and the background stitches.

Machine knit lifted increases

After the edge stitch is moved out by, in this case, 1 needle, insert a transfer tool through the purl bar at the base of the adjacent stitch and lift it onto the empty needle.

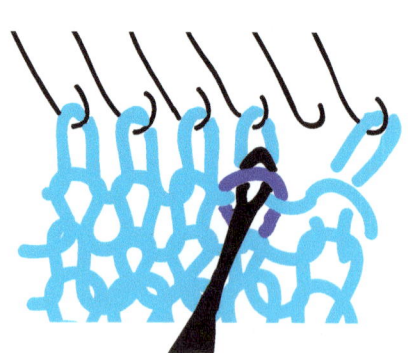

Knitting the Front and Back of the Same Stitch

After moving a stitch(es) out towards the edge of the fabric, leave the empty needle in WP. Insert a transfer tool from right to left, under the right half of the adjacent stitch at left, twist the tool to the right and deposit the twisted loop on the empty needle. To work a Make 1 at the right of the empty needle, just insert the tool under the left side of the right-most stitch.

Machine knitters do not usually deal with the front and back of a stitch, but twisting the right edge of the adjacent stitch and hanging it on the empty needle will satisfy that particular increase.

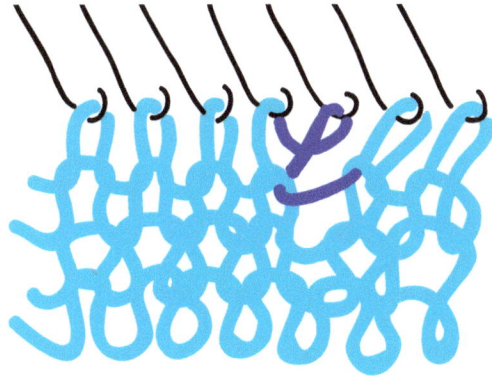

Ladders

If, on the other hand, an empty needle is returned to NWP, purposely or by mistake, a ladder forms as the knitting continues. Ladders do have decorative uses if that is your intention. Otherwise, make sure the needle remains in WP after you transfer its stitch to the next needle. Remember, not all mistakes are bad. If you know what you did and can do it again, you have the beginnings of a pattern and you could easily use a repeating pattern of ladders as part of the increase scheme. When you want a ladder to end, simply do a lifted increase and continue knitting.

Increasing multiple stitches

e–Wraps

You can increase multiple stitches at the edge of your knitting by using a latch tool to work a chain over the extended needle shafts or by e–wrapping additional needles on the carriage side. At the end of the next row, you can repeat the increase at the other edge of the knitting if needed.

e–wrapping is always done on the carriage side

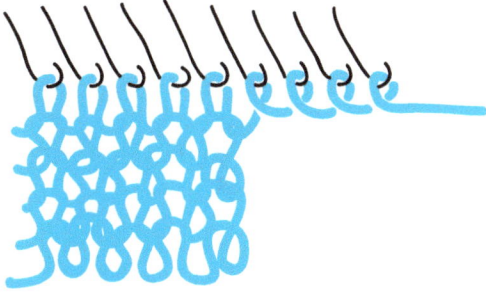

Hanging a "Rag"

It doesn't sound very glamorous, but "hanging a rag" is a great way to increase a large number of stitches all at once so that there are live stitches you can access later on.

Specifically, when I knit sideways sweaters and want to increase stitches from the sleeve to the body of the sweater, I hang a pre-knitted piece of fabric over the needles I need to increase and knit 1 row across them all so that the open edge is even. If the sleeve widens as it joins the garment, I place all but a few of the needles into holding position to shape that area by short row increases, gradually bringing needles back into work.

These "rags" are nothing special and sometimes I do not even bother to actually hang them stitch by stitch on the needles. Rather, I just poke some fabric onto each needle so that there is a "stitch" there to engage the yarn as the carriage moves across the bed. Sometimes I manually knit each stitch back first with ravel cord by manually moving each needle in its slot to form a stitch.

You can also hang the edge of a crocheted chain, previously worked with a piece of contrasting yarn, over the needles to be increased. You can hang a rag or a crocheted chain at both edges of the knitting, regardless of where the carriage is, although you may have to cut and restart the yarn if you do. This method allows you to retain live stitches that can be bound off as a group later on or incorporated into seaming or trimming.

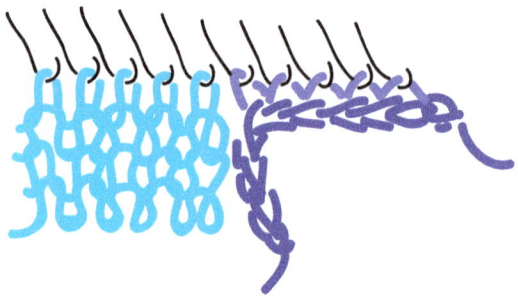

A yarn chain, hung on the needles, is enough to start forming stitches with the next pass of the carriage. Bring all those needles to HP (if you can) to assure that all of the stitches knits cleanly.

Increasing Evenly Across a Row

Increasing stitches across a row isn't a problem for hand knitters, but on a machine you need to make a needle available for each and every stitch. If you have multi-prong transfer tools, you can sometimes move the stitches in a couple of groups to make room for an extra stitch or two.

Most of the time, however, it is just easier and faster to remove all of the stitches from the machine on a GB (page 71) or by scrapping off.

When you return the stitches to the needles, just skip a needle wherever you need to make an increase and after all the stitches have been returned to the machine, go back and make lifted or Make 1 increases.

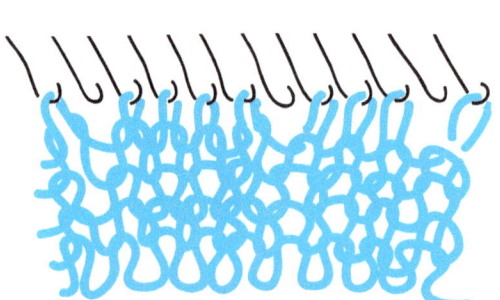

Increasing stitches across an entire row requires first scrapping off or using a garter bar to remove all the stitches from their needles. Then, when you return the stitches to the machine, simply skip a needle wherever you need an increase. After all the stitches have been re-hung, go back and make lifted increases to fill the empty needles.

Decreasing

The very process of knitting two stitches together introduces direction to the stitches. In hand knitting, this directionality is controlled by the kind of decrease used and determines which stitch slants towards the other. On a machine, the direction is determined when you transfer a stitch to the needle at left or right of the stitch to be decreased.

Many times, hand knit decreases are described as left or right slanting. As I said earlier, it is important to know which stitch is on a needle first when deciding which decrease methods to use on the machine. The following illustrations and text explain the difference between one and two-step decreases.

Left Slanting Decreases

k2 tog tbl, SKP, S1K1PSSO, SSK, etc.

The same chart symbols are used to describe all of these variations. You usually have to depend on the text of a pattern to know if a specific left slanting decrease is required.

The fabric depicted in the illustrations that follow will look the same, whether hand or machine knit, but the symbols used in pattern charts are reversed. When a hand knit pattern calls for "SKP" or "SKK" you need to make a left slanting decrease.

Hand knit symbol for left slanting decrease

Machine knit symbol for left slanting decrease

When the machine knit fabric is viewed from the knit side, it echoes the hand knit chart and slants towards the left *only* if worked with a two-step decrease. The slant on the one-step decrease is hidden on the purl side of the fabric.

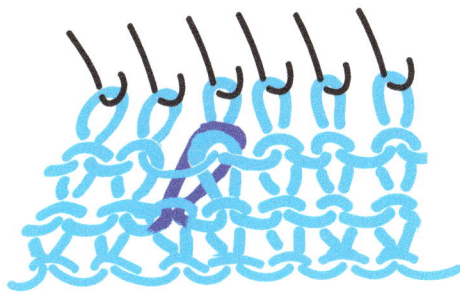

When viewed from the knit side, this 2-step decrease (top) will slant to the left. The 1-step decrease (below), however, is hidden on the back of the fabric.

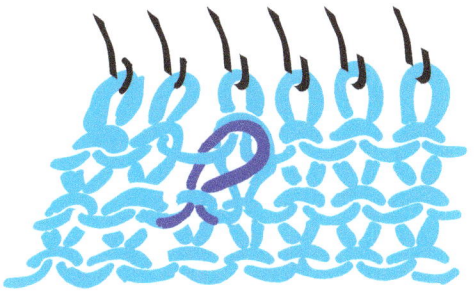

To make a two-step decrease, use a single-prong transfer tool to move the right stitch to the left needle and then move both stitches back to the right needle. When repeated every so many rows, the face stitch remains constant and creates a strong line on the knit face of the fabric.

The one-step decrease is done by transferring the left stitch to the right needle and looks like the second illustration above.

The one-step decrease, which is usually the one shown in machine knitting manuals, actually hides the transferred stitch behind the front stitch so that the slant does not show or contribute to the design. And, as the decrease is repeated over the length of the garment, the face stitch changes regularly. This is a subtle difference but an important one when working lace designs or decorative raglans.

The two-step decrease definitely requires more time and there are times when it is essential. On the other hand, for a textured knit, where the decreases won't show, the one-step method is perfectly fine.

Right Slanting Decreases

K2tog

The following two illustrations show one and two-step right slanting decreases. When a hand knit pattern calls for "K2tog", you need to make a right slanting decrease.

The two-step right slanting decrease is done the same way as the left slanting decrease, except that you need to transfer the left stitch to the right needle, then return both stitches to the left needle.

For the one-step right slanting decrease, simply transfer the right stitch to the left needle.

S1, K1, PSSO

The two swatches on the next page are nearly identical; distinguishable from each other by the bound off edge and the obvious difference in my hand knit gauge. All of the decreases were worked full fashioned, several stitches from the edges, following the chart.

2-step right slanting decrease

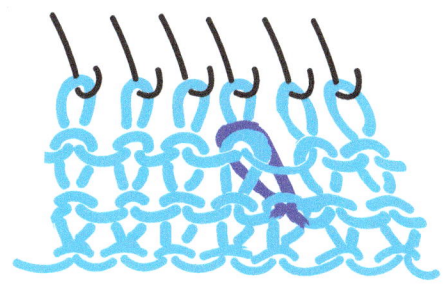

1-step right slanting decrease

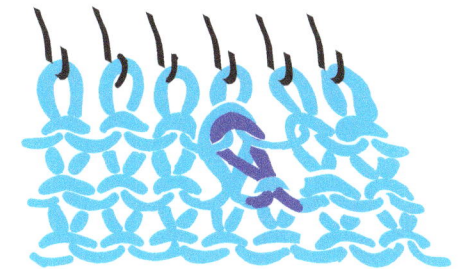

Hand knit symbol for right slanting decrease:

Machine knit symbol for right slanting decrease:

Hand Knit S1K1PSSO

Machine Knit S1K1PSSO

Only the right edge of the hand knit swatch below was worked as S1K1PSSO (slip 1, knit 1, pass the slipped stitch over), which is a left slanting decrease. The left edge was worked with K2tog (knit 2 together), which is a right slanting decrease, so that the decreased edges both slant towards the center.

This decrease can be duplicated by machine and worked at either edge, respecting the relative position of the 4th and 5th needles to each other at opposite sides. The procedure is a little different than other machine knit decreases and requires both a latch tool and a transfer tool. For a full fashioned decrease, you will need a 2- or 3-pronged transfer tool.

Slip the 4th needle from the edge(s) by placing it in HP with the carriage set to hold. Knit the row and then drop *only* the slip (float) from the 4th needle.

Use the latch tool to remove the stitch from the 4th needle and let it slide behind the latch of the tool. Bring the 5th needle to HP and hook the latch tool onto the hook of the needle. Manually push the 5th needle back to WP so that its stitch slides into the hook of the tool.

Pull this (the 5th stitch) through the stitch that was behind the latch (the 4th stitch) and place it on the 5th needle. Use a 3–prong transfer tool to move the three edge stitches in by one needle. Make sure you put the empty needle in NWP.

The next three swatches use paired, complimentary decreases at their centers and edges so that the end result is one of balanced symmetry. The first swatch is hand knit; the other two are machine knit.

The two machine knit fabrics are quite different. However, unless the decreases are supposed to contribute to a pattern of some sort, both examples are correct.

Increasing and Decreasing 41

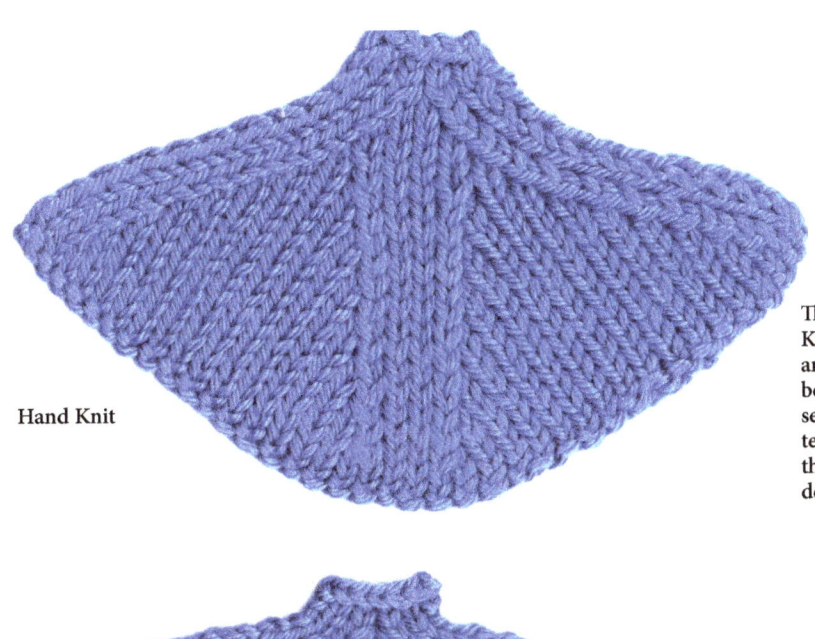

Hand Knit

The right edge used an SSK decrease; the left edge is K2tog. However, the right-center decrease is K2tog and the left-center decrease is SSK. This seems to be reversed until you view each side of the swatch separately. Then it becomes clear that the right-center decrease, for example, is actually on the *left* of that side of the swatch and required a right leaning decrease.

Machine Knit

The corresponding machine knit swatch, at left, worked both edge decreases as two-step decreases and both center decreases as one-step decreases. All of these are full fashioned decreases that require either a multi-prong transfer tool or moving the stitches over to fill the gaps in several steps. Because the four center stitches never moved, they remain on the knit face of the fabric.

Machine Knit

The swatch at left is also machine knit but reverses the use of one and two-step decreases. In this example, the edges were worked with 1-step decreases and the centers with two-step.

Any decrease can be worked as a full fashioned decrease using multi-prong tools, holding two tools together in one hand or making additional transfers right or left.

When knitting lace, the empty needles are left in working position so that they cast on with the next pass of the carriage, forming a yarn over. When shaping garment sections, you normally decrease towards the garment body to narrow the knitting.

There are also some traveling stitch designs that utilize decreases and then increases to fill the empty needles. So, one way or the other, whenever you make any kind of a decrease you need to deal with the empty needles by moving stitches over to fill them, putting them in NWP, making increases or allowing yarn overs to form.

Double Decreases

Vertical Double Decrease
Move one stitch from the left and one from the right onto the same, center needle. The center stitch will show on the face of the fabric.

Whenever this symbol is shown, it indicates a stitch being transferred from both left and right onto a central stitch.

One of the ways that hand knitters do this is by slipping two stitches together, as if to knit, from the left needle. Then, they knit the next stitch and pass *both* slipped stitches over it.

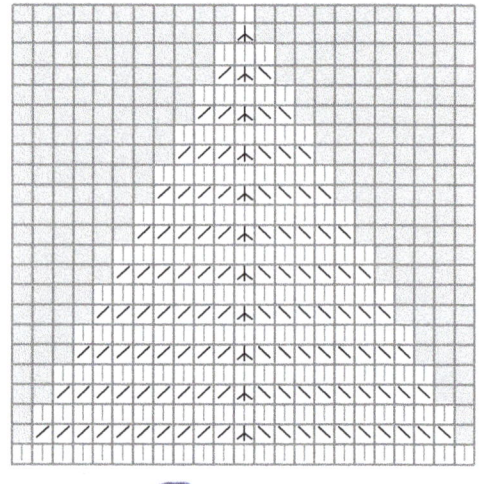

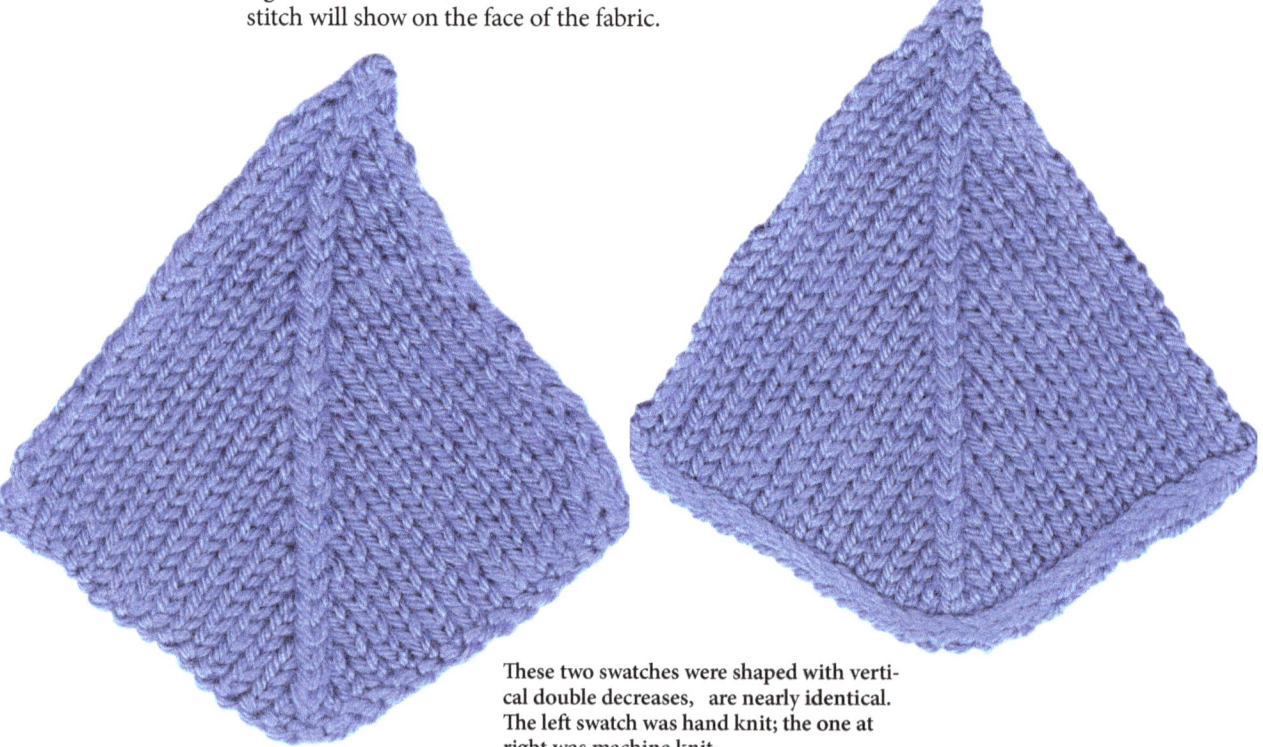

These two swatches were shaped with vertical double decreases, are nearly identical. The left swatch was hand knit; the one at right was machine knit.

By machine, all of the stitches at left are moved over by one needle. Then all of the stitches from the right are moved over by one needle. The center stitch holds three stitches and remains on the knit face of the fabric, where it creates a sharp vertical line.

Left and Right Slanting Double Decreases

Rather than letting the center stitch in the decrease dominate visually, a double decrease can slant left or right.

Hand knitters work a right slanting decrease by slipping 1 stitch knit–wise, knitting the next stitch and then passing it over the slipped stitch. Then this stitch is returned to the left needle where the second stitch on that needle is passed over it and then returned to the right needle. It requires a couple of steps, as does the machine knit version.

Working left to right, move the 1st stitch to the second needle and then move both of those stitches to the right-most needle. Now move all three stitches back to the 1st needle (left). This will leave two empty needles next to each other, which must be filled either by moving additional stitches over to fill the gap or making lifted increases in combination with eyelets.

A machine knit left slanting decrease is worked the same way, reversing left for right in the instructions. Unless a pattern calls for both left and right slanting decreases, paired or on opposite sides, etc. it may not really matter which one you use. If, however, the direction of the slant contributes to the overall stitch design, it is essential to match what the instructions call for.

This chart shows a hand knit right slanting double decrease. If a machine knitter used this chart, the decreases would slant to the left–not to the right–on the knit side.

Both of these fabrics feature right slanting double decreases. The swatch at the bottom was hand knitted, the one at the top was machine knitted.

Hand Knit Slanting Double Decreases

⅄ Left Slanting

⼂ Right Slanting

Machine Knit Slanting Double Decreases

⼂ Left Slanting

⅄ Right Slanting

Decreasing Evenly Across a Row

A garter bar (see page 66) is usually essential for knitting sweater yokes, bands that reduce lots of stitches in a single row or garments where all the decreasing is done far from the edges. All of the stitches are removed on the garter bar (or waste knitting), the number of needles to be reduced is pushed back to NWP at each side and then the knitting is replaced on the working needles. Some of the needles will hold doubled stitches.

The same increases and decreases (and their charted symbols), when paired with yarn overs, are also used for lace knitting. Lace patterns sometimes have very elaborate ways of adding or eliminating stitches; be aware that you may not be able to exactly duplicate *every* transfer and decrease on the machine. Double decreases, for example, are always vertical. If you are especially fond of lace knitting, you should know that many standard gauge machines are capable of automatically transferring stitches with an accessory lace carriage. (See pages 108).

Short Rows

When a hand knit pattern reads "Knit 26 stitches, turn, wrap and work back to the beginning of the row" you can be pretty sure that the work is being shaped by short rows. Short rows are easily worked on all machines by placing needles in HP and setting the carriage to leave them there so that they do not knit.

While not technically increasing or decreasing the number of stitches on the machine, short rows do increase and decrease the number of *actively working needles* so I have chosen to include the technique in this chapter.

All knitting machines are capable of holding stitches in one way or another and the information is always included in the machine's manual. All of the needles can be returned to working position by the flip of a lever or you can return just a few at a time by nudging individual needles back to UWP, thus allowing some needles to remain in hold. You can also return needles directly to WP with a transfer tool.

Some machine manuals use the term "short row" while others talk about "partial knitting". They are the same thing and can be used to increase or decrease the length of the rows being knitted, which, in turn shapes garment sections.

Short rows are typically used to shape shoulder slants, necklines, sock heels and shaped

This jacket is garment #19 from the Winter 2007/08 issue of *Vogue Knitting Magazine*. It's an excellent candidate for knitting on the machine. Worked sideways, the gores, knitted in four colors for added impact, create an easy, swinging fit. Photo courtesy of *Vogue Knitting Magazine*.

hemlines, but the technique can also be used to knit intarsia color blocks, darts, gores, ruffles and a variety of textured effects. It is also the basis for the method I call "Bridging" and opens up all kinds of creative possibilities for machine knitters.

Placing needles into HP acts like decreasing in that the row length gets shorter and shorter while the stitches themselves remain live and available. Gradually returning needles to WP serves to increase the row length. The live stitches remain on the needles and can be bound off or scraped off as group.

You can increase or decrease by a single stitch regardless of which side of the bed the carriage is on, but you can only move two or more needles in or out of hold on the side opposite the carriage. Otherwise, you will have large loops of yarn wrapped around the needles–and ultimately, around the stitches. Because needles in holding position visually define the groups of stitches being short rowed, the process is very easy for machine knitters to understand and even novices use the technique to shape shoulders and necklines very early on.

Hand knitters must rely on counting the stitches in each row and placing movable markers as they work because it is often difficult to distinguish the stitches being held from those still working. I know that I never really understood knitting short rows by hand until I had learned it on the machine - and then it was crystal clear to me. It is one of the techniques that is definitely easier by machine than it is by hand.

Preventing Holes

If you hold some needles and then just knit up to them and then knit back, there will be a small, but very noticeable, hole wherever the knitting changes direction. So, just as in hand knitting, it is necessary to wrap the adjacent stitch to prevent a hole. Machine knitters can wrap manually or automatically and although some patterns don't specifically mention wrapping the turning stitch, it is usually required and understood — unless the holes are included as a design element. The abbreviation "KWK" means to knit, wrap and knit back for both hand and machine knitters.

Hand knitters wrap the turning stitch by passing it, un–knitted, from the left needle to the right. Then they move the yarn in front, replace the stitch on the left needle and return the yarn to the back. The wrap appears around the "neck" of the stitch where the knitting turned.

Most knitting machine manuals explain the basics of short row knitting and show a manual wrap. That is, the free yarn (the yarn between the carriage and the last knitted stitch) is caught around the shaft of the adjacent needle in HP before knitting back to the starting side.

It is also possible to do an automatic wrap, as explained in the directions that follow for decreasing or increasing with short rows.

Decreasing with Short Rows

Many times, unless a manual wrap is specified in the directions, it is faster and just as effective to do an automatic wrap. When holding needles to *decrease* working stitches, bring one *less* needle than required to holding position. Knit 1 row and before knitting back to the starting side, bring one more needle to hold. In other words, if the directions say to hold 4 needles, you would initially just hold 3, knit 1 row and then hold 1 more needle before knitting back. The end result will still be 4 needles in holding position and you will not need to interrupt the work to manually wrap.

Increasing with Short Rows

When *increasing* stitches with short rows, you must return the first needle or group of needles on the side opposite the carriage to WP by nudging them back to UWP. In this case the automatic wrap is achieved by placing one *more* needle than called for in UWP, knitting 1 row and immediately returning the last, extra needle to HP. So, if the directions tell you to return 4 needles to work, you would initially nudge 5 needles from HP to UWP, knit 1 row and then return the last needle to HP.

In the example below, the light blue area was knitted first. The angle was created by holding two needles EOR on the side opposite the carriage. For the first half of the work, I used a manual wrap to prevent a hole later on. The remainder were done with the automatic wrap and I think the difference is quite clear. When short rowing large groups of needles, the effect is bound to be somewhat stair–stepped regardless of which wrap you choose. However, when short rowing just one or two needles at a time as I did here, you can create a much smoother line by using the automatic wrap.

If, instead of color blocks, I had been shaping a shoulder with the light blue, I would have scrapped or bound off after all of the light blue was worked. In that case, I would have first knitted one "smoothing" row over all the needles. However, for this example, I chose to bring the fabric back to level by filling in with dark blue. I returned 2 needles to UWP then KWK. The light blue was decreased by 2 stitches EOR to shape it, while the dark blue was increased by 2 stitches EOR.

Exceptions

I stated earlier that all machines were capable of knitting short rows and that all machines could hold needles. There is a major exception–or variation–that needs to be clarified. Passap machines use a totally different needle system than any other domestic knitting machine.

It is related to the way that semi–industrial machines operate as the needles are always in either WP or NWP. Patterning is controlled by a row of "pushers" directly below the needles and sharing their slots on the bed. Because of the pusher mechanism, Passaps are able to hold needles that *appear* to still be in working position–except that they have ceased working.

Some very simple, plastic machines may not have levers to automatically return needles from HP and you may have to use transfer tools, rather than relying on UWP to return individual needles to work.

The Silver Reed lace carriages will not allow you to put needles into HP, but you can still work short row shaping by manually knitting the stitches you want to hold with ravel cord. These stitches need to be enlarged enough to push their needles back to NWP. It isn't as fast as using HP, but it works and is well explained in the manuals.

Shoulder slants and short rowed intarsia are worked exactly the same except that for one you bind off and for the other, you fill in with second color.

Binding Off

The most common machine knit bind off is nearly the same as the decrease bind off that hand knitters use: Move the first edge stitch to the next needle, manually knit the two stitches together, then move the new stitch to the next needle. This is repeated across the bed until all of the stitches have been bound off. You can also do a latch tool bind off (in several different ways) that is the same as a hand knit crochet bind off. Every knitting machine manual describes these methods in detail.

Binding Off Around the Sinker Posts

The trickiest part to binding off – by hand or machine – is to create a reasonably stretchy, but firm edge and to prevent that edge from being so tight that a neckline, for example, won't fit over your head. Many machine knitters catch the yarn or the stitches being bound off around the sinker posts (gate pegs) between the needles to prevent this.

On machines that do not have metal posts between the needles, you can use an empty needle in holding position instead. After removing a stitch and transferring it to the adjacent needle, leave the empty needle in HP and catch the yarn around the empty needle before laying it in the hook of the next needle to knit the two stitches together.

In the photo below left, a stitch has been removed from its needle and transferred to the adjacent needle to the right. However, the stitch was moved *behind* the sinker post, rather than in front of it as it would normally be done for a decrease. Then, as shown in the photograph at right, the yarn is laid in the hook of the needle and the two stitches are knitted together.

By the time the entire edge has been bound off, all of the stitches will have been caught behind the sinker posts which will support the fabric and prevent the last few stitches from stretching and enlarging.

Whether you transfer stitches behind the sinker posts or wrap the yarn around the sinker post or an adjacent, empty needle,

When binding off around the sinker posts, you can either pass the stitches behind the posts (1) as you transfer them or you can transfer the stitches in the usual way and catch the yarn behind the post before knitting the two stitches together (2).

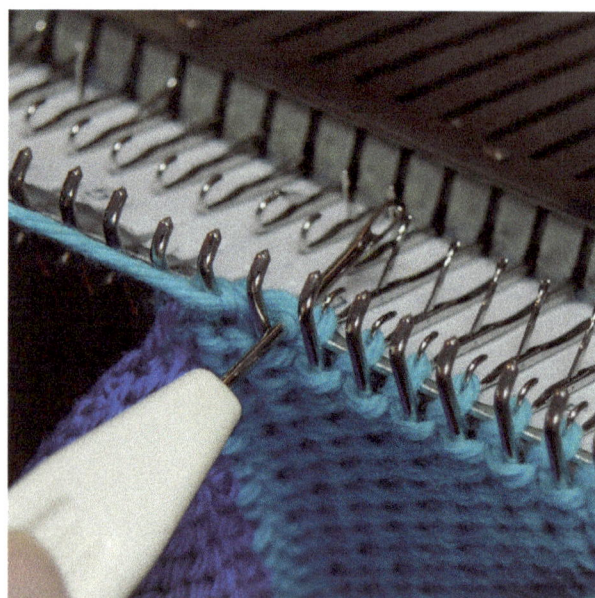

you are only adding extra length to the space *between* each of the bound off stitches, not making new stitches. In addition to enlarging the stitches, this method supports the work evenly as you bind off so that it doesn't hang from fewer and fewer needles. When the last stitch has been bound off, simply cut the yarn and pull the end through the last stitch to secure it. Then lift the fabric off the sinker posts or the needles in HP.

Three-Needle Bind Off

The 3-needle bind off that hand knitters use for joining shoulder seams can be handled two ways on the machine. For either one, you need to rehang both sets of shoulder stitches on the same needles. The live stitches can be held on sections of a garter bar or just scrapped off on waste knitting and you can hang bound off or selvage edges as well.

Rehang the stitches for the first shoulder (for example) on the machine with the right side facing you; then rehang the second set of stitches with the wrong side facing you. For light weight yarns, you can just bind off the two sets of stitches as one, using whatever bind-off method you prefer.

Fold back the scrap and rehang the stitches for the first shoulder with the right side facing you.

Push the needles to HP so that the stitches for the first shoulder slide behind the latches. Then, with the wrong side facing you (i.e. right sides together) hang the stitches for the second shoulder in the hooks of the same needles.

Use the flat side of a needle pusher to close the latches and slowly ease the needles back to WP so that the stitches behind the latches slide off the needles as you do so.

Bind off the stitches by whatever method you prefer. In the photo at left, the stitches have been transferred to adjacent needles behind the sinker posts to maintain an even bind off.

For heavier yarns, most machine knitters prefer pulling the second set of stitches through the first as shown in the photographs on the previous page. This reduces bulk before binding off and makes a somewhat finer seam. It is especially helpful with bulky yarns.

To do this, after hanging the first set of stitches, push the needles to HP so that the stitches slide over the latches and sit on the shafts of the needles. Hang the second set of stitches in the hooks of the same needles and then carefully push the needle butts back to WP with the straight edge of a needle pusher so that the first set of stitches slides over the closed latches, leaving just a single stitch in the hook of each needle. Then just bind off.

Either of these methods helps reduce bulk and produce a firm shoulder seam whether your shoulder has been short rowed or knitted straight. I always work the bind off around the sinker posts to prevent the seam from pulling in. I often scrap off hand knit shoulders and join them on the machine by this method.

Picot Bind Off

This edge looks very different when worked with the knit or purl side facing you so I recommend trying it both ways to see which you prefer. In order to work with the knit side facing you, you'll need to remove all of the stitches from the machine with a garter bar or waste knitting and re-hang them with the knit side facing you.

Begin with COR, set to hold needles in HP and all needles in HP except for the first 2 on the right edge. *Knit 4 rows and then move the first stitch onto the second needle. Use a transfer tool to move the next 3 needles from HP to WP. Bind off 3 stitches. E-wrap 1 needle at right so that there are 2 needles in WP ** and repeat from * to **. This is the method I used for the swatch below left, worked with the purl side of the fabric facing me.

Popcorn Picot Bind Off

You can also knit a picot edge the way bridged popcorns are knitted, which is how the swatch at right was worked with the knit side facing me. Begin COR, set to hold needles in HP and with all needles except the first 2 on the carriage side in HP. Knit 6 rows over these 2 needles. *Push the next 5 needles to UWP and knit 1 row. Hold all needles except the last 2. Knit 5 more rows over these 2 needles and then** Repeat from * to ** to the end of the row. Break the yarn. Each pair of needles that knitted the 6 extra rows will form a popcorn or bobble on the edge of the fabric. Beginning at the right edge, use the latch tool to catch a loop at the base of the first popcorn (6 rows below). Then remove both of the popcorn stitches in the hook of the tool and pull them through the first stitch together. *Chain off the next 3 stitches. Then catch a stitch at the base of the next popcorn group and pull it through the stitch on the tool. Catch both popcorn stitches together in the hook and pull them through.** Repeat from * to ** across the work.

Because this variation uses a yarn-less latch tool bind off, you need to increase the stitch size so that the work doesn't pull in. That is, the stitches are just pulled one through the next, with no additional yarn fed into them. This kind of a bind off usually tightens and always requires a larger stitch size. I worked the entire row (including the extra rows for the popcorns) with stitch size 10.

This picot bind off was worked with the purl side of the fabric facing.

The latch tool bind off creates a strong chained effect between each of the popcorns. This edge was worked with the knit side facing.

Scrapping Off

Rather than always binding off pieces, machine knitters remove work from the machine by "scrapping off" instead. They knit 8-10 rows with waste yarn and then just drop the work–unbound–from the machine. This is a useful option when you want to join and bind off shoulder seams with live stitches, pick up edges for ribs or trims or work a hand-sewn or crochet bind off instead. Scrapping off, however, is not a bind off. It is just an interim solution for stitches that will be dealt with later.

Hand Sewn Bind Off for Ribs

This method takes a little extra time and effort than some other methods. Although I do occasionally use it for finer gauge knits, it is most suitable for mid–gauge and bulky ribs. It produces a beautiful edge which, incidentally, happens to match the tubular rib cast on edge.

Also, although this method is normally used for binding off ribbed edges, I have occasionally used it to bind off single bed fabrics as well. Sometimes I will reform every other stitch in the very last row, but not always.

I prefer starting garment pieces on waste knitting so I can knit my ribs down, sometimes reducing the number of stitches from the sweater to the rib, though not always. All of my rib edges match - at cuffs, neck and hem because they are all bound off edges. I think this edge has the best elasticity and, when working with inelastic yarns like cotton and linen, you can use the channel in the edge of the rib to insert elastic thread to add some memory to the rib.

Leave a long tail of the main yarn attached to the work - about twice the width of the knitting. With waste yarn, knit one row alternately knitting 1 stitch then slipping 1 stitch, followed by 6-8 rows of stockinet. Drop the work from the machine and press the scrap knitting so it lays flat and is less likely to ravel. This prep row can also be worked in reverse if you start a garment piece on scrap and then switch to the main yarn. Just work the last row of the scrap as (knit 1, slip 1) and then change to the main yarn.

Unlike most bind off methods, this one is worked by threading the yarn through a yarn needle and sewing each and every stitch.

Depending on your machine and its capabilities, you may have to manually select every other needle to holding position and set the carriage to slip to accomplish this set–up row. You may also be able to program it into your selection system, but there are just too many variables from machine to machine for me to address it further than that. At the very least, you can always manually knit every other needle across the bed, skipping the needles in between. This row is important because, when you fold the scrap knitting back, it makes it possible to see the stitches so much more clearly.

Thread the yarn through a blunt tapestry needle and then make a figure eight, stitching back and forth through the end stitches in both rows to begin. Then follow the series of photographs on these two pages. Once you have worked a couple of stitches on each row, you probably won't even need the photos to guide you.

When working on the upper row of stitches, Always insert the needle down through the last stitch worked in that row and up through the next un–worked stitch: always think "down the old and up the new".

These photos illustrate working the upper row of stitches.

1 The needle goes down an "old" stitch first, the second stitch that was worked in the previous upper row.

2 Next, insert the needle up through the next stitch. This is a new, un–worked stitch. It will be the first stitch worked in the next upper row.

Fold back the scrap knitting to expose the tops of the stitches in the last row of the main knitting and you will see that they appear to be in two separate, alternating rows. This is because of the way the prep row separates the stitches.

You will alternately work on these two "rows" of stitches held by the scrap. The first stitch of each new sequence is always taken through the last stitch that was worked on that row. Think "in the old stitch and out a new one" as you work. (1) For convenience sake in these directions, I will continue to refer to these stitches as two separate rows even though it really is just an illusion.

3 When both stitches in the upper row have been worked, tighten the yarn just enough to remove any excess.

Binding Off 53

When working stitches in the lower row, let the yarn lie over the work as shown in the photograph below (4) and take the first stitch up through the last stitch you worked in that row and down (5) through the next. Pull the yarn through each pair of stitches as you form them, but just enough to remove excess slack (6) and form a neat stitch. Do not tighten the stitches or the bind off will be too tight to be useful. For the lower row of stitches, think "up through the old stitch and down through the new".

Remember, each stitch will be worked twice: as the last stitch of one sequence and the first of the next. Stitches in the upper row are worked down and then up; those in the lower row are worked up then down.

Hand knit directions for this bind off show working directly from the hand knitting needle, but I have never been able to manage that. Instead, I usually work a scrap header (by hand or machine) on my hand knit pieces to work this bind off. With the scrap header, it is easy to see what appears as two distinct "rows" of alternating stitches.

5 Next, insert the needle down through the next stitch to work it for the first time.

4 First, carry the yarn across from the upper row and insert the needle up through the last stitch worked in the previous bottom row.

6 When both stitches have been made, tighten the yarn just enough to remove any excess.

Once you have finished sewing through each row of stitches, just remove the scrap knitting. The edge is rounded, closed and very finished looking.

I-Cord Bind Off

I-cords are usually worked over 3-5 stitches, knitting them in one direction and slipping them in the other. In addition to a multitude of decorative uses, you can use I-cord as a bind off or a trim on live stitches, selvage edges or even up a column of stitches on the front of a garment. You can also hang two garment pieces together on the needles, wrong sides together, and use this I-cord bind off to both join and decorate a seam.

Set the carriage to hold needles that are in HP and place all needles except the first 3 on the carriage side in HP.

Set the carriage so that needles in WP will knit in one direction to slip in the other–some machines accomplish this with simple carriage settings, but others require a hand manipulation prior to every two rows. If your carriage does not have levers or settings to automatically knit I-cord, you may have to knit one direction and free pass the carriage to the other side or hold needles when knitting in one direction and allow them to knit in the other by flipping a lever or nudging them back to UWP.

*Knit 2 rows (1 row knitted and 1 row slipped). Move the 4th stitch (from the first needle in HP) onto the 3rd (working) needle and then move all 3 stitches over to fill the empty space.** Repeat * to ** until only 3 stitches remain. Cut the yarn and gather off the remaining 3 stitches.

You should recognize this as a 2-step decrease. A simple, 1-step decrease will not join the I-cord to the edge of the fabric neatly because the face stitch keeps changing with every decrease. I use a 3 and 1 transfer tool so I always have the right tool in my hand.

I-cord creates a lovely, narrow edging that I especially like for finishing off necklines. I normally knit 1 smoothing row across all the short rowed neckline stitches before scrapping them off. With this method you can sew both shoulder seams and then fold back the scrap and re-hang some of the neckline stitches, work the trim and add more of the neckline stitches as you go.

The front and back of the fabric look a little different where the I-cord meets the fabric and I personally feel that the fabric rolls a little less if I work this edge with the knit side facing me.

Keep this in mind when re-hanging stitches on the needles for any I-cord trim, but be especially careful if you use this method to apply trim to the surface of a garment or to join decorative sleeve or shoulder seams. Make sure that you always re-hang pieces so that the roll of the cords match from one to the next.

I sometimes use I-cord to work decorative seams along the top edge of two-piece sleeves. I make sure that I always rehang the back of the sleeve first and then the front piece (wrong sides facing). Because I prefer working left to right, I seam one sleeve from cuff to shoulder and the other from shoulder to cuff to be sure they match.

Binding Off

With the carriage set to knit circular and all needles except the first three on the carriage side in HP, make two passes of the carriage. It will slip in one direction and knit in the other. (1)

Transfer the stitch from the fourth needle to the third needle (2).

Then move all of the stitches over by 1 needle to fill the gap. The third needle holds 2 stitches. (3)

An I-cord edge is an excellent alternative to ribbing for neck bands and cuffs.

Picking Up Stitches

There are lots of times when it is necessary to pick up live stitches, selvage edges and maybe even the surface of a fabric to re-hang on the machine for finishing or trimming purposes and there are several of ways to do this.

Picking up Live Stitches

Live stitches can be transferred to the machine with multi-prong transfer tools or a garter bar if you have pre-knitted a trim or surface texture that you want to hang on the needles so it knits into the surface of your fabric. For example, you could pre-knit several four stitch I-cords to use for cardigan ties and remove them all from the machine as they are knitted, just stacking them up on the same 4-prong tool. Then, you can feed each one back onto the needles, when and where you need them.

Picking up From Scrap or Waste Knitting

Scrap (or waste) knitting is often used to preserve live stitches the way hand knitters use stitch holders. Although you do not have to bind off the scrap rows, I often do for extra security when I plan to take the knitting with me for hand finishing or if the yarn tends to ravel easily. At the very least, I always press the scrap knitting with an iron to help set the stitches and make them less likely to run.

Many knitters think of scrap knitting as a way to avoid binding off stitches – and it can be that – but I tend to use it mainly to retain live stitches for joining, finishing later on or leaving myself the option to change my mind about finishing details once the garment is assembled. It is the ultimate, limitless, flexible stitch holder.

Most Japanese knitting machines provide ravel cord as part of the basic accessory package. Ravel cord is used to knit a single row between the main knitting and the scrap. It serves two purposes. First of all, it prevents any possible fuzz or color from the scrap yarn from transferring to the main yarn. Second, it makes it very easy to separate the scrap from the main knitting later on by just pulling it through the stitches.

When picking up stitches from scrap, simply fold the scrap knitting back (or forward) to expose the tops of the main stitches. You can do this with either the knit or purl side facing you. Then just insert a transfer tool through each stitch and place the stitch on a needle. Once you are comfortable doing this, you will be able to use a 3-prong transfer tool and pick up and re-hang three stitches at a time. If you want to reduce stitches across the row, simply hang two stitches on the same needle every so often. I always press my scrap knitting (not the main knitting – just the scrap) so the it is less likely to curl and the main stitches are more secure and easier to handle.

Picking up 3 full selvage stitches

Picking up Selvage Edges

Picking up selvage edges is a little different. If you need to re-hang a selvage edge on the machine to continue knitting from it, you only need to pick up some of the selvage stitches. Because stitch and row gauges are seldom the same, you are likely to have more edge stitches than you need. You can do the math, converting numbers of rows to inches and back to stitches or you can use take the old rule of thumb and pick up just 2/3 of the edge stitches.

Let's assume, for example, that your gauge is (conveniently) 5 stitches and 7 rows per inch, and you want to pick up a side edge to knit a drop shoulder sleeve from shoulder to cuff. If the armhole is supposed to be 9" deep, I would tag the edge stitches of the front and back 63 rows (9" x 7 rows per inch) before the shoulder while knitting the piece. If you forget to hang the yarn tags, you can always measure carefully and tag them later on.

When it comes time to hang the piece on the machine, according to the stitch gauge the space between the two tags should be re-hung over 90 needles (5 stitches per inch X 18") even though there are a total of 126 rows between the tags. Hanging 2 out of every 3 stitches would actually bring me pretty close to this with about 84 stitches, but doing the math is a bit more exact. The coarser the gauge, the more important it is to figure accurately. Very fine, standard gauges provide a little more flexibility as the difference between 7 or 8 stitches per inch isn't going to make as much of a difference as it would with 3 versus 4 stitches per inch.

Sometimes you can just "poke" the edge to distribute the stitches and avoid counting while you pick up. To do this, determine how many stitches you need by multiplying gauge times width. In my example above it was 90 stitches. I would bring the 45th needle on each side of zero out to hold and hang the stitch next to each yarn tag onto them. Then I would poke the transfer tool through the stitches on either side of the shoulder seam and place them on needles #1 at each side of zero. From then on, I pinch what feels like the middle of a section, poke the tool through a stitch and hang it on the approximate middle needle above. My sections keep getting smaller and smaller until all of the stitches have been hung. It works every time. Just one word of caution: make sure you pick up a whole stitch and don't jump from one stitch column to the next or the seam will look ragged.

As you look at the selvage edge of the fabric, each stitch has two sides to it, alternating with a tighter bump or knot for the place where the carriage turned and knitted back the other way. For join-as-you knit methods like modular knitting and entrelac, there may be times when the work looks better if you just pick up half of an edge stitch instead of a whole one. It may even be necessary, when picking up a lot of stitches, to pick up a stitch from the small bump.

When knitting entrelac, for example, I don't find that picking up a whole or half stitch reduces any of the color "grin through" that results when changing color. However, I do think that picking up half stitches creates a looser, somewhat softer fabric. For the most part–unless directions specify–it is your choice which you do.

Picking up half a stitch for join--as-you-knit

Picking up Surface Stitches

In addition to picking up live stitches and selvage edges, you can also pick up stitches from the surface of the fabric to add textural details or pocket flaps.

Depending on your needs, you can pick up along a single column of stitches or allow the tool to travel across the surface of the fabric as I did in the example below.

You can pick up stitches from the surface of a knit fabric to add textural details or pocket flaps by inserting a transfer tool through individual stitches or small groups of them.

This stockinet curl was added later by picking up stitches from the surface of the fabric.

Crochet Hook Pick Up

There are times, however, when neither a full nor a half selvage stitch quite works. For example, when knitting modular log cabin blocks, you need to pick up live stitches *and* selvage stitches next to each other in the same row. Regardless of whether you choose full or half selvage stitches, there will be a jog in the edge of the fabric.

To combat this, I leave long tails at the beginning and end of each section so that I have yarn I can use to pick up and make stitches along the edge with a crochet hook the same way hand knitters pick up stitches.

One of the things I especially like about this crochet hook pick-up method is the fact that I can see the knit side of the fabric as I pick up the stitches to make sure I work along the same column of stitches and get a nice, crisp edge that never wavers.

Hold the work so that you can see the knit side of the fabric and insert a crochet hook from the knit side through to the purl side and pull up a loop of yarn to form a stitch. Let the stitch slide back on the crochet hook as you insert the hook through the next

The stitches for the curl in the photo above were picked up from half stitches.

selvage stitch and pull up another loop. Work your way across the fabric, forming even, regular stitches and sliding them along the length of the crochet hook as you work. Once you have picked up (and checked) all of the required stitches, use a transfer tool to move each stitch from the crochet hook to a needle on the machine.

I don't always use this method because it takes a few extra minutes to do, but I do use it when blocks of color need to stand out cleanly from each other, as they do for the log cabin blocks on page 155.

Combination Method

Sometimes very specific situations require creative or combination methods. When I started working with log cabin modular knitting (page 15), I realized there was a problem where I needed to pick up both live stitches and selvage edges side by side.

Regardless of whether I picked up a whole or a half selvage stitch, there was still a jog in the work where I switched to picking up live stitches.

Work from the right side of the fabric, inserting the hook 1 full stitch from the edge of the fabric to pull up loops. Hold the stitches on the crochet hook–or an afghan hook for very large projects–until you are ready to hang them on the needles.

Because you work from the right side of the fabric, you can be sure that the stitches are all picked up along the same column of stitches.

Use a transfer tool to remove the stitches from the crochet hook and hang them on the needles of the machine.

I knew that I needed to pick up a little differently in this case. I used the crochet hook pick up method first, picking up the selvage edge from the light blue (in the photo below), feeding those new stitches onto the hook.

Then I transferred the stitches from the crochet hook to the machine and folded back the waste knitting at the top of the dark blue section to pick up each of the live stitches.

On larger pieces of log cabin, where I needed to use the crochet hook method at both edges of the fabric, I used the hook to make stitches at the right edge and then just passed the hook behind the next group of live stitches to use it on the left side.

I had one group of stitches at either edge of the fabric picked up on the crochet hook with some live stitches, held on waste knitting, between them.

First I transferred the group of crochet hook stitches from the right edge of the fabric onto the needles. Then I folded back the waste and picked up the live stitches. Lastly, I transferred the second group of crochet hook stitches to the machine.

First use the crochet hook to pick up stitches from the selvage edge of the light blue.

Hanging Hand-Knitted Ribbing

If you own a simple hobby machine with no ribber, rather than latching up stitches, you may want to hand knit your ribbing. Knit the required number of rows and then hold the knitting needle close to the bed and use a transfer tool to individually lift each stitch off the needle and onto the needles of the machine. If you want to increase stitches for the

Next, transfer the stitches from the crochet hook to the machine using a transfer tool.

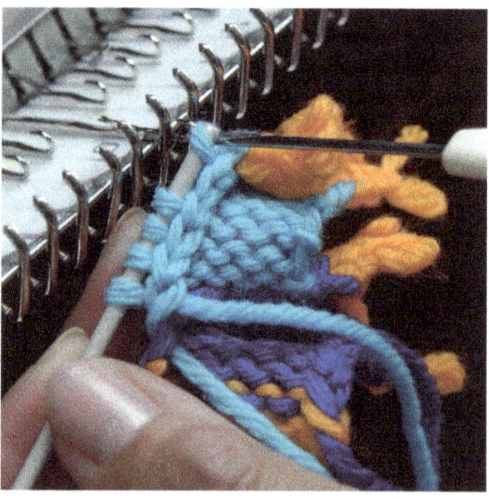

Then pick up the live stitches from the scrap.

body of the garment, just skip a needle every so often and continue transferring the stitches to the remaining needles. After all the stitches have been hung on the machine, use the tip of the transfer tool to pick up the purl bar of an adjacent stitch to fill each empty needle so that there are no holes in the first row.

Pretty much anything you can hang on the needles of the machine can be used to start or embellish a knit.

In addition to hanging pre-knit ribbing on the machine, you can also hang the edge of a woven fabric or a length of commercial lace or trim on the needles of the machine to create an edging. It usually helps the machine knit more smoothly if you bring the needles to HP for the first row with the carriage set to knit them back to regular WP. In some instances, you may even need to manually knit each of the needles for the first row, but if the fabric or trim has openings that the needles can poke through, you can find a way to use it on the machine. Knitted-on trims work especially well with hand woven fabrics.

Weaving in Ends

You can save lots of finishing time if you learn to weave in your ends as you work. Although this method is not suitable for Fair Isle or purl-side-right fabrics, you will be able to use it more often than not.

Leave an 8–10" tail when you begin working. Knit 1 row and then bring 12–14 needles to HP on the side where the tail is hanging. Weave the tail over and under the shafts of the extended needles, set the carriage to knit needles back from HP (or nudge them to UWP) and knit the next row.

When changing colors or starting a new yarn, I weave in the ending tail, knit the first row with the new yarn and then weave in that tail. It makes stripes a breeze!

When you finish knitting, check the knit side of the fabric to be sure there is no unsightly "grin through" and then go ahead and clip the tails close on the reverse of the fabric.

Weaving in the ends while you work is a huge time saver when knitting fabrics that have lots of color changes like intarsia, entrelac and modular knitting. When knitting intarsia, just make sure you weave the yarn tails behind the open latches of the needles.

Hand knitted ribbing is easy to transfer to the machine. Just insert a transfer tool through each stitch, slip it off the HK needle and deposit it on a needle on the machine.

After knitting the last row of the dark blue, bring some needles at the edge out to HP and weave the cut end of the yarn over and under them.

Knit the first row of the light blue.

Bring the needles at the edge out to HP and weave the tail of the light blue over and under them.

Knit a few rows and then clip the tails close to the surface of the fabric so they do not tangle or pull.

Loose Ends

Some things your manuals *should* explain, but seldom do.

Most of the knitting machine manuals I have ever seen did an excellent job explaining *what* to do, but none of them ever adequately explains *why*. Also, there's a lot of very useful information that is never included at all in those manuals and would be so helpful for beginners to have. So, in these last few pages I will try to share some of that information with you. I don't want to re-write the books that are already available, but I would like to give you an overview and a frame of reference for some skills I think are well worth having.

The Garter Bar

The garter bar is an especially useful accessory and because it is comprised of lots of prongs that fit onto the needles, it must be the same gauge (needle spacing) as your machine. The only exception to this is the 4.5mm (standard) gauge garter bar, which is usable on every-other-prong on a chunky 9 mm machine. The eyes in each prong are on the small side, which makes it a little awkward, but it can be done.

Garter bars have been produced with 4.5, 6.5, 7, 8 and 9 mm spacing and I highly recommend having one for your machine. They do show up used, but see page 184 for a source for excellent new garter bars in a variety of gauges.

The Needle Stabilizer

Complete garter bar sets include 2 or 3 sections that can be coupled together to accommodate all the needles on the bed of the machine. They also include (or offer as an option) a needle stabilizer. This is an adjustable, rectangular device (usually in two sections) that secures the needles in holding position by catching the needle butts underneath one long edge and the front of the bed with the other.

There are a couple of screws that can be loosened and then tightened to adjust the width of the stabilizer so that it grips the needle butts securely. Once you have adjusted the stabilizer for your machine, you shouldn't have to change it although the screws do sometimes loosen after a while.

The needle stabilizer is placed on the bed when you need to move stitches onto the prongs of the garter bar and then back onto the machine. It must be removed from the bed before you can resume knitting. Using the stabilizer does add some additional steps, but initially it offers great security in removing so many stitches from their needles all at once. After you have some experience using a garter bar, you'll find that you don't always need to use the stabilizer, but it certainly reduces the learning curve if you start with one.

Apart from using it with the garter bar itself, the needle stabilizer makes it fast and easy to rip back multiple rows of stitches by locking the needles in HP. Then, all you need to do is firmly

The needle stabilizer prevents the needles from moving in their slots. By pulling the yarn to one side and then lifting back, you can rip out an entire row in a second and row after row with very little effort or fear of dropping stitches.

pull the yarn to the side so that the stitches un-knit and the previous row of stitches remain in the hooks of the needles. You can rip back 20 rows in the time it would normally take to rip out one so it is worth owning a needle stabilizer for this purpose alone!

Garter bars are useful for removing the work from the machine to check the knitting on the knit side of the fabric and for all kinds of decorative and specialized techniques, but they are used primarily for turning all of the stitches over for garter stitch and for decreasing or increasing stitches evenly across an entire row.

Garter Stitch Effects

In hand knitting, the fabric is turned over after every row so that the purl and knit faces of the fabric alternate. To compensate for those turns, stockinet is worked by knitting the knit stitches or purling the purls as each side faces you. When all the rows are knitted (or, less commonly, purled) regardless of which side faces you, the result is garter stitch.

However, every row on a knitting machine is worked with the same, purl, side of the fabric facing you and because the carriage can form stitches from right to left and then from left to right, the resulting fabric is stockinet. In order to produce garter stitch, the fabric needs to be turned over after knitting each row.

So, while garter stitch is one of the easiest stitches to do by hand, it is surprisingly time-consuming and cumbersome by machine. Having to turn the work over after each and every row is knitted makes garter stitch more practical for portions of designs or accents than it is for an entire sweater.

There is, however, one exception worth mentioning here. Brother machines had an automatic garter carriage available and many are still in circulation. This is a motorized carriage that, as it chugs across the bed, actually un-knits each stitch and transfers it to a needle inside the carriage. Because that accessory needle faces the opposite direction to the needles on the bed, the stitches that it re-knits are reversed and the G-carriage knits row after row of automatic garter stitch as well as beautiful knit/purl combination stitches.

Because it operates quite slowly, the G-carriages is affectionately known as "The Turtle". People often turn on the G-carriage and walk away to do something else while it works its magic – unless, of course, they need to shape garment sections along the way.

G-carriages were manufactured only for Brother standard gauge machines until the mid 90's. If you really like the looks of garter stitch and knit/purl combination stitches and you own a Brother machine, you should keep your eyes open for a G-carriage on the used equipment market. Do, however, make sure it is in working condition.

Knitting Garter Stitch with a Garter Bar

Every two turns with the garter bar (and the two knitted rows that accompany them) account for a single ridge of garter stitch. On the simplest level, knitters often use a single ridge of garter stitch as a fold row where a hem turns back on itself or to crease a doubled band. I often use a garter ridge above a rolled stockinet edge (see page 31) to prevent the edge from rolling too high or to accentuate and outline bands of a particular pattern or color within the body of a garment.

Instead of turning the work after every row you knit, you can also opt to turn it over every 10 rows, for example, to create stripes of reverse stockinet; every four rows to create large-scale mock-garter stitch; after building up an area with short rows to fill in with reversed stitches. The possibilities are endless, governed only by your patience and the acquired skill of using a garter bar.

Begin by removing the yarn from the carriage yarn feeder and free-passing the carriage to the opposite end of the bed. Then use the needle stabilizer to secure all of the needles in HP and push the fabric back against the bed.

Make sure all of the latches are open and then hook the garter bar onto the needles. (1) It's usually a good idea to center the GB on the needles, rather than beginning at one end and having lots of un-used prongs at the other. If you are using an old style, Japanese garter bar, make sure you *always* begin with the horizontal ridge facing up. The newer style GBs are the same on both sides.

Way back when many machines only operated in intarsia mode, they came with a handy little latch opener and you may still find some available. Most people find that a plastic letter opener or an expired credit card with a notch cut out of it works just fine to open all the latches in one smooth motion across the bed. Also, try to leave some weights on the knitting so the latches remain open and the stitches transfer more easily.

With one hand, firmly hold the garter bar even with the needles and with the other hand; pull the fabric over the needle latches and straight onto the prongs of the tool. (2) Always begin at one edge and work your way across the fabric. Under no circumstances should you work part way from one side and then begin at the other or you will find that the stitches at the center catch on the needle latches and will not transfer cleanly.

Once all of the stitches have been transferred onto the garter bar, hold it with both hands and, still even with the needles, nudge it back just enough to open all of the latches. (3) Then lift the tool off the machine. Turn the entire business over to return the stitches to the open hooks of the needles.

2

1

3

With the new style GBs, pictured here, after turning the work over, position the GB in front of the hooks of the needles and just high enough above the needles that they can slip into the slot below each stitch. (4) The slots in the garter bar are visible above each stitch and also for a short bit below the stitches. Make sure all of the latches are still open.

The head of each needle should be aligned with one of the slots. The stabilizer helps keep the needles straight and aligned so this is easier to do than it sounds. Although he needle stabilizer can compensate for slightly wonky needles, you should have replaced any badly bent needles before you started.

Once all of the needles are aligned with the slots, tip the GB forward and down just enough to catch each stitch in the hook of a needle. (5) Then return the GB to perpendicular to check for accuracy. If one or two stitches failed to catch, just use a transfer tool to lift them onto the prongs. For more than that, tip the bar forward to release the stitches and try again.

If all of the stitches are caught on the needles, just pull the tool straight down and away from the work. (6) Remove the stabilizer and knit the next row.

The old style GBs work a little differently, as I have illustrated on the next page. First of all, in order to be able to turn the work over and return the stitches to their needles, you *must* begin by holding this GB with the side

5

4

6

that has a raised ridge along its length facing up. For some things it doesn't matter, but it's a good idea to get into the habit of always using it this way to avoid problems later on.

Remove the stitches the same way I described on the previous page, with the ridge facing up, and nudge the GB forward to open all the latches before removing the prongs from the needles and turning the work over. (7) Make sure all the latches are open.

Hold the GB perpendicular to the needles with the heads of needles resting in the *grooves* (rather than slots) below the stitches

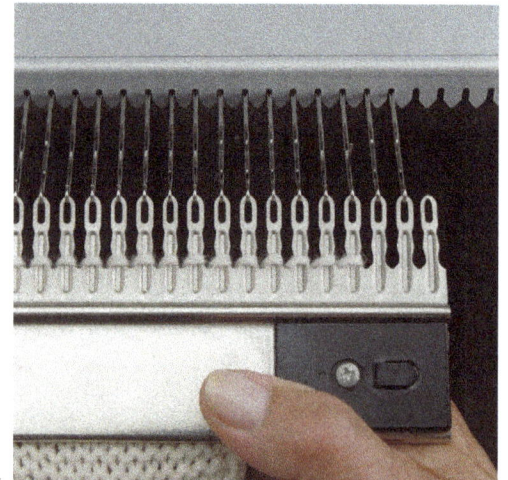

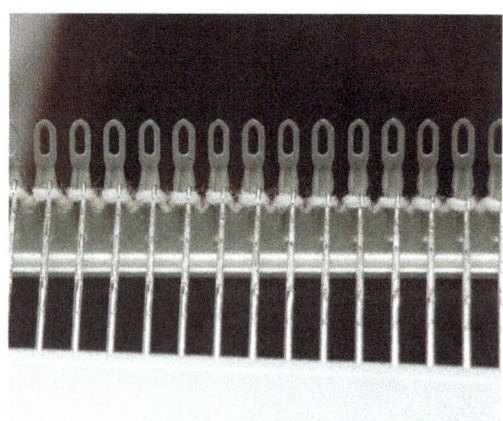

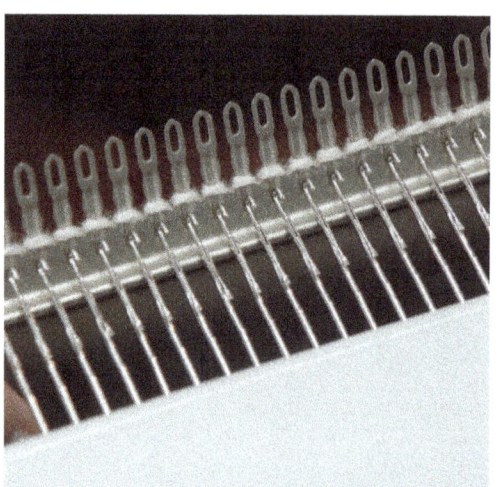

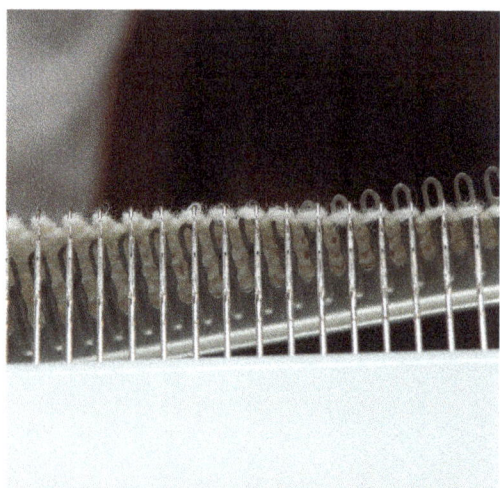

on each prong. (8) Pressing the GB firmly against the needles, slowly rotate it until it is nearly flat on top of the needles and then give a slight tug towards you. (9) You should feel the stitches catch in the hooks of the needles.

Tip the bar back to perpendicular to make sure all of the stitches have been caught in the needles. (10) If they have, carefully remove the GB by tipping it slightly back towards you to clear the needle hooks and then pull it straight down and out of the stitches. (11) As with the new style GB, if you have not caught all of the stitches, rotate the tool again and try once more.

Don't be in too much of a hurry to remove the GB from the work because you run the risk of catching it in the hook of a needle or two and then it is practically impossible to remove it without dropping the work from the machine. In general, the fastest, easiest way to use a Garter Bar is slowly and deliberately.

A word of caution is warranted here. Turning 50 or 100 stitches over all at once is not an easy maneuver to master and requires practice - preferably not while you are working on a precious project! Also, if you are careless pulling the tool away, its possible to trap it behind the stitches on the needles and then there is nothing to do but start over. If ever there was a reason to knit practice swatches, the garter bar is the one.

As I said, all Garter Bars come in sections so that you can turn over 50 stitches, for example, without having to handle an accessory long enough for 150. When you work with a full length GB, you need to apply a little more pressure towards the center to overcome the tendency of the long GB to bow slightly at the center.

I have a couple of the old–style garter bars and a new one for the 6.5 machine. Granted, I've known how to use a garter bar for years, but I think the new ones are definitely easier to manage. Aligning the heads of the needles with the open slots is much easier than positioning them in the groves and having to always remember to start with the ridged side of the old bars facing up.

Increasing and Decreasing with the garter bar

Once you have removed the stitches from the needles, you can bring additional needles to WP or nudge some back to NWP, depending on whether you are increasing or decreasing. It is usually a good idea to add or subtract an equal number of needles at each edge prior to returning the stitches to their needles. This keeps the work centered on the bed, which makes it easier to keep track of edge increases and decreases and also provides equal space at each end of the bed for the carriage to safely pass all the working needles.

With both increasing and decreasing, after you have removed all the stitches on the GB, you need to work your way across the bed a little at a time. You'll nudge some of the stitches onto the needles and then lift the bar away slightly to shift its position before moving any more stitches back onto the machine.

In the example below, I've left an empty needle after every 5th stitch. Rather than tipping the tool to return all the stitches at once, I just use my index fingers to nudge a few stitches at a time back onto the needles.

Each of the empty needles will be filled (at right) by picking up the purl bar of an adjacent stitch. You will need to remove the needle stabilizer to do this.

If you start replacing stitches onto their needles at the left, in order to make space for an increase, you'll need to shift the garter bar two needles to the right to skip an empty needle before returning the next group of stitches to the machine. After all the stitches have been returned from the GB to the needles on the bed, you should pick up the purl bar of adjacent stitches to create stitches on the empty needles unless large eyelets figure into your plans.

For decreasing, you need to shift the bar *back* towards the needles already holding stitches so that the next stitch you nudge off the bar and onto the machine lands on the last needle already holding a stitch.

For double decreases like the ones I used to create the tulip edging below, I find it easier to make all my decreases first and then remove the stitches on the bar. Then, when returning

After working two rows of double decreases, this trim reduces down to 1/3 the original number of stitches cast on. It was knitted using the lace chart on page 105 except that, instead of allowing eyelets to form, the stitches were moved closer together to eliminate the empty needles and 1 stitch was latched up between each repeat to help the "tulips" stand out.

the stitches to the machine, I only need to lift and shift the GB enough to make sure that stitches are placed on every needle and that there are no empty needles and no doubled stitches in addition to the decreases.

Beaded Knitting

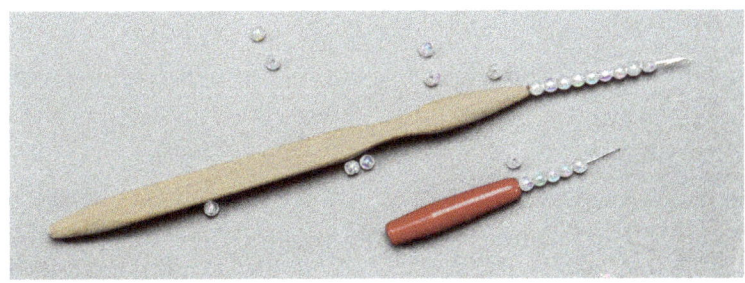

When hand knitters want to add beads to a fabric, they usually thread them all onto the yarn first and then feed them into the stitches as they work across the rows. That pre-threaded method doesn't work very well on a knitting machine. First of all, the beads will probably get caught passing through the tension unit. If they do manage to get that far, they still need to pass through the carriage yarn feeder and allow the yarn to form stitches in each of the needles.

Instead, most machine knitters add beads by one of two methods. The most direct method involves using a tiny latch tool or crochet hook that fits through the holes in the beads to place the beads on exactly the right stitches. There are special beading needles sold for this very purpose (see page 184) and you can sometimes find tiny latch tools on sewing notions counters where they are sold for fixing pulls in knits.

If your beads have large enough holes, you can just use a standard gauge latch tool to apply the beads. In that case, you can just hook the latch tool onto the hook of each needle to transfer the stitches to the tool and to return them to their needles after slipping a bead onto them.

Depending on the length of the shaft of the beading needles, you should be able to stack up several beads behind the latch of the tool. Then, after knitting a row, you can simply remove a stitch from its needle on the machine with the hook of the beading tool, slide a bead over the closed latch of the tool and onto the stitch. Push the bead down snuggly on the stitch and then return the stitch to its needle.

You probably won't be able to hook a beading tool onto the needles on the bed to transfer stitches to and from the tool as you would with a regular latch tool. Beading needles are fairly delicate because they are so tiny and you need to be careful not to damage the latch itself.

So, It is usually best to insert the beading needle directly into a stitch (just below the needle) and then push the needle to HP and back to WP so that the stitch drops from its needle onto the beading tool. By the same token, returning the stitches to their needles is easiest if you just hold the beading tool tautly above the needle and then poke the needle through the back of the stitch before removing the tool.

To add a bead to a knit stitch, insert the tip of the beading tool through the stitch and then move the needle forward and back in its slot so that the stitch slides off the needle and onto the beading tool.

To bead a tuck stitch, insert the tool in the second stitch below the needle so that when you drop the stitch onto the tool there is a float directly above it as shown in the photo below. Lift the float back onto the needle along with the beaded stitch. Beaded tuck stitches are useful with larger size beads.

Close the latch on the beading tool and slide a bead over the latch and onto the stitch. Tug lightly on the tool as you push the bead forward with your fingers.

Catch the stitch in the hook of the beading tool and lift it back onto the needle *or* just hold the stitch taut with the tool and poke the needle through it. Then remove the tool. Standard gauge yarns are more likely to fit comfortably in the hook of the tool than are bulky and mid-gauge yarns.

The second method of beading is useful for all-over and more random effects. The beads are all threaded onto a fine yarn or doubled strand of sewing thread before you begin and are woven through the stitches as you need them. The thread usually disappears into the fabric and the beads can be popped through to the knit side as you work or later on.

Many machines are able to automatically work knit-weave, with the pattern controlled by electronics or punch cards. In this case, dictating which needles the weaving yarn passes over or under as the carriage carries it in front and weaves it through the stitches that the main yarn forms at the same time. Depending on how closely the weaving is interlaced, you might be able to use purchased strands of beads and sequins. These yarns usually stabilize the beads by twisting two strands of thread or fine yarn together in a way that regularly traps the beads between the plies so that they stay put along the length of the yarn.

However, with large beads or those that you string yourself and are free to slide along the yarn, you will probably find it is easiest to manually weave the beaded strand through needles in HP prior to knitting any rows where you want to place some beads. You can feed the beads along the length of the thread as needed and space them however you want.

Chances are you will only want just so many beads, intermittently placed – certainly not in every single row – so this doesn't have to be a very time consuming manipulation. You can also periodically catch the weaving strand around an edge needle to bind it to the edge of the fabric. Just take care not to pull the thread holding the beads too tightly or there will not be enough slack for the beads to easily pop through to the knit side and for them to remain there.

In addition to beads, you can use these methods for working sequins, paillettes and decorative buttons into your fabrics. I like to use a double strand of matching thread and I usually wind up as much length as I can manage on a bobbin to keep it from tangling while I work.

Socks, Mittens and Hats

Hand knitters love small projects that work up quickly and make useful gifts and machine knitters are no different. Socks, mittens and all kinds of hats, scarves and shawls can be knitted on any machine. While ribbing does have its place for bands and the occasional ribbed toque, most knitters tend to rely on single bed machines for these projects.

First of all, it isn't possible to knit circular, seamless rib on any of the domestic machines. And, with the possible exception of the Passap, you cannot knit patterned fabric in the round either unless you are willing to do a whole lot of hand manipulations. Single bed machines have fewer of these limitations.

The obvious exception to this, of course, is a circular sock machine. Lots of hand knit sock enthusiasts eventually gravitate to these fascinating little machines so it is definitely an option if you want to quickly knit lots of socks. However, the method for knitting a sock on a cylindrical machine is totally different from the methods used on flat bed machines and not something I will include here. There are also circular hat machines if you want to knit lots of circular ribbed hats, but they do not knit automatic Fair Isle patterns either.

The following information is just a summary of information on knitting socks, mittens and hats on a machine. Please check out the free downloads (Tips & Techniques) on my web site (www.guagliumi.com) for patterns and more specific information.

Socks

You can knit socks on any knitting machine. The foot can be worked circular on a double bed machine or flat and seamed on a single bed machine. However, ribbing always needs to be seamed because it takes both beds to produce the rib structure and there is no possibility of working ribbing in the round.

Circular socks require the least amount of finishing and have a smooth, comfortable fit. However, with careful grafting and seaming, you can still knit beautiful, comfortable socks on a single bed machine. In addition to knitting the ribbing on a double bed machine, you do have the option to begin your socks on waste yarn and then pick up the top edge on double pointed needles to work the ribs by hand.

Heels and toes are shaped by short rows, just as they are by hand. You can take advantage of all the patterning capabilities of your machine, add cables or other hand-manipulated textures and play with color to your heart's content. Christmas stockings are great fun to make by machine because you can easily incorporate intarsia details or angora Fair Isle snowflakes and you don't have to confine yourself to special reinforced sock yarns.

If, however, you prefer to wear your socks, rather than hang them once a year, you should use a reinforced yarn to prevent the heels and soles from walking away after a few wearings. Many sock yarns are reinforced with some nylon, which also helps the washability. Most typically, sock yarns knit on standard gauge machines but there are also some heavier sock yarns now that are suitable for mid-gauge and bulky machines.

The method for knitting the foot of a sock is the same for ankle socks or knee high socks so in the following descriptions I'll assume that you plan to knit the ribs by hand on double pointed needles or by machine with a side or center back seam. Also, the longer the leg section, the more likely it is that you will want to shape it for a better fit, especially if it is worked in stockinet.

Double bed socks, worked in the round, are very similar to hand knit socks. The heel is turned on half the stitches, the instep/sole knitted for the desired length and then the toe is shaped by decreases or short rows and grafted closed.

Single bed socks are constructed a little differently as shown by the schematics on pages 78 – 79. The first two methods require grafting the heel and seaming both sides of the foot as well as the back of the rib. The third method is a little different because it produces a left or right sock with one continuous seam along one side of the foot and rib.

Regardless of whether you work single or double bed, the heel is turned in exactly the same way. You can use hand knit sock patterns for numbers of stitches, but will have to convert inches to row counts and you will either have to match the gauge in your hand knit pattern or be prepared to re–chart the pattern for *your* gauge.

Once you understand the basic methods for knitting socks on a machine, you should be able to follow most hand knitting patterns without too much difficulty. Granted, there are some unusual variations in heel gussets and other details (especially in ethnic patterns) but if you are able to understand what needs to be done by hand, the machine knit method should not seem all that different.

Tips & Techniques #37 is one of the free downloads on my web site and it explains how to size and chart socks according to your own measurements and your own gauge. T & T #15 is dedicated to Christmas stockings.

Heels and toes are usually (but not always) shaped on half the total number of stitches. By machine, that means scrapping off some of the other stitches (the first two methods) or placing them in hold (third method).

With the carriage on the left, I have just wrapped the last needle I placed in HP prior to knitting the last row and have brought 1 more needle to HP on the opposite side in preparation for knitting the next row.

After reducing down to 1/3 of the stitches, I began increasing by placing 1 needle on the side opposite the carriage into UWP prior to knitting each row.

Basic Socks

After knitting the leg portion of the sock, ¼ of the stitches are scrapped off at each side, leaving half the original number of stitches for knitting the instep, toe, and sole and then the heel. The toe and heel are shaped with short rows. Scrap off all the stitches at the end. After sewing the leg seam at center back, fold back the scrap at the sides of the leg and the end of the heel and graft the heel to the side sections. Sew the two side seams in the foot.

Gusseted Heel

This method is nearly identical to the first, except that the sole increases by 1" at each side over the last 3" of its length to form heel gussets. You will need to multiply by your gauge to know exactly how many stitches and rows to work. Scrap off the gusset stitches before shaping the heel itself with short rows. After shaping the heel, the gussets are joined at each side of the heel by picking up 1 gusset stitch and hanging it on the edge needle every row until they have all been hung. (see page 58) Scrap off the heel and finish this sock exactly like the first example.

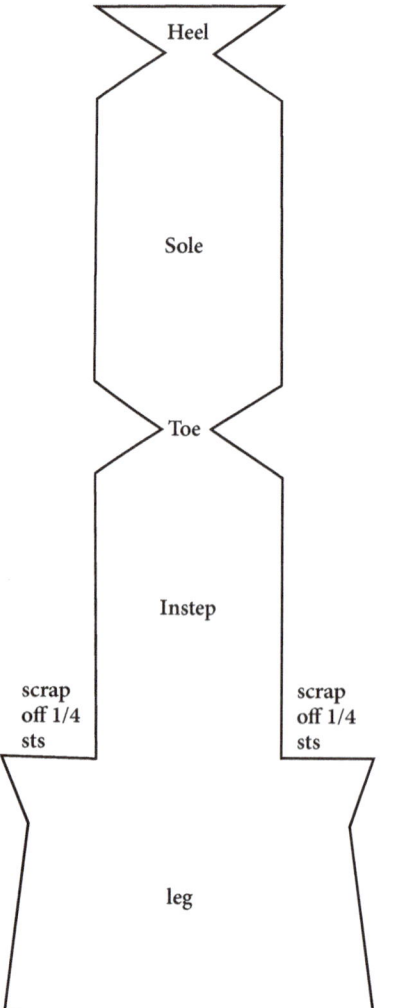

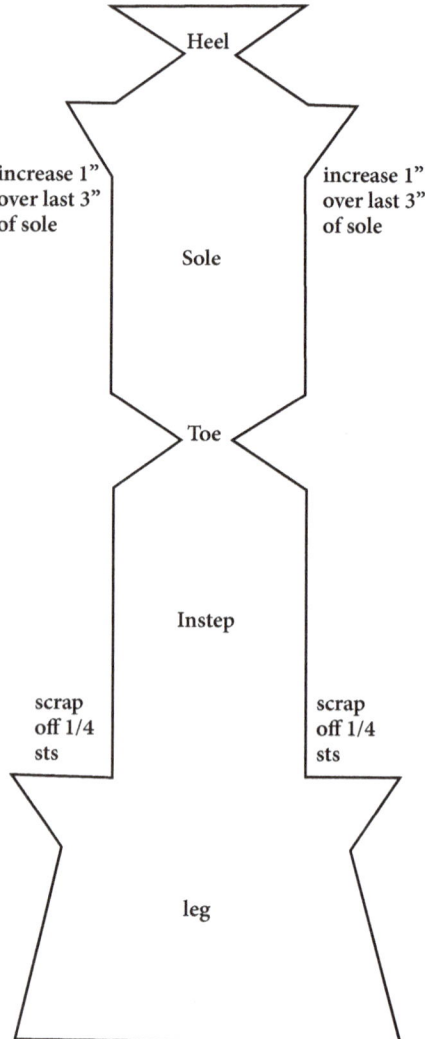

One Seam Sock

After knitting the leg portion (with or without shaping), half of the stitches (at left in my diagram) are placed in HP while the remaining stitches are used to short row the heel (at right). Once the heel is completed, all of the needles are returned to work to knit the instep and sole at the same time. The toe is shaped on half of the needles at the side opposite the heel and the remaining half of the needles are placed in HP while the toe is short rowed. Scrap off all the stitches. Fold the piece in half and graft the toe stitches to the sole stitches and then sew a continuous seam along one side of the foot and the leg. The second sock should be knitted with reversed shaping. The socks are worn with the seam on the inside of the leg/foot.

The side view of this turned heel shows the short row shaping quite clearly.

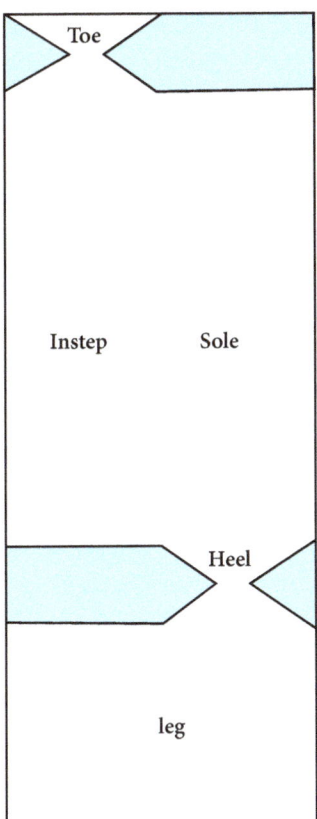

Turning a Heel

First, set the carriage to hold needles in HP. Heels are usually short rowed until only 1/3 of the heel stitches are still in WP and they are always short rowed equally at each side. You can begin with the carriage on either end of the bed for the first two construction methods described at right. For the third method, you should begin shaping the heel with the carriage on the right; the toe with the carriage on the left.

*Hold 1 stitch on the side opposite the carriage. Knit 1 row, wrap. Hold 1 stitch on the side opposite the carriage. Knit 1 row, wrap.** Repeat from * to** until 1/3 of the needles remain in WP. This sequence will decrease the heel by 1 stitch at each side every two rows.

When the heel has been short rowed down to the last third of the stitches, begin increasing with short rows as follows: *Return 1 needle on the side opposite the carriage to UWP, knit 1 row, wrap.** Repeat * to ** until all the heel needles are working again.

When short rowing either toes or heels, keep a claw weight underneath the working needles to make sure that all of the stitches knit cleanly. This is especially important when knitting double bed because you cannot see all of the stitches as clearly between the beds.

Mittens

Like socks, mittens can be worked single or double bed, but the ribbing will always have a seam. You can hang pre-knitted rib or just start on scrap and do the ribs later by hand.

Double Bed Mittens

To knit double bed mittens, you can begin on scrap or you can knit the ribs first, transfer all the stitches to one bed and then remove half of the stitches to rehang them opposite the first set of stitches on the other bed. Unless you have a decker comb with a snap-on cover to move the stitches, you'll need to scrap off and rehang the stitches.

Once you have stitches on both beds, you can knit the hand portion of the mitten circular. However, you need to make allowances for adding thumb stitches later on. I like using a strand of ravel cord or heavy cotton to manually knit across just the thumb stitches once and then tuck the ends of the cord down between the beds to continue working circular. The ravel cord stitches act as markers where you can pick up the stitches later to work the thumb. You can also work some rows half-circular and later pick up thumb stitches along the side edge of the mitten.

I've always felt that double bed mittens involved a lot more fussing that most mittens justify. So I always knit them single bed with two short side seams. It is much faster and easier. Again, please check my web site for Tips & Techniques #6, which gives detailed instructions for charting and knitting mittens in any size or gauge.

Single Bed Mittens

The diagram at left shows the basic shape of a single bed mitten. Note that the thumb stitches are increased at each side so that they stack up over each other in a straight line. I do this with full fashioned increases, moving 1 stitch over for the first increase, then 2 stitches for the second increase and so on. When complete, the thumb gusset is scrapped off to continue knitting the length of the hand. Later, the gusset stitches are picked up and rehung to finish knitting the thumb.

To finish the mittens, there is one seam that runs the length of the thumb and the ribbed cuff and another seam to close the remainder from the top to the point where the thumb joins the hand.

The tops of the thumb and the hand can be reduced by decreasing stitches gradually over the last few inches of the hand or the last few rows of the thumb. You can also knit straight to within 4 rows of the total length, double all the stitches by transferring every alternate stitch to its adjacent needle. Then place the empty needles in NWP and knit the next row with a reduced stitch size, twice. You could also use the garter bar to move all the stitches in to eliminate the empty needles.

Knitting mittens on a single bed is fast and easy and allows you to take full advantage of the patterning capabilities on your machine for Fair Isle and intarsia patterns, crossing cables and making popcorns. Well stitched seams disappear into the fabric.

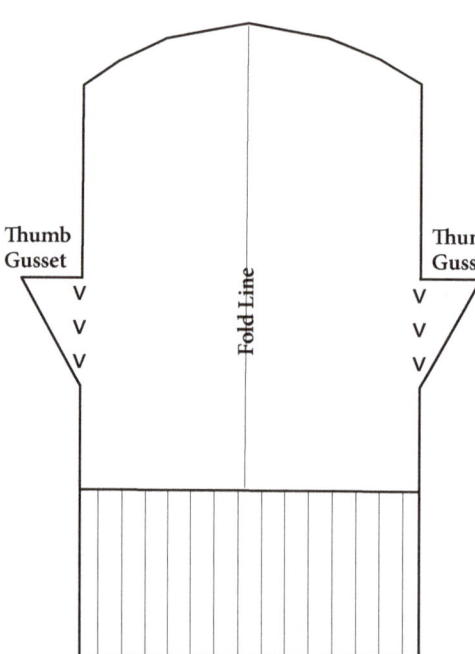

Single bed mittens have a seam that runs the length of the thumb and through the cuff. There is a second seam to close the side of the upper hand. The thumb gussets ensure a comfortable fit; once complete, the gussets are scrapped off. When the body of the mitten is complete, re-hang the gusset stitches to complete the thumbs.

You can also knit mittens (and socks and hats) with textured yarns or 100% wool that can be felted. Just make sure you take your gauge information after felting the swatch, not before!

Hats

There is no end to the shapes and styles that people put on their heads for fashion and warmth. However, the only hats that can be knitted seamlessly, in the round are those knitted in stockinet. Because it is not possible to work Fair Isle or Tuck or ribbing in the round, the majority of machine knit hats are knitted flat on single beds and then seamed.

For years, many of the hats sold for ski-wear were knitted by cottage industry knitters, working on single bed machines in their homes. Some of the best ones were knitted with deep hems, rather than ribs, that were knitted with 100% absorbent cotton on the inside. Not all hats need to begin with a ribbed band, but you can, of course, knit ribbed bands by machine or by hand if you do not have a ribber or if you want to work the rib as a circular band with no seam.

The crowns of machine knit hats can be shaped by the same methods that hand knitters employ. You can shape them gradually by well placed decreases, using a garter bar to distribute them across the row. You can also reduce just the last few rows of stitches to every other needle and then gather the last row of stitches tightly together.

Some hats, like berets, are knitted sideways with short rows. Tips and Techniques #22 gives a pattern for a textured hat with ear flaps. There is also a free pattern entitled "Loopity Lou" on my web site that utilizes an unusual construction method and is loaded with interesting techniques. Even if neither of these two hats is your cup of tea style-wise, don't just skip over them. Both patterns are loaded with techniques and information, which is the most important thing about any pattern.

Scarves and Shawls

Scarves and shawls are some of the simplest project to knit and they provide an easy format for showcasing all kinds of techniques.

Double bed scarves tend to lie flat because of the underlying rib structures you can use to knit them. Even just a few well-placed rib stitches near each selvage edge–formed with a ribber or by latching them up– will prevent the fabric from rolling back on itself.

Single bed scarves, on the other hand, are plagued by rolling edges and unless you want to knit your scarves twice as wide and seam them up the back, you do need to take action to prevent the roll.

You can always add a crocheted edge to your scarves. I usually find that a row of backwards crochet does the best job of stabilizing the curl, but there are lots of stitches – some decorative, some not so much – that will do the trick.

Machine knitting books and patterns are loaded with suggestions to prevent rolled edges and everyone has their favorites. The two that I use most often and with the greatest success are I-cord edgings and cabled selvages. In addition to keeping the fabric flat, I-cord doesn't detract from the body of the project while cabled selvages add a decorative element.

I-Cord Edges

I use two different methods for I-cord edges. The first knits the corded edging (at one or both selvages) while the body of the garment is knitted. The second method is applied later.

The integrally knitted I-cord edge is fast and automatic on machines with needle selection because you can program the machine to slip the first 3 or 4 needles at each edge when the carriage travels in one direction and to knit them in the other.

However, even if you work on a simple manual machine, you can work an integral I-cord edge by setting the carriage to hold needles in HP when traveling in one direction and to knit them back on the return pass. Then, just move 3 or 4 needles at each edge to HP and knit 2 rows. If your carriage cannot automatically return needles from HP, knit 1 row and then just nudge the edge needles back to UWP so they return to WP with the next pass of the carriage. Alternating this two-row sequence will create I-cord at the edges as the slips are absorbed into the edge stitches.

Depending on the yarn, this edge may not roll at all even though the I-cord tends to pull towards the purl side of the work. To be sure, knit and then steam or wash your swatch before you commit a whole garment to this method. I find that the edges lose any tendency to roll if I latch up a single stitch adjacent to the I-cord as shown in the photographs below.

You can also apply I-cord by re-hanging the edge of your finished scarf on the machine and following the directions for the I-cord bind off on page 54. Rather than just picking up a single edge stitch from the selvage of a finished piece to join it as the I-cord is knitted, I find that it causes less strain on the stitches to hang the whole edge (or as much as you have room for) on the machine and then place needles into HP and treat it as a bind off instead. I usually find that an applied I-cord edging looks best when worked with the knit side of the scarf facing you. But, as always, do a swatch.

I worked a 3-stitch I-cord at each edge of the swatch below. However, I latched up one adjacent stitch next to the I-cord stitches at the right edge as seen from the knit side of the fabric (left side in back view). This single latched up stitch eliminates any tendency of the edge to curl; the edge without the latched up stitch lies fairly flat, but still wants to turn under slightly.

Cabled Edges

For years, out of habit, whenever I placed a cable at the edge of a scarf or other flat project, I always allowed two extra stitches for a latched up stitch on the second needle

from the edge. I think I figured that these two stitches would act as rib and prevent the fabric from rolling. Which they did, but required extra time and effort.

Not so long ago I decided to eliminate the two extra stitches and to try involving the edge stitches themselves in the cable. I was delighted to find that it worked even better in preventing the fabric from curling under and that the edge was far more decorative because it takes on the curves of the cables.

If you try to cross edge cables on the carriage side, you will trap the free yarn (the yarn between the carriage and the first stitch) on the front of the cable unless you bother to lift it out of the way every time you return the second set of stitches to the needles. The float is unavoidable on the carriage side because the edge stitch remains connected to the carriage by the free yarn and once you cross the stitches, the first stitch is then 3 needles (for example) from the edge of the knitting and so is the free yarn. It lies underneath the first 3 empty needles and if you just replace the second group of stitches on those needles, the yarn remains trapped on the front where it shows.

If, on the other hand, you only cross cables on the side opposite the carriage, there are no floats to worry about. The cable crossings at each edge will be one row off from each other, but probably not detectable by the keenest eye.

In my example below, you might notice that the left edge of the fabric does not lie quite as flat as the right edge. This is because the cable at that edge was crossed out and then in, while the better cable crossed in, towards the fabric, before crossing out. It is a small difference that has to do with the tension on the stitches. The cable at left was also peskier to cross.

So, when crossing a 3 x 3 stitch cable, for example, at the right edge of the work, the right–most group of 3 stitches should cross to the left (in) and then the second group of 3 stitches to the right (out towards the edge). Conversely, when crossing a cable at the left edge, cross to the right (in) and then to the left (out). Or, to put it another way, always cross in towards the center of the fabric and then out towards the edge, regardless of which side you are working on.

Sandwich Bands

One of my favorite finishes for bound off, selvage and "cut and sew" edges is a band that totally encloses the edges in a sandwich of fabric.

Cut and sew is an especially useful way of working lots of pattern without having to interrupt anything to shape the neckline. Instead, you just knit straight to the shoulders and after blocking the garment piece, mark the neckline with chalk or a basting stitch. Then you stitch along the marker with a regular zig–zag sewing machine or a serger and cut away the extra fabric. It's a method that is employed in industry – even with some high priced cashmere knitwear.

Needless to say, a cut and sew edge isn't beautiful and needs to be hidden somehow and a sandwich band is the usual answer.

I scrapped off this band so you could see the details more clearly. In practice, you would knit the whole band and leave it on the machine to join it to the garment.

However, there are other times when a doubled band like this adds body and shape to bound off edges as well. With the addition of some buttonholes, a sandwich band makes an excellent finish for a cardigan and a narrow band with a picot edge is sometimes a better neckline finish than ribbing. You can even apply these bands to the edge of a woven fabric if you'd like to try combining knits and wovens for a special project.

If you want to try a sandwich band with buttonholes, there are detailed directions in Tips & Techniques #26 on my web site. The following directions and photographs detail the method for joining any sandwich band to a garment right on the machine.

Knit the band first, over the number of needles necessary for hanging the fabric edge. I usually just poke the edge of onto the needles to determine the number of needles, but you can measure the neckline and then multiply by your stitch gauge to see how many needles it translates into. Keep in mind that you need to join one shoulder seam first and then knit and apply the band to the entire neckline. The back neckline usually requires fewer needles than the front so you need to either poke or do the math for the entire neckline.

This band was only knitted for 3 rows. Then I worked a row of eyelets to create a decorative fold before knitting 3 more rows for the inside of the band.

This band is wider (7 rows on each side) and uses a garter ridge to create the fold.

Begin the band with waste yarn then change to the main yarn and knit enough rows for the inside depth of the band. To create a sharper fold line, you can work two turns with the garter bar, a row of picots by transferring every other stitch to the adjacent needle or one row with a very large stitch size. Then knit the outside of the band and leave the band on the machine. Do not cut the yarn.

Some people knit the inside of the band with a slightly smaller stitch size to help the band lie flatter and to pull it slightly to the inside so it can't flare. Work a sandwich band on one edge of your gauge swatch so you can work out the details before you begin the garment.

Before you begin joining the band to the garment, cover the needle bed with some paper towels or fabric to avoid getting oil on your garment. (I didn't do this for my photos so you could more clearly see what I was doing, but I *would* do this for a full garment.)

Lay your garment on top of the needle bed with the right side facing up and the neckline even with the front of the bed. Begin poking a few needles through the fabric, about ¼" from the edge, pushing them out to UWP so the band will enclose any sewing machine stitching and to be sure there is enough "meat" in the sandwich to support the band.

I specified bound off edges and working 1/4" from the edge because although you *could* attach a sandwich band to live stitches held on scrap, it wouldn't look or function very well. The band will out-weigh the edge of the fabric and flop around.

I usually begin by poking a couple of needles through the fabric at the center and at each edge first to position the fabric and then I poke the remaining needles through. (1) If you want, you can poke the fabric over the sinker posts/gate pegs first and then push the needles through. You'll just have to lift the fabric off the posts in a later step.

Once all of the needles are poked through the neckline and in UWP, fold back the scrap on the lower edge of the band to expose the first row of stitches. Hang them on the needles above (2) and then pull the needles out to HP.

With the yarn that is still attached to the band, manually knit each of the needles back to a position half way between NWP and WP to create over-sized stitches for the bind off.(3)

To keep the stitches even, I lay a ¼" wooden dowel across the back of the bed, in front of the needle butts in NWP. Then, as I manually knit each of the needles, I push them back until they bump into the dowel. This ensures that all the stitches are the same size. You have to reach under the garment with one hand to move the needle butts back while the other hand feeds yarn into the hook of each needle.

Make sure there *is* yarn in the hook of each needle before the latch closes so that you don't drop any stitches in the process. Don't try to put yarn in several needle hooks to knit them back as a group. It seldom works without dropping stitches and when it does, the stitches are too tight to be useful.

4

Once all of the stitches have been knitted back, cut the yarn, leaving a 6" tail. Carefully lift the garment off the bed and flip it towards you so that you can see the stitches in the needles. (4) If you initially poked the fabric onto the sinker posts, lift it off now, using a transfer tool if necessary so that you don't drop any of the enlarged stitches from their needles. Beginning on the side opposite the yarn tail, use the latch tool to chain one stitch through the other, locking the end of the chain by pulling the cut end of the yarn through the last stitch.

You can work this chain with the needles in WP, but I find it faster and easier to manage if I bring the needles to HP first. Then I just poke the hook of the latch tool through the next stitch, push the needle back to WP so the stitch lands in the hook of the tool and I pull the new stitch through the old one.

Normally, a yarn-less chain like this would be too tight to be useful, but this works because the stitches are manually knitted to a much larger size (than the carriage could knit with any stitch size). The chain effect is normally positioned on the inside of the garment and the "back-stitched" effect used on the outside, but if you want to switch that, just position the garment with the wrong side facing up when you start.

If you want a more decorative band, you can add lace or another trim by poking it onto the needles on top of the garment edge, before hanging the second edge of the band. Lots of commercial trims have holes or open work that will fit nicely over the needles or you might want to add a trim you crochet or knit yourself.

Hand-Manipulated Textures

I don't want to re-write *Hand-Manipulated Stitches for Machine Knitters,* but I do want to give you some basic information about three of my favorite texture stitches: popcorns (bobbles), cables and twisted stitches.

Popcorns or Bobbles

Let me begin by saying that the following method is probably the easiest to understand when it comes to knitting popcorns. It is a good place to start, but it is not the method I generally use. Instead, I use a method that involves bridging from one group of needles to the next so that I don't have to knit any of the stitches manually. The "Loopity Loo" hat pattern, which is another free download on my web site, explains that method in detail.

Although I knitted my sample with yellow popcorns, unless I wanted the contrast, I would normally knit them in the same yarn I use for the body of the garment. If you look at the photos carefully, you might see a little color "grin through" between the popcorns. Depending on the yarn and your gauge, there could be more or less of it, but when worked in one color throughout, you won't see any.

Loose Ends 87

These popcorns were all worked by manually knitting a separate strand of yarn back and forth across 2 needles. Because I wanted to work across the bed from one popcorn to the next, I knitted an odd number of rows (5) for each popcorn, then carried the yarn across the back of the work to the next one.

The last row of the main knitting (before the popcorn rows) needs to be lifted back onto the needles, forcing the 5 popcorn rows out to the knit side of the fabric and creating the signature bump of a bobble. You can lift each popcorn as you go or wait and do them all at once after the last one is completed.

To finish each popcorn, use a single prong transfer tool to lift the stitches that were originally on the needles back into their hooks. It is almost like the yellow rows never happened when you look at the purl side. However, those 5 extra rows are pushed out on the knit side as popcorns.

I have already completed a row of popcorns at the bottom of this swatch and one at the left in the current row. I've knitted the first of five 2–stitch rows over the pair of needles at right. Note the lifted float in the row of popcorns below.

To help the popcorns pop, once the fabric is off the machine, use the tip of a transfer tool to give each popcorn a gentle tug.

All 5 rows have been knitted on the 2 needles at right.

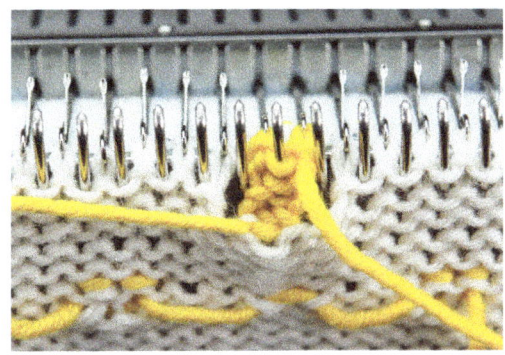

Because my popcorns were 7 needles apart, I lifted the float between each one onto an empty needle to bind it to the back of the fabric. This is the stitch that causes the "grin through" on the front of the fabric. With contrasting bobbles, you can eliminate hanging the floats to avoid the grin through if the floats are not more than and inch or so.

Cables

The most important thing to know about crossing cables on a machine is that *the first stitches returned to their needles will show on the knit side of the fabric and define the direction of the cross.* When working from a hand knit chart, remember that the chart shows the stitches that are on the front of each cable and that the direction is actually reversed when working on a machine.

So, a hand knit chart that shows a cable crossing from lower right to upper left will be worked on the machine by crossing the left group of stitches to the right needles first.

It often doesn't matter whether a column of cables crosses right or left as long as they all cross the same way. However, when individual cables join to form larger motifs or when they are placed to highlight other patterning or texture, the direction does matter.

Initially, you will find that 2 x 2 or 3 x 3 cables are the easiest to manage on a machine. You will also find that cables knitted in wool and wool blended yarns cross more easily than do those worked in cotton, linen or many synthetics. With experience, you will be able to cross really large cables in almost any fiber, but initially you can make things much easier on yourself by sticking to stretchy yarns and 3 x 3 cables at the most.

When I cross cables, I generally replace the first set of stitches on the needles and leave those needles in WP. However, when I replace the second set of stitches, I use the transfer tool to pull those needles out to HP so that the carriage can knit them back more easily on the next pass. This is especially important when working with very wide cables or less stretchy yarns.

Keep in mind that when you cross cables on a machine, the needles are somewhat flexible. Although the stitches do stretch and give a little, they tend to pull the needles together, which makes them a little harder for the carriage to knit.

With extremely tight cables or unforgiving yarn I bring all the needles holding crossed stitches out to HP and then I nudge them back to UWP where they are not drawn as closely together and knit even easier.

Some knitters advocate leaving an empty needle along each side of a cable, but I have never found it necessary and I don't like the way a ladder looks there. I do, however often latch up a stitch at each side of my cables.

That said, 4 x 4 and larger cables will probably require some extra tricks to make sure they knit smoothly and easily, without snapping

One stitch at the left of this cable was reformed to help the cable stand out from the background.

The hand knit chart below left indicates the stitches that will show on the front of the cable with the darker, unbroken lines. The machine knit chart at right represents the same cable by showing the dark, *broken* lines for the first stitches placed on the needles. This is how the stitches appear as you look at the purl side of the fabric.

Loose Ends 89

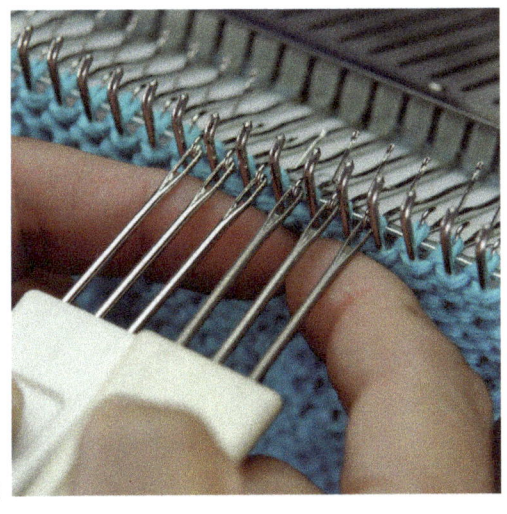

1

2

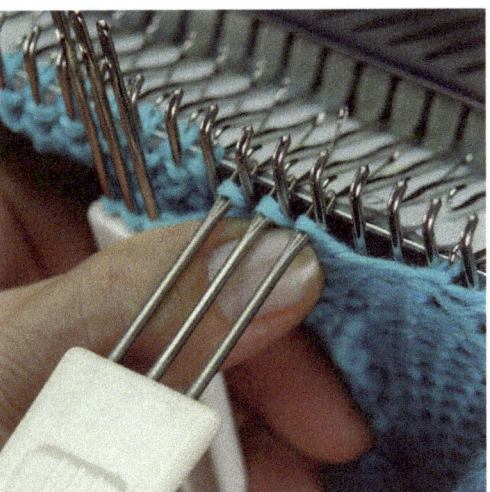

4

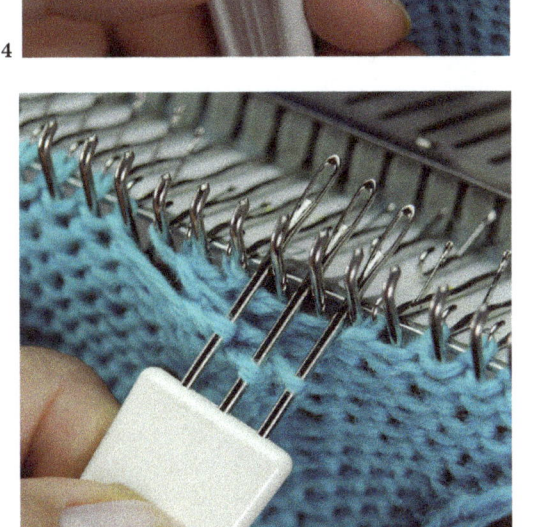

5

(1) Whenever I remove stitches with transfer tools, I use my index fingers to keep the fabric back against the bed as I move the needles forward and back to transfer the stitches onto the tools

(2) For safety sake, always keep the stitches as far back on the tools as you can.

(3) Hold the left tool off to the side while you move the stitches from the right hand tool onto the left group of needles. Sometimes I even hook the left tool onto the needles at the side so I can use two hands to manage the other tool. Then I just unhook the left tool when I want to move those stitches.

(4–5) Depending on how many stitches you move in each group there will be some resistance as you replace the second set of stitches. A little tension is actually a good thing as it helps shape the cables

(6) When you place the second set of stitches on the needles, use the tool to pull the needles right out to HP. If the needles are *very* close together when you do so, just nudge them back to UWP before knitting the row.

3

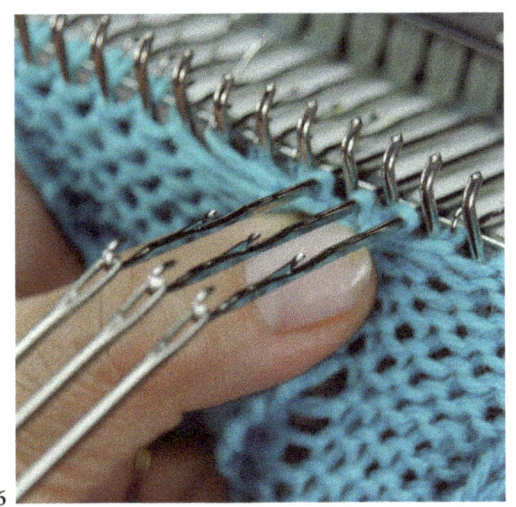

6

stitches or jamming the carriage. Once you have had some experience with cables, you might find the information in my book, *More Hand-Manipulated Stitches*, helpful for crossing larger, more elaborate cables. That book focuses exclusively on "bridging" a technique that enables you to control the size of each and every stitch on the machine and to do things you didn't know were possible by machine!

Twisted Stitches

This is probably my favorite ways to manipulate stitches on a machine. It's fast and easy and you get an awful lot of texture for very little effort. The end result looks like little 1 x 1 cable crosses, but the method is very different from crossing cables. It also very different from the way that hand knitters work twisted stitches by knitting the second stitch on the left hand needle and then the first stitch, releasing them both at the same time.

Please keep in mind that there are lots of ways to twist stitches on a machine, but they do not all equate to hand knit twisted stitches. I covered twisted stitches in detail in *HMS*, but the following guidelines should be enough get you started with the kind of twisted stitches that are the hand knit equivalent.

First of all, you'll need two 2-prong transfer tools to twist the pairs of stitches. The basic method is pretty straightforward: Remove two stitches on one tool (1), insert the second tool from above the stitches (2) and then remove the first tool. (3)

In order to return the stitches to the needles, you will have to rotate the tool either to the left or the right (4) for the prongs to face in the correct direction. That twist of the tool de-

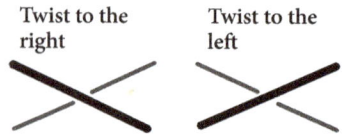

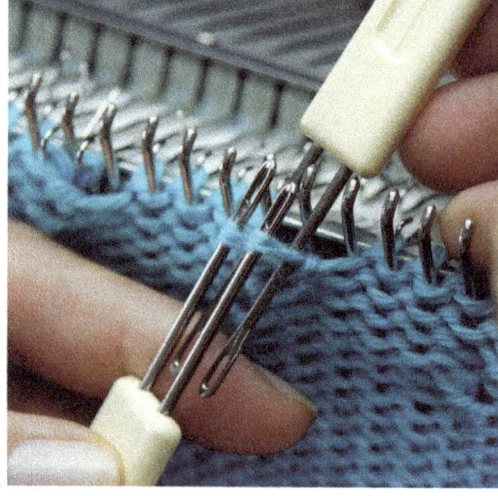

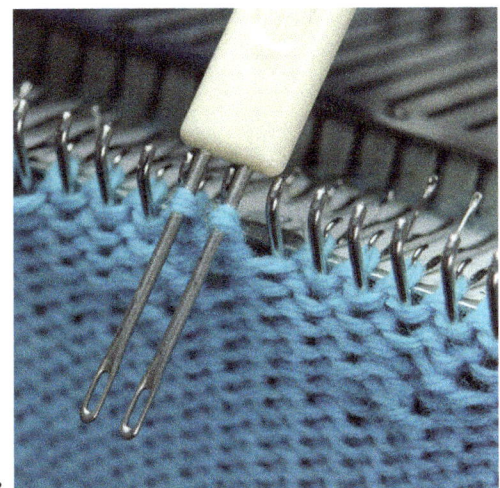

3

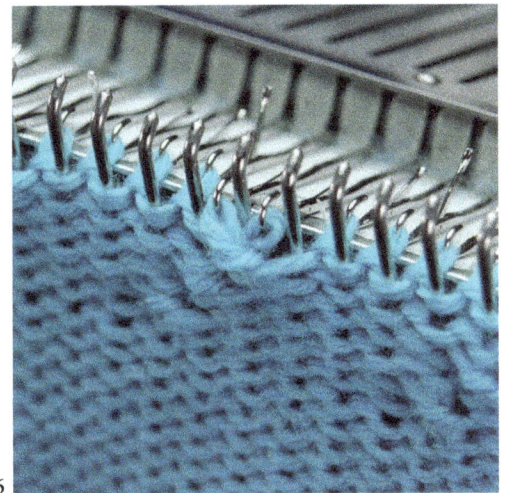

6

4

5

fines the twist of the stitches. Once the stitches are returned to the needles (5) knit two rows.

When working vertical columns of twisted stitches, it won't matter whether they twist to the left or to the right. However, if you want the stitches to travel across the face of the fabric, you must rotate the tool in the direction the stitches travel (as viewed from the purl side of the fabric as you work). So, if your stitches are moving towards the right, you should always rotate the tool to the right, which will produce a *left* twist while rotating the tool to the left will produce a right twist on the knit side of the fabric.

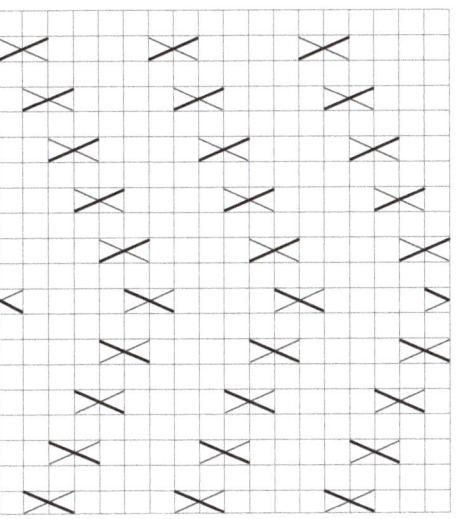

The darker line indicates the stitch you can see on the purl side of the work, while the lighter line is the stitch that shows on the knit side. Although the stitches are traveling to the right (bottom of chart) the dark lines slant left. However, the front stitches are in agreement with the direction: both the traveling and the slant of the stitches is to the right.

You will be able to follow what you are doing by looking at the purl side of the work, but if the twists look really good on the purl side of the work, chances are they are wrong on the knit side. The effect on the purl side is more of a ghost impression – there are no smooth lines. (6)

In order to make stitches "travel" in a continuous line, each successive pair of stitches that you choose to twist should include the last stitch of the previous twist and a new stitch to the right (for example).

Using Hand Knit Patterns

Most of us are drawn first to the looks of a particular sweater and photos of the garment can often give you a rough idea whether or not a particular design can be worked on the machine.

Chances are, however, that you'll need to start reading the pattern itself to find out what is required. First and foremost is the yarn that the pattern calls for. Is it a yarn that you think will knit on your machine? If not, are you prepared to substitute a thinner, thicker or less textured yarn and to re-chart the pattern accordingly?

Is the stitch pattern one that your machine is capable of doing automatically? Can it be hand manipulated instead? Will it require any special equipment, like a ribber or an intarsia carriage or any specialized tools? If you don't have a ribber, can you work the ribbing by hand or substitute another kind of band?

In the first chapter of this book I explained some of the capabilities and limitations of various machines so you should be able to determine if a particular pattern falls within the range that you or your machine are capable of doing. For example, with Fair Isle pattern knitting, the number of stitches per repeat may be a problem if you work on a punch card machine. Still other pattern stitches may not be possible at all on a machine, but there might be alternatives that are more doable.

Sometimes it is a simple matter of not having enough needles on the bed to accommodate pattern pieces and, in that case, you'll need to re-chart the garment in sections. A garment knitted in the round will have to be reworked with a separate front and back.

Matching Gauge

These are some of the most basic questions you'll need to ask yourself, but the issue I encounter the most often is that of matching gauge. Assuming the yarn a pattern calls for is appropriate for your machine, you will probably be able to match the stitch gauge without much difficulty. Row gauges are not so easily matched and will probably cause you the most concern.

Hand knitters can tweak their row gauge by changing needle size and sometimes it is as simple as changing from a metal needle to a wooden one the same size. On a machine, you can adjust the tension on the tension unit and vary the number of weights that you use, but if those measures don't help, you will probably need to re-chart the pattern for *your* gauge.

For years, machine knitters relied on charting attachments that made it possible to knit absolutely any shape you could draw. Known as Knit Leaders, Knit Contours and Formas, these are ingenious devices that allow you to follow an outline of your garment in ¼, ½ or full scale, depending on the brand and style of the attachment. Some machines even had these devices built into them because they were really indispensable in the days before computers.

Since the introduction of programs like Garment Styler and DAK, these old-school charting attachments seem to have gone out of favor, but there are several things that charting attachments and computer programs have in common. They all rely on you to enter accurate stitch and row gauge information and they utilize a visual schematic to guide you.

You don't have to be a math whizz to make adjustments to knitting patterns, but you do have to be comfortable thinking of stitches and rows as inches (or centimeters). If you are not mathematically inclined, you should probably invest in either a charting attachment or a computer program to help you because you are bound to find that you will have to re-chart many of the hand knit patterns you want to knit on the machine.

Schematics

I rely heavily on having a schematic diagram of any garment I want to knit. If a pattern doesn't supply a schematic as part of the directions, I create one by sketching a large outline of each garment piece and then supplying all the information I can glean from the verbal directions. When I do this, I am not interested in stitch patterning, just those directions that affect the size and shape of each piece.

Once I have written all the information on my schematic, I turn any length measurements into row counts by multiplying the number of inches by my stitch gauge.

In any instance where a number of rows is listed, rather than a measurement, I first divide by the pattern's row gauge to determine the measurement and then multiply by my gauge if it is different from the pattern's.

Knitters sometimes convince themselves it sometimes won't matter very much if a sweater ends up being an inch or two too long or short and they often reason that it "will fit somebody!" The truth is that row gauge is crucial not just for knitting garments the correct body length, but, more importantly, to guarantee that you are able to increase sleeves where the increases are distributed evenly along the length of the sleeve; to make sure that necklines are neither too short nor too long to fit correctly. Row gauge is, in short, a big deal.

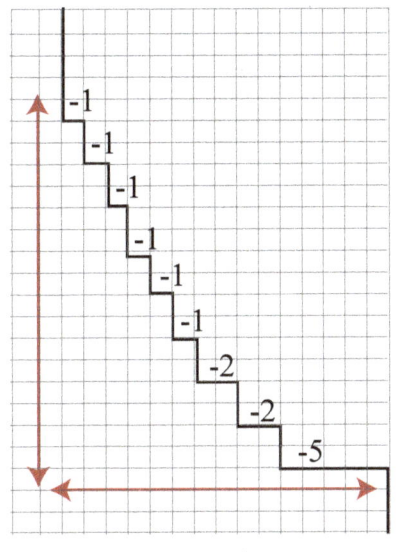

$$\frac{18 \text{ rows}}{7 \text{ rows/inch}} = 2.57"$$

$$\frac{15 \text{ stitches}}{5 \text{ stitches/inch}} = 3"$$

There are whole books about charting sweaters (my favorite is *Designing Knitwear* by Deborah Newton) but there are a couple of things you can do to accommodate variations in row gauge.

First of all, determine how deep and how high the armhole of a garment is supposed to be. For example, if a pattern's gauge is 5 stitches/7 rows per inch and the armhole is shaped by decreasing a total of 15 stitches (maybe -5, 2, 2, 1 x 6) with the decreases made every other row, you can determine the size of the armhole quite easily.

To find the depth of the armhole, dividing 15 stitches by 5 stitches per inch tells us that the armhole is 3" deep. The decreases in this example were made in 9 steps, with a row between each, totaling 18 rows. Dividing 18 rows by 7 rows per inch tells us that the decreases need to be made over a total length of 2.57".

Now, whatever row gauge I use to knit my sweater I know exactly how deep and how high to make the armhole and only have to multiply these measurements by my gauge.

You can round off the measurement of the armhole depth from 2.57" to 2.5". However, I have gotten into the habit of never rounding off *any* measurements or stitch or row counts until the very end of my calculations. A calculator makes it effortless to do the math so you can easily work with fractions until the very last step. You can't cast on 120.5 stitches and it won't matter whether you round it up or down by 1 number.

An extra stitch or row (or a couple less) won't change the size or shape of the garment enough to notice when you work with a finer gauge like 8 stitches/10 rows per inch. However, *the coarser your gauge, the more important it is to be as accurate as possible.*

Necklines are re-figured the same way, but make sure you determine how many inches below the end of the knitting to begin shaping the neckline as well as how many rows the decreases are spaced over.

The Magic Formula

Re-figuring increases along a sleeve can be challenging, but the "Magic Formula" is the best way to do it. I understand the *how* of the math involved here, but I can honestly tell you that I don't exactly understand the *why*. I will also tell you that there are several Magic Formula calculators on the Internet that will do all the math for you. Just do a search for "Magic Formula calculators" and take your pick. Obviously, if you use Garment Styler or DAK, this is part of the calculations these programs do automatically.

That said, here is the Magic Formula the way that I first learned it. In this example, I need to increase 16 increases (at each side) over 100 rows. Because there shouldn't be an increase on either the first or last row, you actually need to account for 17 spaces.

So, the first step is to divide 17 into 100. The answer is 5 times. The "85" (5 x 17) is subtracted from 100, with 15 left over. This is pretty standard long division so far.

```
      5
17 ) 100
     -85
      15
```

From here on, however, the math takes a couple of strange turns and this is where the "why" of it all eludes me. First, you need to subtract 15 (the remainder) from 17 (the divisor), leaving 2.

```
         5
    17 ) 100
  -15   -85
    2    15
```

You also need to add "1" to the answer at the top so 5 & 1 = 6. The plus 1 has to do with providing spaces before and after the first and last increases.

```
         5 + 1 = 6
    17 ) 100
  -15   -85
    2    15
```

Connecting things up, we find that we need to increase 1 stitch every 5th row twice (+1 5/R x 2) and 1 stitch every 6 rows 15 times (+1 6/R x 15).

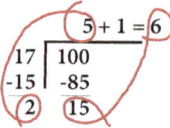

However, we need to make the last number 14 instead of 15 because of the extra 1 we added at the beginning. Like I said, I understand the How, but not all of the Why. Nonetheless, it works every time.

To double-check myself, I just add up the
number of stitches and the number of rows:

+1 5/R x 2 =   2 stitches increased   5/R x 2 = 10 rows
+1 6/R x 14 = 14 stitches increased   6/R x 14 = 84 rows
              16 stitches increased   94 rows with 6 rows
                                                    after the last increase

PART TWO

Lace

Mosaic Knitting

Entrelac

Modular Knitting

Lace

lace

lās/noun

1. a fine open fabric, typically one of cotton or silk, made by looping, twisting, or knitting thread in patterns and used especially for trimming garments.

It's really amazing what a few well-placed decreases and yarn overs can create! In hand knitting, there are endless ways of increasing and decreasing stitches and forming eyelets in the process. The options are a little more limited with machine knit lace and there is a big difference between hand-manipulated lace and the fabric that an automatic lace carriage can produce.

Most of the Japanese standard and fine gauge machines had lace carriages available as an optional accessory, but the European machines never did. That said, all machines are capable of hand manipulated lace and there are lacy *effects* that can be achieved by transferring stitches from one bed to the other, skipping needles or by knitting a thread along with a heavier yarn. While these fabrics look lacy and are covered in most manuals, they are not the equivalent of hand knitted lace, which is built upon increases, decreases and yarn overs and they will not be addressed here.

Many hand knit lace patterns can be knitted by machine and although we may tend to think of lace as "delicate" knitting, when worked on mid-gauge and bulky machines, the garments are bold and extremely fashionable. However, because there have never been lace carriages available for mid-gauge or bulky machines, all lace must be worked with hand transfers on these machines.

Charts vs. Verbal Directions

In order to convert hand knit patterns to the machine, you simply must have a chart to work with. Verbal directions can be very confusing, especially when you need to read them as hand knit and then convert them to the machine. If a pattern is not charted, use the hand knit verbal directions to make a chart for the hand knit version first.

In an effort to make lace charts less dense and easier to read, some hand knit charts leave empty squares to represent the knit, background stitches. For machine knitters, the purl stitches form the working background. So, there is often a lot of white space on lace charts because they commonly indicate only the actionable stitches, not those that remain in the same position throughout

Most hand knit patterns show only the lace transfer rows because the rows between are understood to be plain purl rows. However, if there are knits and purls in the same row to create a background or an outline for the lace, they are usually shown on the chart. The chart (or verbal directions) will also indicate how many rows to knit between transfer rows.

In the hand knit chart at 107, purl stitches are indicated at each side of the cable and lace columns. In order for those stitches to be purls on the *right* side of the fabric, they must be re-formed as knit stitches on the machine.

In hand knitting, the yarn overs are formed in the same row with the decreases; on a machine, whether you make the transfers by hand-manipulations or a lace carriage, the emptied needles remain in WP so that they can form yarn overs with the next pass of the carriage. Silver Reed Simple Lace is an exception because the eyelets and decreases are knitted in the same row.

Many times a decrease and the eyelet it forms are several stitches apart. The eyelet and the decrease can both be made in the same row with hand manipulated lace, but this requires numerous transfer rows when using a lace carriage. The chart must be expanded to account for these extra rows which is why lace charts converted from a hand knit pattern often bear little resemblance to the original chart.

Keep in mind that hand knit lace charts always show the knit side of the fabric and that the design will be reversed if you convert it for a lace carriage without reversing it first. Most of the time, it won't matter, but if a design simply *must* face left or right to be correct, I find that the fastest and least confusing way to reverse a chart is to scan it into the computer where I can reverse it with the click of a mouse. Copy machines can also reverse images, which saves time and prevents possible mistakes in re-copying a chart by hand.

Limitations on Machine Knit Lace

The Number of Stitches Counts

There are a couple of things you need to evaluate as you choose hand knit lace patterns to convert for the machine because not all lace designs will be suitable.

First of all, patterns that have a different number of stitches from one row to the next are a problem for automatic lace carriages because they do not make increases–only decreases and yarn overs. Neither do they return unused needles to NWP.

There are, however, some patterns in this category that are quite doable when worked as hand-transferred lace. The lace leaf trim on page 120 is a good example, but if you study the row-by-row directions for this 18-row pattern you will see that it promises to be slow, intense work. Then again, even by hand, this is not speedy, mindless knitting; it would not be possible at all with a lace carriage.

The leaf trim is meant to be picked up or added to a garment edge so you only have to knit enough repeats of the pattern to span the bottom edge of a sweater, for example, or to en-circle a neckline. An all-over design that required this much intervention would be much less practical.

The second thing to consider is the number of stitches in each repeat of the pattern. This is important if you use a punch card machine and lace carriage because the design *must* satisfy the repeat requirements of the punch card. Electronic machines are able to accommodate any number of stitches while hand-manipulated lace is governed only by your patience and dexterity.

Centering motifs and repeats on a machine is actually a lot easier than it is by hand because you can rely on the numbers on the bed when working hand-manipulations. Also, punch card and electronic machines have isolation cams or pins that can be positioned on the bed or on the back rail of the machine to center and/or limit the repeats. These cams/pins are also essential in making sure that the edge stitches of the fabric are not transferred to non-existent needles beyond the established edge of the fabric.

Knit and Purl stitches

Some, though not all, lace patterns visually benefit from having purl stitches surrounding knit stitches to make the motifs stand out clearly. Unfortunately, none of the lace carriages can be used with a ribber for double bed knitting. This means that any hand knit lace designs with both knit and purl stitches in the same row will require re-forming select stitches. If the stitches can be reformed in a straight column, like the example at 107, it is easy to do at reasonable intervals like every 10–12 rows.

If, rather than vertical columns of ribbed stitches, the placement of the re-formed stitches keeps changing, you will likely need to reform some stitches after every row to ensure that you still have access to them. That is typically the case when motifs widen, thus blocking access to the stitches below them.

Most people find it difficult to see what they are doing when they perform hand transfers with the ribber bed raised, but it is an option that might be worth exploring if there are more ribbed stitches than transferred stitches and if you are knitting on a mid-gauge or bulky machine. Keep in mind, however, that the ribber is only helpful if the same stitches are always ribbed. None of the machines are able to automatically convert stitches from knit to purl from bed to bed, row after row.

Let me caution you about latching up stitches next to an eyelet. Pay special attention to how the yarn interlaces and crosses next to the eyelets as you drop the stitches or column of stitches so that, when you latch them back up, their position doesn't change and affect the shape of the eyelets.

Obviously, there is a point where the number of stitches requiring re-forming is just not practical for an all-over design. Like the leaf example, however, it might be just fine for a border or trim. The practicality will be defined by your needs and patience, but it is a factor that needs to be considered when choosing lace designs beyond those that are provided specifically for machine knitting and it is an issue that arises fairly often.

Yarns

For hand transferred lace stitches, you can use whatever yarn is suitable for your machine. Mohair, ribbon and some novelties knit beautiful lace on bulky and mid-gauge machines, although you may need to bring needles holding more than one stitch to HP to make sure they knit cleanly. Wool/rayon blends, fine mohair and cashmere can be used on the standard gauge machines. However, on some machines, you may not be able to rely on the lace carriage to knit needles holding several fuzzy stitches back from HP so check your manual first.

Regardless of the fiber content, all lace carriages work best when the yarn has some elasticity (although some of the new yarns with stainless steel fibers do make beautiful, very open lace fabrics). Initially, I suggest that you steer clear of yarns like rayon that run like wildfire when stitches drop. My samples are all knitted in smooth yarns mainly so that you can clearly see the structure of the lace.

Hand-Manipulations and Automatic Lace Carriages

Although lace carriages make knitting lace much faster and easier, you can actually create a wider variety of lace fabrics with hand-manipulations. This is because, with hand-manipulations, you can replicate many more of the hand knit decreases than a lace carriage is capable of doing.

With a transfer tool in your hand, you have the ability to control which stitch is on the front of every decrease and you can move two or more stitches to an adjacent needle without difficulty.

Lace carriages cannot move two (or three) stitches from one needle to the next without dropping them. Therefore, ***they only make a simple left or right decrease, where the stitch being decreased always lies on the purl side of the fabric; all double decreases are vertical decreases where the center stitch is on the knit face of the fabric.*** This means that as you re-work hand knit charts for lace carriages you need to simplify the decreases that are called for in the hand knit pattern. This may or may not change the pattern from the original.

Also, whether you work manually or with a lace carriage, you can never have two empty needles next to each other in the same row. Neither of them will ever cast on and form a regular stitch and the problem compounds with each advancing row. With hand manipulations, however, you *do* have the ability to

When reforming a stitch next to an eyelet, pay attention to the way the bars of the ladder extend from the adjacent stitches to make sure you latch them up in the correct order.

twist a stitch to form an e-wrap or to pick up the purl bar of an adjacent stitch to fill one of the empty needles.

A definite advantage to working hand manipulated lace on a machine is that you do not usually have to convert the chart because one row of the hand knit chart is still equal to one row of hand manipulations on the machine. There may be some esoteric decrease that you will need to find an alternative for, but most of the time it is fairly straight forward as long as you remember this: *the stitch that is placed on a needle first shows on the knit side of the fabric* and may (or may not) contribute to the overall design. Make all transfers first and then knit the row indicated on the chart as well as any plain rows that follow.

I find it helpful to make multiple copies of any hand-manipulated stitch charts I use so that I can check off each completed row as I work. Sometimes I put a check mark next to the row the first time through the list. Then, for the next repeat, I might make an additional mark to turn the check into an "X" and maybe the next time will just cross out the previous marks. I never, ever rely on just the row counter and what I *think* I did previously.

Hand Transferred Lace

As I said earlier, most hand knitting charts can be used just as they are for hand-manipulated lace transfers. When eyelets are formed on the needles adjacent to the decreases, you can use a single pronged transfer tool to make the decreases. However, when there are several stitches between the decreases and the eyelets, you should use multi-pronged transfer tools to speed things up. Because I usually find myself using a 5-prong tool for some decreases, 3 and 4-prong tools for others, I keep an arsenal of tools on a small table next to me so they are handy and ready to use.

If any of your decreases are two-step decreases, you will have to use a single prong tool for the first step and then a multi-prong tool to move the group of stitches as required. Most machines have a transfer tool with a single prong on one end and two or three prongs on the other. This makes it much faster to do the two-step decreases because you can just flip the tool end to end. For larger groups of stitches, changing tools so often does take a few extra moments, but it is still faster than trying to make all of the transfers with a single tool. By now, you should be getting the idea that lace knitting is not a speedy business and that having the right tools can make all the difference.

This luscious scarf is from Berroco book #337, "Kodiak". The yarn is fairly thick and would suitable for a mid-gauge or chunky machine. Because these machines do not have lace carriages, the pattern must be worked with hand transfers. Photo courtesy of Berroco.

All of the decreases were described in Chapter 3 so please refer to that information for symbols and methods. Any unusual symbols will be addressed along side the chart where they appear.

In addition to reforming stitches in lace designs, you can also add cables and popcorns to the plain sections of hand-manipulated lace (and lace produced by a lace carriage). It is usually a good idea to position these details and textures so that they are followed by a plain row of knitting, rather than a transfer row, and to avoid tightly crossed stitches that may cause the carriage to jam.

The example at the bottom of this page features simple columns of alternating eyelets, but the details are very different between the patterns at left and right because of the decrease methods used.

The samples on the next page illustrate two different applications of one hand knit chart.

Worked as a single repeat across the bed, this pattern forms a lovely curved border for the lower edge of a garment. In an all-over fabric (knitted with a lace carriage), the vertical decrease lines become an important design element.

The chart can be used just as it is to work it as a hand-manipulated pattern on mid-gauge or bulky machines. All of the decreases are made with transfer tools and you have the ability to choose between vertical or slanted double decreases.

With a lace carriage, all of the double decreases must be vertical and, as I will explain shortly, one repeat of the pattern requires many passes of the lace carriage to make all the transfers.

While hand manipulated lace is well suited to mid-gauge and chunky machines, there is really no substitute for a lace carriage when it comes to knitting lots of standard gauge lace.

The wider column of eyelets at left was formed with 2-step decreases; those at right with one-step decreases. It's interesting that, although they were both worked with the same number of stitches, the one at left appears wider and has a more interesting, over-all texture. The 2-step method is only possible with hand-manipulated lace.

The stitch chart below features a fairly straightforward arrangement of eyelets. In the first row of the chart, the eyelets are 4 stitches away from the double decrease that formed them. In the following pattern rows, the decreases and eyelets are separated by one less stitch each time until, in the last row, the eyelets are finally adjacent to the double decrease at center.

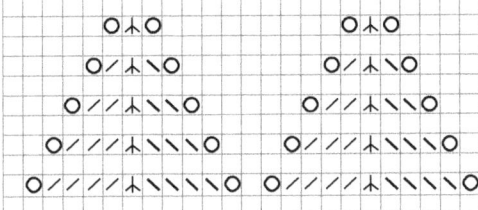

Knitted with a lace carriage, the decreases create a strong vertical effect in contrast to the zig-zag rows of eyelets.

Both of the triangles in the photo at right were created by manually moving the stitches on each side towards a central stitch. The first decrease was made by moving 5 stitches, the next by moving 4 and so on. The triangle at the right was worked with vertical double decreases, while the example at left utilized right slanting double decreases. The slanting decrease is only possible with hand transferred lace.

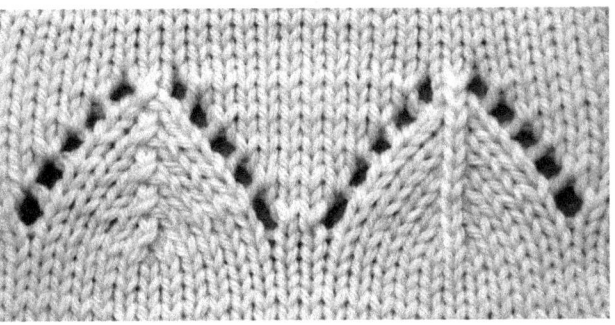

This lace border creates a gently curved edge at the bottom of a garment.

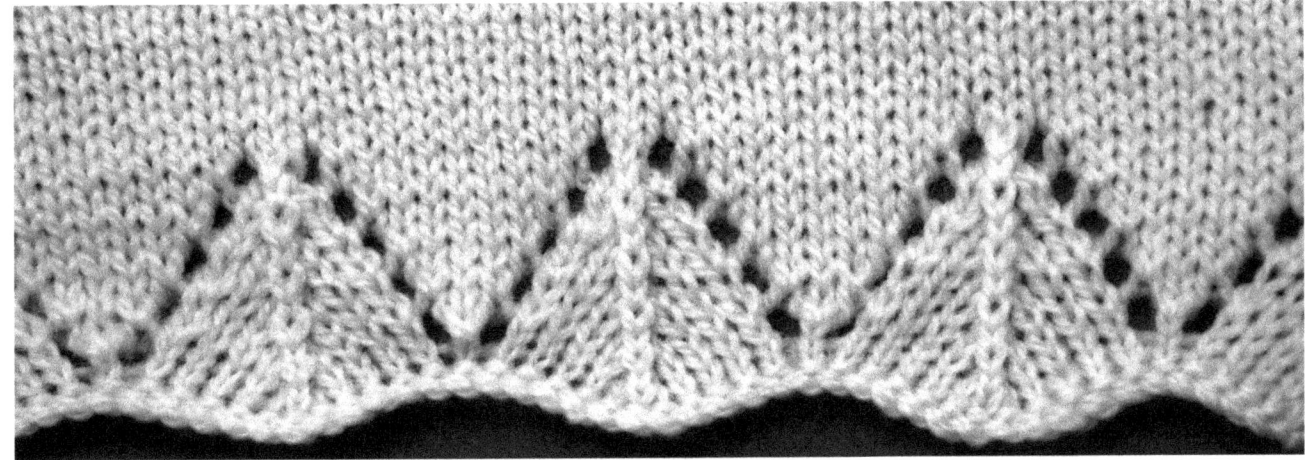

The bottom half of the hand-manipulated swatch below was worked with 1-step decreases, while the top was worked with 2-step decreases. In this instance, the one step creates a stronger vertical effect at the edge of each triangle, while the 2-step decrease adds nice texture to the diagonal lines within each motif. Either one is correct, but you must be consistent from one repeat to the next.

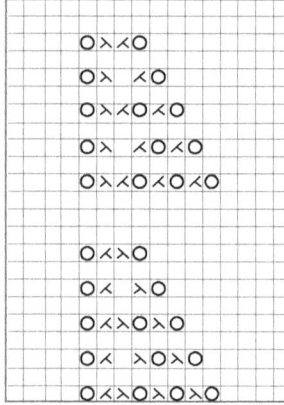

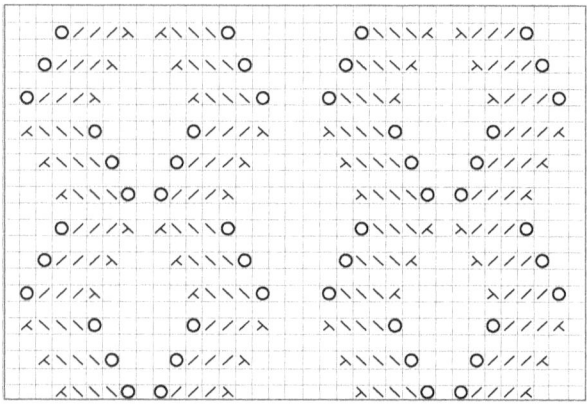

The zigzag lines that define the design on the left of this swatch were shaped with 2-step decreases. Those at the right were worked with 1-step decreases and you should notice that the outer edges of those lines are not as clearly defined as they are at left. The 1-step decrease is your only option with an automatic lace carriage, but with hand-manipulations you do have a choice.

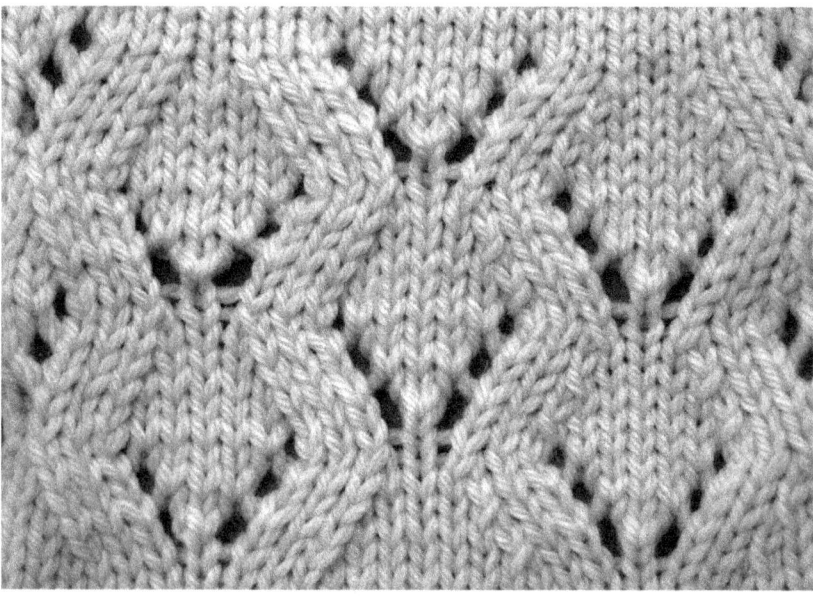

Lace 107

The two hand–manipulated swatches above were worked from a shortened version of the chart below, creating just three rows of eyelets in each repeat, instead of five. Both of these swatches have lots of movement in the stitches because of the difference in tension across the rows where cables are crossed and stitches transferred for lace. The swatch at top–right was knitted using 2–step decreases and the swatch at left created the pairs of eyelets in each row with a single vertical decrease. The two stitches between each repeat were latched up every 20 rows with a double latch tool. This is a pattern that really requires the purl stitches between the repeats to help the stitch pattern stand out.

The swatch below was knitted with a standard gauge lace carriage so all of the decreases are 1-step decreases. The purl stitches between repeats were latched up by hand, which is a little more time consuming on a standard gauge machine than it is on a mid-gauge, but quite doable every 10-12 rows.

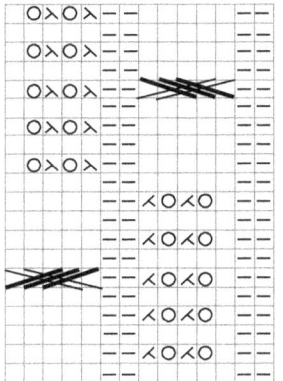

Lace Carriages

All lace carriages are manufactured for use on specific machines. In today's active used-machine market, it is important to know that machines have changed over the years and that some carriages may only be usable on specific models. Find out before you invest!

The lace carriages most commonly still in use are those manufactured by Brother and Silver Reed for both their punch card and electronic machines. The mechanics of these two companies is totally different and the equipment is not interchangeable.

"Iwi" is an asymmetrical design by Emily Nora O'Neill for Berroco Book #344, "Folio". The sweater features a lace panel that could be knitted with a lace carriage (with slightly thinner yarn) or with hand manipulations. Photo courtesy of Berroco.

What they do have in common is the way that they knit lace. The carriage arm (or sinker plate) on the front of the carriage literally forces the selected needles to cross each other and, in a perfectly orchestrated way, return the needles to working position so that some of the needles return to WP empty, ready to take on yarn and form yarn overs; other needles return to WP with two stitches in their hooks to form a decrease. How the machines select those needles is where the difference lies from one brand to another.

Also, a*ll lace carriages transfer stitches only in the direction they are traveling.* So, all needles that are programmed to transfer in a given row will be transferred in the same direction.

When the carriage travels from right to left, all programmed stitches are transferred to their adjacent left needle. When the carriage moves left to right, it makes right leaning transfers.

For this reason it is imperative that you begin with the transfer/lace carriage on the correct end of the bed. If you are not sure where to begin, look at the first row of transfers in the original pattern (not on the design card) and determine which way the stitches are being moved. If all else fails, knit swatches beginning at each end of the bed and compare the results. The fabric never lies. Decreases made in the wrong direction look ragged and interrupt the flow of the design.

If a HK pattern has stitches transferred in both directions in the same row, it will take two carriage passes to transfer those stitches to their adjacent needles – many more rows if the eyelets are not adjacent to the decreases.

Two plain rows between each transfer row is common, but sometimes (*only* on Silver Reed) there is just one and sometimes there are several. The important consideration here is that the carriage(s) always travel in the correct direction, which I will discuss a little further on.

You don't have to be expert with all the other kinds of knitting your machine can do in order to knit lace, but you must have a strong comfort level with the machine itself because lace knitting can be frustrating and trying if you are not up to the challenge. Make sure you are 100% comfortable with your machine and not bothered by an occasional dropped stitch or jammed carriage. Believe me, picking up dropped stitches is considerably more trying when there are yarn–overs involved.

Before you begin converting hand knit lace charts, you should already have some experience with your lace carriage and a firm understanding of how it works. The following information is intended to supplement the directions in your manual – not to replace them.

Silver Reed Lace Carriages

Silver Reed machines have been sold under the name Studio, Studio by White and Singer in the U.S. and Canada, Knitmaster and Empisal in other parts of the world.

Silver Reed lace carriages are complete units that, in addition to making lace transfers, are capable of knitting stockinet as well as the plain rows between lace transfers. You cannot, however, place needles in HP when using these lace carriage. Your machine's manual explains other ways of holding stitches.

Silver machines are always one row ahead of themselves. That is, as the carriage knits across the bed, the leading end of the carriage guides the needle butts through the carriage cams and knits the pattern for that row. As that is happening, the trailing end of the carriage (which will be the leading end for the next row) is learning the pattern for the next row. At the end of each row, all of the needles are back in WP.

These carriages knit two kinds of lace. "Simple Lace" is not simple *looking*, but it is the fastest and easiest kind to knit. The carriage transfers and knits stitches all in the same row and can do so row after row. This method is only suitable for patterns where all of the decreases are adjacent to the eyelets they are paired with.

However, when there are any stitches at all between the decrease and its eyelet, you need to chart and knit the pattern as "Fashion Lace".

This is a little more involved than Simple Lace because the carriage must be unthreaded and the cam lever changed to make as many empty passes across the bed as necessary to move the stitches to the proper needles. It's kind of scary the first time you do it because we've all learned, early on, that an empty carriage usually means dropped stitches.

The cam lever is set to "P" for all of the yarn–less transfer rows and to "L" for the plain knit rows. If you forget to thread the carriage for the "L" rows, you will drop the work from the machine; if you leave the yarn in the carriage when set to "P" you can cause a serious jam. Between threading and unthreading the carriage and flipping the cam lever each time you do so, Fashion Lace knitting requires all of your attention.

Your manual will supply the specifics, but electronic machines can be programmed to beep at the end of a repeat and to signal when to change the cam lever and the threading. On punch card machines, you have to rely on markings on the side edge of the punch card to guide you.

Fashion lace requires some fairly involved re-charting from hand knit or original designs because the eyelets are not formed next to the decreases. Rather, there can be any number of plain stitches between them and, the more stitches there are, the more passes of the carriage are required to complete a single row of transfers before you can rethread and knit those stitches.

Assuming you start on the right end of the bed, the first pass of the carriage transfers any and all left leaning decreases (as seen from the purl side) in that row. The next row, traveling from left to right will make any right leaning decreases in the same row. These first two rows accomplish the actual decreases and you will see that some needles now hold two stitches, with an empty adjacent needle at one side or the other.

The following transfer rows move single stitches one needle per row closer to the decrease and always in the direction the carriage is traveling. When all the transfer rows are complete, the eyelet will be so many stitches away from the decrease and then the carriage is re-threaded and two rows knitted. The series of photographs and charts on page 114 shows exactly how this happens.

Brother Lace Carriages

Brother machines were sold as Brother and Knit King in the U.S. and Canada; Jones and Jones Brother in other parts of the world.

The Brother system is very different from Silver Reed's. First of all, Brother machines use a separate transfer carriage in tandem with the regular carriage. One is referred to as the LC (lace carriage) and the other as the "K carriage" (knitting carriage). The machines are supplied with extension rails for the bed so that each carriage can be moved beyond the last working needle at each side and all of the needles on the bed can be used. The lace carriage is *usually* parked at the left end of the bed and the K carriage on the right.

Brother carriages all pre-select patterning needles and shoot them out to UWP in the row prior to the actual patterning row. This allows you to see exactly where the patterned needles are and even gives you the opportunity to re-arrange some of the needles if you want to by nudging them back to WP - or out to UWP to change the pattern.

As these lace carriages move across the bed they transfer the needles that were selected in the previous pass and at the same time, select the needles for the next row to UWP. The K carriage is only used for knitting the (usually) two plain rows in between. Both carriages must make an even number of passes in order to end each sequence on the correct end of the bed.

When charting your own designs, you need to pay close attention to this, especially when the LC doesn't transfer in both directions. You may need to program an extra "dead pass" in order to return the LC to the left end of the bed.

Brother lace carriages also knit two kind of lace. "Fine lace" is an interesting variation where only half of the transferred stitch is deposited on the adjacent needle and half remains on the original needle. The end effect is one of a slightly open, patterned fabric, but there are no true eyelets formed. The transfer carriage makes two passes, followed by two passes of the K carriage. Although you can knit patterns like this in hand knitting, it rarely shows up in stitch patterns and I will not address it here.

The "Normal Lace" that Brother knits is worked like the Fashion Lace on Silver machines. The lace carriage makes the initial two decrease passes and then as many more passes as required to move the stitches so that the eyelets are not adjacent to the decreases. Instead of changing the cam lever and rethreading the carriage, you simply alternate using the two carriages on the bed.

Live and Learn...

I came to Silver Reed machines after having knitted for several years on Passap and Superba machines, neither of which have lace carriages. Needless to say, lace was a big attraction and I rushed right in.

I had already mounted the ribber onto the machine and the lace directions in the manual said something like "If using the ribber, cover the bed with a ribber bed cover and bring the fabric in front of the ribber bed."

I figured I would go one better and just remove the ribber bed from the machine, but I left the main bed elevated on the ribber clamps. I reasoned that it was better than risking the fabric getting caught on the needles or sinker posts because I didn't have a proper ribber bed cover. Well, I spent the next two days picking up dropped stitches and wondering why I couldn't knit lace, no matter what I tried.

Turns out, the manual should have said "You MUST bring the fabric in front of the ribber bed in order to maintain the proper angle of the fabric to the bed for transferring stitches." It could also have suggested that I return the machine to the flat, single bed position on the table because, with the bed elevated, the fabric hung down at an angle that simply alluded the transfer mechanism in the lace carriage. The fabric needs to be absolutely perpendicular to the bed for trouble-free lace knitting as I eventually found out for myself.

Unfortunately, the manuals seldom say "why". They usually just dictate what to do so you need to follow the directions to the letter until you have some understanding of what the equipment is doing. In my case, it was a lesson well learned and never forgotten!

Even patterns that are knitted as Simple Lace on Silver machines are worked this way on Brother because of the two carriage system.

Brother lace carriages are capable of incorporating Fair Isle and other patterned stitches between rows of lace. Once you are competent with the basics you may want to try that. Also, unlike Silver, you can place needles in HP when knitting lace on a Brother machine.

Lace carriages work the same way on punch card or electronic machines. The advantages to the electronics, once again, have to do with there being no limits or requirements on the number of stitches per repeat and only having to draw or input a single repeat, rather than punching a whole card.

Some people like the idea of being able to knit Simple Lace in a single pass on a Silver; others value the two carriages employed on a Brother so that they do not have to re-thread and change cam settings. Because I worked for the U.S. importer for Silver Reed machines for so many years, all of my lace experience has been on those machines, but I wouldn't venture to tell you that one system is superior to the other. The truth is that the very best machine for you is the one that you understand and that you actually use. All of these machines have more potential than most of us ever realize and the real creativity comes from the user, not the equipment.

Converting Charts

Although it may be tempting to start designing and converting your own lace designs right off the bat, I'd advise you to first try some of the stock design cards that came with your lace carriage. They are usually explained in a step-by-step way in the manual and leave less to chance than do original designs. Once you have a little experience under your bet, you can play as much as you want because by then you will be able to determine why things work or don't and why stitches drop or form improperly, etc.

Whichever machine and lace carriage you use, there are bound to be some guidelines and standards unique to that equipment so make sure you consult your manual. As I said earlier, there are some differences from brand to brand in how lace is knitted. Also, punch cards require full length repeats so that the cards' ends can connect and rotate endlessly through the machine while electronics only require one repeat and some properly set controls or marks on the card.

Other things, however, are pretty standard from machine to machine. As I said earlier, all lace carriages transfer stitches in the direction they are traveling. When a carriage travels from right to left, selected stitches are transferred from their needles to the adjacent needle at left. You cannot transfer two adjacent stitches in the same row so you should never show two adjacent eyelets in the same row of a chart.

You can only move stitches over by one needle per pass of the carriage. So, if a decrease (doubled stitch) is supposed to be separated from its eyelet by 5 needles, it will take a total of 6 passes of the transfer carriage moving in that direction to move the stitches over. This means that there would also have to be 6 passes traveling in the opposite direction and the entire sequence would be 12 rows on the punch/design card.

The first two transfer passes a lace carriage makes are always the ones that doubles the stitches to form the actual decreases, leaving empty needles in WP adjacent to them. All the transfer passes that follow are just to move the individual stitches that are supposed to sit between the decrease and the resulting yarn overs.

Purchased lace cards are usually marked to show the direction the carriages should travel, which carriage or setting to use, etc. In order for visual reminders to be useful, they need to be placed a specific number of rows above the row being read by the machine, which is why the markings sometimes seem at odds with the cards at first glance.

All punch cards and electronic cards are read down inside the machine so the portion of the card that you can still see while you work is never the row that is currently knitting. On Silver punch card machines, the active row is 5 rows down inside the machine; on the EC-1 it is 10 rows. For Brother punch cards, the drop is 7 rows and for their electronic machines it is 1 row. Keep this in mind when you begin creating your own design/punch cards so that any reminder marks you make on the cards remain visible when you start knitting.

Electronic machines can be programmed to beep when it's time to change the cam lever or to knit with the K carriage. These auditory reminders are easier to work with than counting rows and reading the pattern as you work.

When designing your own patterns or converting hand knit charts, it is always a good idea to plot out at least two vertical and two horizontal repeats of the pattern to make sure it connects correctly from one repeat to the next. Patterns can be worked as all-over repeats or isolated in panels. Punch card and electronic machines all offer some kind of isolation pins or cams, which are also used to prevent edge stitches from trying to transfer to nonexistent needles!

The hand knit pattern shown in the chart at right is an 8 row pattern, just as it is when knitted as Simple Lace on a Silver machine.

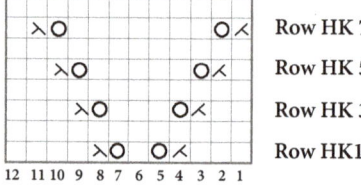

Step by Step Conversion of Hand Knit Patterns

Simple Lace on the Silver Reed

The pattern below left is a "Simple Lace" design where the eyelets lie adjacent to the decreases that formed them. If you examine the HK chart, you will see that there are two transfers in every alternate row and that they slant away from each other. I have broken this pattern down step-by-step to knit it as "Simple Lace" with the Silver Reed lace carriage. (For Brother, you would treat this pattern as "Normal Lace", which I will explain a little further on.)

This sequence begins with the carriage on the right end of the bed to begin knitting row 1 of the hand knit chart (HK1). As the carriage moves right to left, stitch #7 is transferred to needle #8. The next, left-to-right pass transfers stitch #5 to needle #4. Keep in mind that Simple Lace also knits the row as it makes the transfers. These two passes of the carriage complete Row HK1 of the hand knit pattern.

It requires two transfer rows to knit Row HK1 because the transfers need to be made in both directions and, as I stated earlier, lace carriages can only transfer stitches in the direction they are traveling. If all the transfers in Row HK1 slanted one way, the second pass would have a plain knitted row to return the carriage to the right end of the bed.

Rows 3 and 4 on the machine chart will knit Row HK3 by transferring stitch #8 to needle #9 with the first pass; stitch #4 to needle #3 with the second pass.

Rows 5 and 6 will transfer stitch #9 to needle #10 and then stitch #3 to needle #2 to complete Row HK5.

Lastly, Rows 7 and 8 will complete Row HK7 by first transferring stitch #10 to needle #11 and then stitch #2 to needle #1.

I hope that studying the chart will clarify the transfers. Keep in mind that I have just illustrated one width-wise repeat of this pattern to keep things as simple as possible, but remember that any and all left leaning decreases in a row would have been made with the first carriage pass and all right leaning decreases with the second pass.

Although the original hand knit chart shows one plain row between decrease rows, The rows actually get knitted the same time the transfers are made so I don't have to interrupt the knitting to make any changes at all. This is pretty streamlined lace knitting.

To knit this pattern on a Brother machine, you must use the LC to work the transfer rows and the K carriage for the plain rows in between. You would not be able to knit this pattern without two K carriage rows between each set of transfers.

Fashion Lace/Normal Lace

On both Silver and Brother machines, patterns where the eyelets are *not* adjacent to the decreases that formed them require a different approach. The pattern below is the same one I used to knit the hand-manipulated swatches on page 105. The swatch at the upper right on that page was knitted with a lace carriage and the design card that I created by the method that follows.

I developed the electronic design card (shown on the next page) for this pattern by identifying each and every transfer that needed to be made in each of the pattern rows. The series of charts that follow detail that breakdown.

I know this all sounds confusing right now, but once you have worked your way through this process with me–and tried converting a pattern or two on your own–I think you will find it is much easier than it first seems. Ready?

Row 2, shown in detail on the next two pages, represents the first row in the original chart. Row 1, a plain row is not shown. Follow my steps from bottom to top and remember that (1) all transfers in the same must row slant the same way and (2) you can only move a stitch over by one needle at a time.

The first row of the breakdown represents the right to left movement of the lace carriage, transferring the first stitch at the right of the center needle onto that needle. The next pass, from left to right, moves the corresponding stitch from the left of center onto the central needle. These are the only decreases that will be made for row 2. *The decreases themselves are always made in the first two passes of the carriage.* All of the following carriage rows simply move one stitch at a time, one needle towards the decrease until, as shown at the top of my breakdown chart, the eyelets are now 4 needles away from the decrease.

I have highlighted (in blue) the stitches that are moved with each subsequent pass of the carriage. You should note that there are a total of five transfer rows in each direction and that the position of the *eyelets* keeps shifting until the top row looks like the corresponding row on the HK chart.

Nothing is actually knitted until the ten transfer rows are done. Then 2 plain rows are knitted; 12 passes of the carriage are required to complete Row 2 of the original chart. Each of the rows in the expanded chart for Row 2 at left will be represented on the electronic (or punch card) design card by the position of the eyelets.

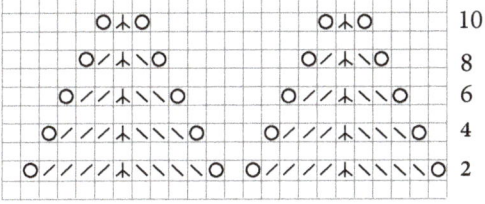

114　Chapter 7

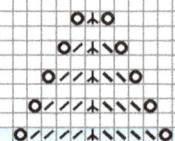

Row 2

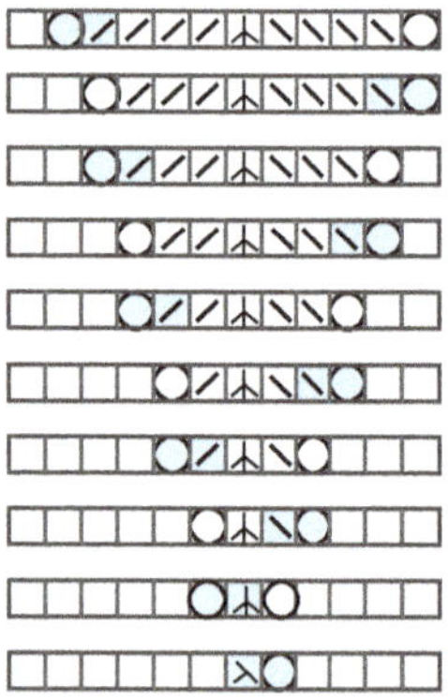

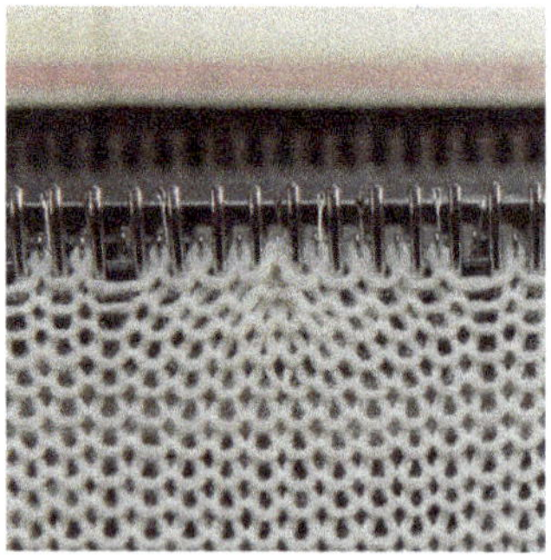

Two rows are knitted after the 10th transfer to complete Row 2.

Row 4

Row 4 of the original chart breaks down the same way. The first two passes of the carriage (as always) are for the left and right leaning decreases at center and then, with every pass of the transfer carriage, stitches are moved one needle closer to the decrease, every alternate row so the carriage is moving in the correct direction to do so.

It will take 8 transfer rows to position the eyelets on the 4th needles at either side from the decrease. These 8 rows will then be followed by two knit rows.

1

2

3

4

5

6

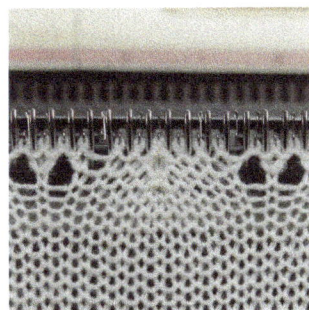
7

8

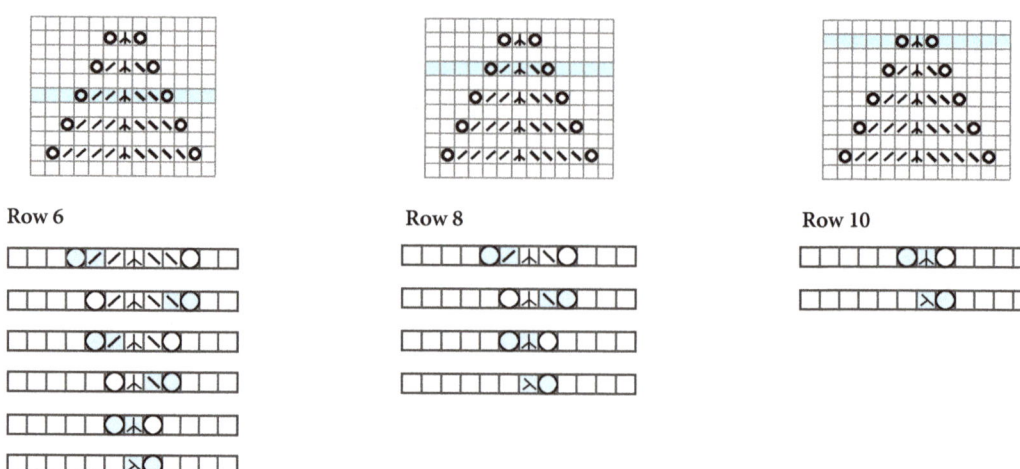

Row 6   Row 8   Row 10

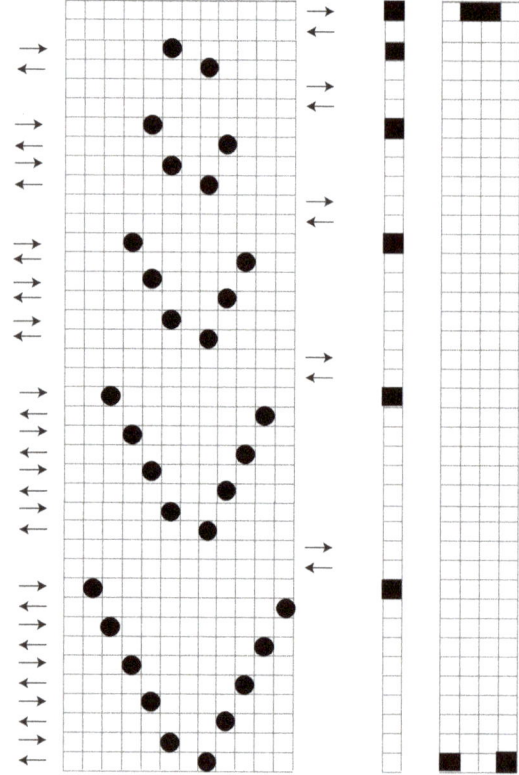

This is the finished design card for the triangular pattern as it would appear for use with the Silver EC-1 or punch card. Each of the blue eyelets has been recorded and the plain knit rows inserted between sets of transfers. Because it is a 12 stitch repeat, it is suitable for electronic or punch card machines. The arrows along side the pattern indicate the direction of the transfer rows and the knitted rows. This card is marked to return to the beginning after each full repeat and to beep when it is time to knit the plain rows. For Brother, the rows knitted from the right would be done with the K-carriage and those from the left with the LC.

The remaining rows of the pattern break down the same way. And, although the subsequent rows of the chart require fewer and fewer transfer rows, this is not true of every pattern. It only happened here because, in this case, the design itself narrows, bringing the eyelets closer together.

Also, there were only two transferred stitches (in each 12 stitch repeat of the pattern) per row of the HK chart. With more detailed patterns, there might be several stitches transferred in both directions.

Lace 117

This pattern is interesting for two reasons. First of all, if you knit on a Silver machine, it can be knitted as a combination of both Simple Lace and Fashion Lace. As shown in the chart at far right, with the knit rows between transfer rows eliminated in the top section, those 10 rows can be knitted with the cam lever on "L". There is no need to thread and unthread the yarn or to change the cam lever, which makes the top portion faster and easier to knit.

The chart at left shows the entire pattern knitted as Fashion/Normal Lace. The chart at right shows the top portion knitted as Simple Lace (Silver).

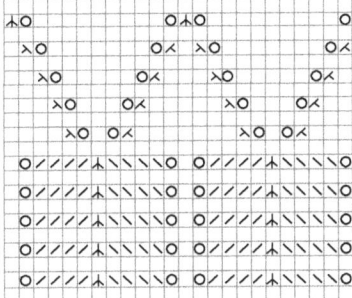

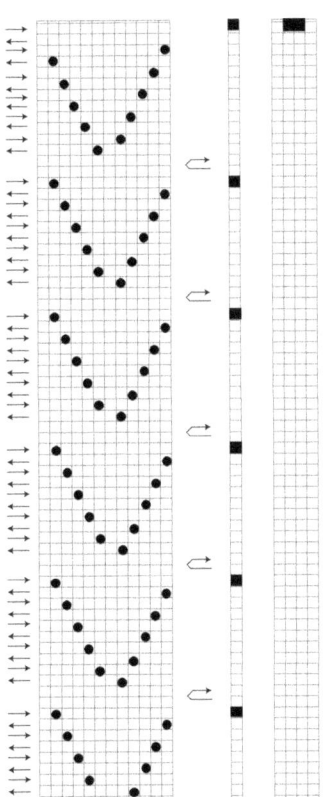

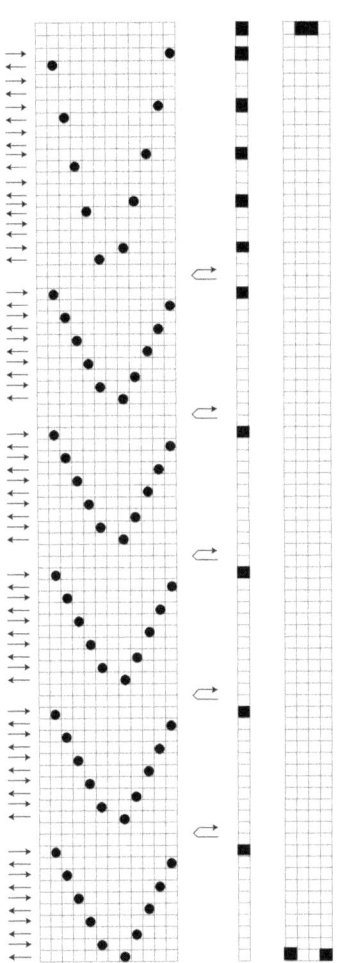

Did you notice that the bottom of this pattern begins exactly like the triangular pattern I just detailed? However, instead of the subsequent sections getting smaller or changing in some way, the same 12 row sequence is repeated five times. If you were knitting this on an electronic, you could draw out just one repeat of this section, mark the card to keep repeating it, knit it five ties and then switch to the top section. You could also use it to knit a vertical pattern of eyelets.

This pattern is also a 12 stitch repeat, suitable for either punch card or electronic machines. The decreases in the hand knit chart are left leaning double decreases, which the lace carriage cannot do. Instead, they need to be treated as vertical double decreases, which changes the fabric slightly, creating a jog in the vertical lines that divide each repeat.

The lower edge of this pattern curves as a result of the decreases and eyelets and would make a lovely edge for a garment. The fabric may roll, but that can usually be controlled by working a row or two of crochet or some other trimming.

The pattern on the next page features a strong diagonal. If the direction the diagonal slants is important, you might need to reverse the chart before adapting it to the machine.

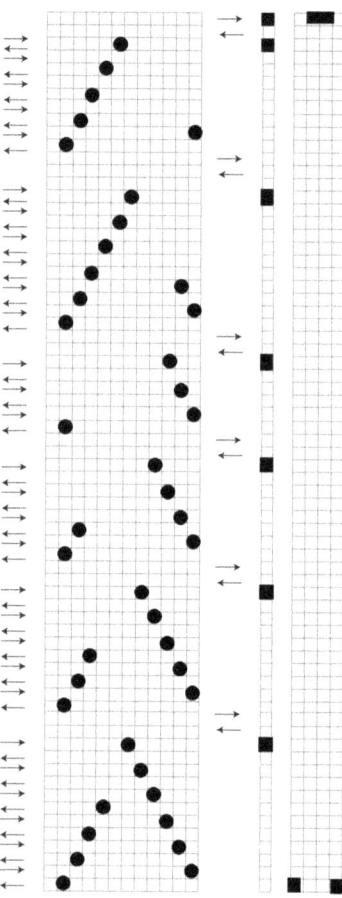

The left leaning double decreases shown on the hand knit chart can only be done with hand transfers on a knitting machine. Lace carriages treat all double decreases as vertical double decreases.

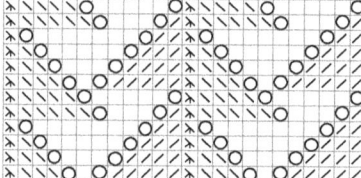

Lace 119

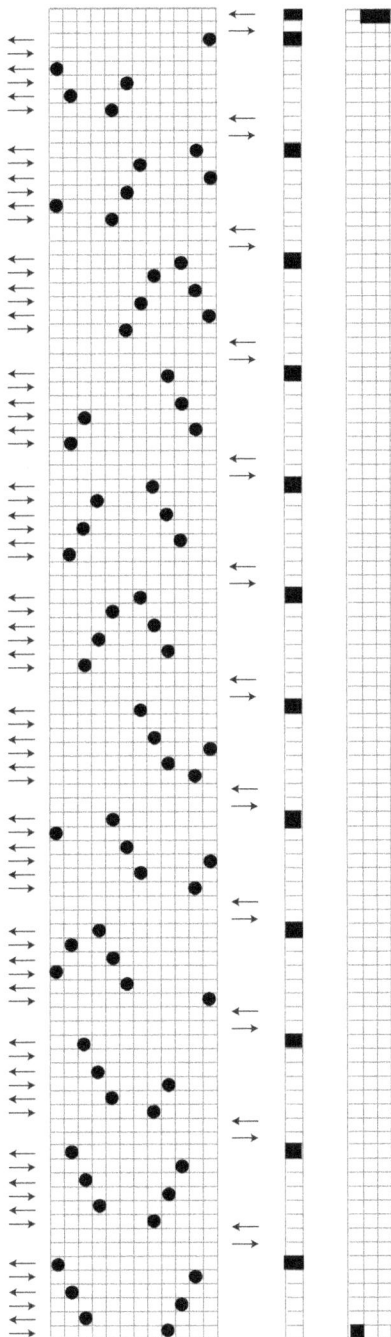

This design card is marked to repeat and to beep after each series of transfers for the Silver Reed machine. The arrows indicate the carriage(s) direction for both Brother and Silver.

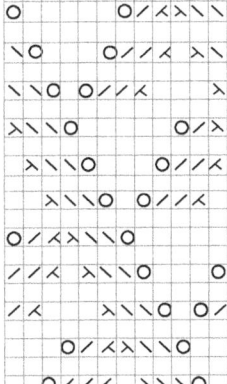

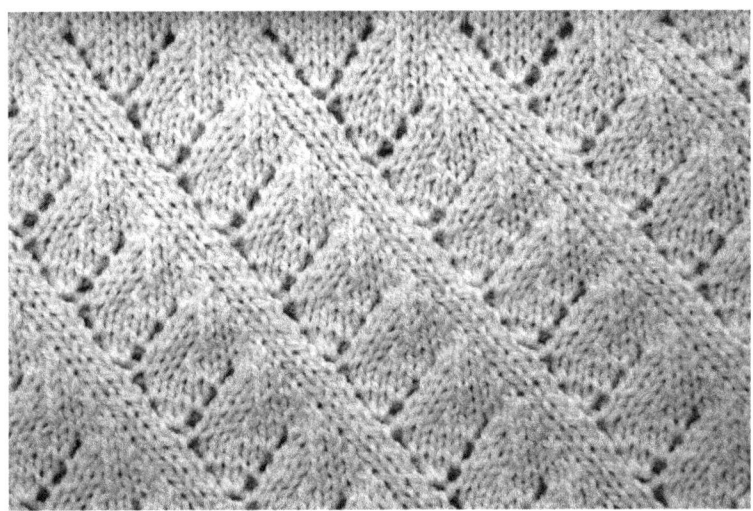

Lace Leaf border

This trim first appeared as part of a hand-knitting pattern in the Spring/Summer 1990 issue of Nihon Vogue, a wonderful Japanese knitting magazine. The text is in Japanese, but all of the patterns are charted with the international knitting symbols, which is really all you need, but it also shows up in other pattern collections.

Lynn McLune, who was one of the educators at Studio by White Knitting Machines, translated the trim for machine knitters and it was first featured in the spring/summer 1993 issue of *Studio by White Design Magazine*.

This isn't difficult knitting, but you do have to pay close attention and check off each row as you work. Several years ago I wrote step-by-step directions that simplified the process a little more and those have been available on my web site as a free download.

However, I was never quite satisfied with the way the leaf stood out from the purled background stitches and I started playing around with some alternate increases to eliminate the problem. Not only did the improved increase sharpen the visual edge of the leaf, it also made it much easier to drop down and reform the stitches that form the purl background.

The original directions called for making lifted increases. The increase that worked for me is actually a *twisted* lifted increase. Normally, when you make a lifted increase, you insert your transfer tool *under* the purl bar of an adjacent stitch at left or right and lift the purl bar onto the empty needle. Instead, I inserted my tool *from above* the purl bar and then rotated the tool to the right to place this now–twisted stitch on the empty needle. The twist is what makes all the difference here. This increase is nearly invisible and the edge of the leaf is sharp and clearly defined.

This trim is a poor candidate for an automatic lace carriage because each leaf repeat begins with 6 stitches, increases up to 18 and reduces back to 6. As I said earlier, lace carriages do not make increases so this band needs to be worked with manual transfers and with certain stitches reformed to create the essential purl contrast to the leaf.

I recommend casting on needles 1–6 to the right of zero so that the numbers in these directions agree with the numbers on your bed. It will minimize counting and errors. If you want to make a trim with reversed shaping, simply work on the left side of center zero.

You must latch up stitches before knitting row 12 because, after that, the 4th stitch should not be reformed. Make sure you leave empty needles within the trim in WP so they can cast on and form eyelets; when decreasing to shape the edge of the leaf, those empty needles are returned to NWP.

If you want to work this edging around a neckline, sleeve or hem, you might want to graft the beginning and ending six stitches together for an invisible seam. If so, begin and end on waste knitting. Obviously, the width of your sweater will be partially determined by the length of the trim strip if you plan to use it for the lower edges of the garment.

When dropping down a column of stitches to reform them for the first time (definitely by row 12), insert the latch tool through the twisted stitch at the base of each column, then drop the stitches to that point and latch up. Do not untwist the stitch.

Lace Leaves Step-by-Step

There is a lot going on in this trim so follow the directions carefully. Knit each row and then check it off the list. After a couple of repeats you will begin anticipating what comes next, but I still recommend checking off rows and following the chart!

C/O 6 sts with scrap and knit some rows, ending COL. Change to the main yarn and knit 1 row to the right. RC 000.

Row 1: 6 ndls in WP. Move sts 5 and 6 to ndls 7 and 8. Move stitch 4 to ndl 5. Leave empty ndls in WP. Knit 1 row to left.

Row 2: Move sts 3–8 to ndls 4–9. Make a twisted/lifted inc from ndl 4 to ndl 3. Knit to right.

Row 3: Move sts 7–9 to ndls 9–11. Move stitch 6 to ndl 7. Knit to left.

Row 4: Move sts 4–11 to ndls 5–12. Make a lifted inc from ndl 5 to ndl 4. Knit to right.

Row 5: Move sts 9–12 to ndls 11–14. Move stitch 8 to ndl 9. Knit to left.

Row 6: Move sts 5–14 to ndls 6–15. Make a lifted inc from ndl 6 to ndl 5. Knit to right.

Row 7: Move sts 11–15 to ndls 13–17. Move stitch 10 to ndl 11. Knit to left.

Row 8: Move sts 6-17 to ndls 7-18. Make a lifted inc from ndl 7 to ndl 6. Knit to right.

Row 9: *Move stitch 7 to ndl 8. Move sts 18 & 17 to ndls 17 & 16. Make a lifted inc from ndl 8 to ndl 7. Knit to left.

Row 10: Knit to right.

Row 11: *Move stitch 8 to ndl 9. Move sts 17 & 16 to ndls 16 & 15. Make a lifted inc from ndl 9 to ndl 8. Knit to left.

Row 12: Reform stitches 3– 8. Knit to right. (After this do not reform stitch #4)

Row 13: *Move stitch 9 to ndl 10. Move sts 16 & 15 to ndls 15 & 14. Make a lifted inc from ndl 10 to ndl 9. Knit to left.

Row 14: Knit to right.

Row 15: *Move stitch 10 to ndl 11. Move sts 15 & 14 to ndls 14 & 13. Make a lifted inc from ndl 11 to ndl 10. Knit to left.

Row 16: Knit to right.

Row 17: Move stitch 11 to ndl 12. Move sts 14 and 13 to ndls 13 and 12. Then move all sts on ndls 13 and 12 to ndls 12 and 11. Knit to left.

Row 18: Reform sts 3, 5–10. Do NOT reform stitch #4. Knit to right. Move stitch 12 to ndl 11. Reform stitch 3. B/O until 6 sts rem to begin next rep.

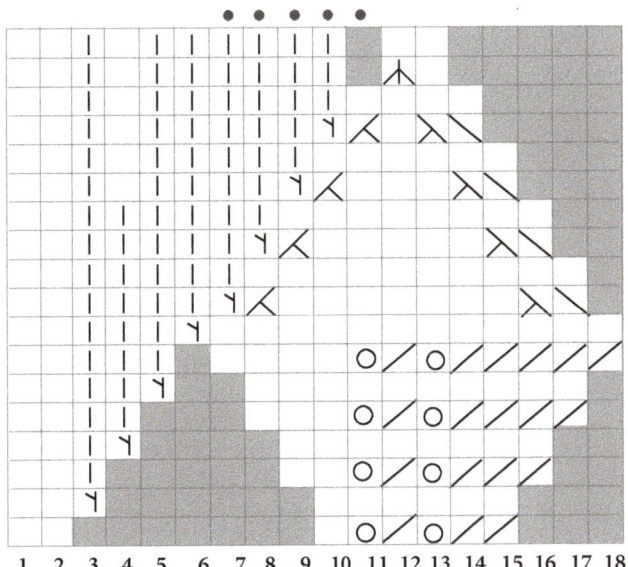

- Bind Off
- Purl Stitch
- Non–existent stitch resulting from transfers

You can use any bind off for the last 5 stitches. I found that I preferred the way they looked when chained one through the next with the latch tool. To make sure the stitches are large enough to do this, they need to be knitted with stitch size 10. With COR and set to hold needles in HP, hold needles 1-6 and change the stitch size dial to 10. Knit 1 row across needles 7-11. Beginning with stitch 11, pull one stitch through the next and then deposit the last stitch on needle #6. Put the empty needles in NWP and move the COR to begin the next repeat. If you reform stitches 7-11 before you latch tem off, the chain effect will be on the back of the fabric. If you don't bother reforming them, it rolls nicely to the front of the fabric and adds a nice detail. Either way is correct, but be consistent from one repeat to the next and remember to return to your regular stitch size before the next repeat.

Mosaic Knitting

mo·sa·ic

mōzā-ik

noun

1. A picture or pattern produced by arranging together small colored pieces of hard material, such as stone, tile, or glass.

2. Striped slip stitch patterning.

Hand knitters use the name "mosaic knitting" to describe the patterning method that most knitting machine manuals refer to as two-color tuck (or slip) stitch. Barbara Walker is credited with naming the hand knit technique "mosaic" and has probably done more exploration of mosaic knitting patterns in her books than anyone else, laying a strong foundation for others to follow.

Mosaic is one of my favorite machine knit stitches because it produces interesting, intricate-looking patterns that are easily knitted on any single bed machine by alternately knitting two rows each of a dark and a light colored yarn. I especially appreciate the fact that two-color mosaic fabrics are lighter weight than their Fair Isle counterparts.

The punch card shown at right satisfies the 24 stitch repeat on most Japanese machines. Note that the first and last two rows are fully punched to allow for overlapping and fastening the ends of the card so it repeats continuously. Also, each row on this card was punched twice so it would not be necessary to use the elongation button. The electronic design at right shows only one repeat of the pattern (12 stitches/10 rows) and each row is only shown once. You would knit this using the elongation button and the color reverser.

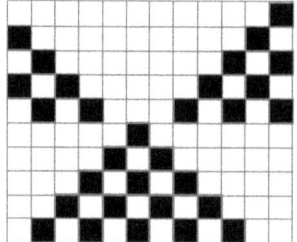

Knitting machines with automatic patterning systems generally include directions for knitting two-color patterns with the cards that come with the machine (usually card #10 for Japanese machines). Once a punch card or electronic card is inserted into the machine and the carriage properly set for slip stitch or tuck, all you have to do is alternately knit two identical rows of black (or a dark color) with two identical rows of white (or any light color) and a pattern - *totally unlike the one on the card* - begins to emerge.

The instruction manuals for simple, manual machines (those without punch card or electronic patterning systems) usually provide charts and directions to hand pull needles for these patterns. The needles pulled to holding position will either collect tuck stitches or, if you are knitting two-color slip stitch, be knitted back from holding position with each pass of the carriage.

The patterns in your manual are a good place to start learning mosaic knitting, but once you realize the patterning potential of this method, chances are you will want to design your own patterns or take advantage of some of the beautiful mosaic stitch patterns available in hand knitting books. Barbara Walker's two books are my favorite sources for mosaic patterns: *Charted Knitting Designs* contains a chapter on mosaic stitches, while *Mosaic Knitting* is entirely devoted to the subject. (Both of these books are available from Schoolhousepress.com and both give full hand knit stitch charts for all of the patterns).

Hand knitting patterns always describe mosaic as a two-color slip stitch, worked on either a stockinet or garter stitch base. By machine, the garter stitch option doesn't exist, but you can knit mosaic with either tuck or slip stitch. I prefer knitting tuck mosaic, rather than slip, for a number of reasons. First of all, machine knit tuck stitch has more texture and better drape than its slip stitch counterpart. Second and more important, while slip stitch fabrics tend to narrow and elongate (as compared to stockinet) tuck stitches cause fabrics to shorten somewhat and to spread width wise. This means that a sweater knitted in mosaic slip will generally require more needles than the same sweater knitted in mosaic tuck, which limits how large a garment you can produce, given the fact that all knitting machines have a finite number of needles to work with. Being able to knit larger sweaters using *fewer* needles is an important consideration if you want to knit large or oversized sweaters. And, if you work on a manual machine, tuck mosaic will require far less (hand) needle selection than would slip mosaic. (1) and (2).

Typical mosaic patterns have a lattice or maze-like appearance with *most* dark verticals only one stitch wide and *most* dark horizontals only one row high. There are always exceptions and a pattern with lots of exceptions will knit more successfully as slip stitch than tuck because you will have difficulty tucking several stitches next to each other. That said, I encourage you to try both methods because it is only a matter of flipping the cam lever to slip or tuck - everything else is the same - on machines with automatic needle selection.

On manual machines, however, I find hand-pulled tuck patterns more intuitive and easier to keep track of than hand-pulled slip. When knitting tuck mosaic, you only need to pull the pattern needles shown on the chart to holding position. However, slip mosaic requires pulling all the *background needles* to holding position so that the carriage can knit them back while the un-selected needles in working position can be slipped to create the pattern. Additionally, slip stitch patterns need to be selected every row, while the tuck selections are good for two rows at a time.

The knit side of a mosaic fabric is usually the right side, but because there are no floats on the purl face of a tuck mosaic fabric (and only small floats when knitted in slip), the purl side can often be quite attractive as well. (3) and (4).

The lack of floats in Mosaic is in sharp contrast to Fair Isle knitting; mosaic fabrics are also generally lighter weight as a result of there being no long floats. On standard gauge machines, the weight of a finished sweater is not usually a major consideration. However, it is a factor when you knit on a chunky or a mid-gauge machine. Also keep in mind that the lack of floats translates into having to buy less yarn to begin with, as compared to other two-color knitting methods.

1 Labyrinth pattern knitted as tuck mosaic.

2 Labyrinth pattern knitted as slip mosaic. Note that this pattern is somewhat more elongated than the tuck example above.

3 The purl side of the slip mosaic labyrinth has short floats.

4 The purl side of the tuck mosaic fabric is defined by texture, rather than floats.

Because mosaic patterns always alternate two rows of a pattern color with two rows of a contrast color, a color changer is a very useful accessory to have if one is available for your machine. All Japanese color changers are mounted on the left end of the bed, while Passap color changers mount on the right. This means that all pattern sequences must begin on the left for Japanese machines and on the right for Passap in order to knit two identical rows of pattern in the same color.

Without a color changer, you will need to develop a rhythm to smoothly change yarns every two rows. If, for example, you start knitting on the right end of the bed, you will always change color when the carriage returns to the right. The yarn threaded through the right side of the tension mast can be tucked under the right end of the bed when not in use. However, the yarn that is threaded through the left side of the mast will pass below and in front of the needles to the left end of the bed when not in use. Don't worry - it won't knit or get caught in the needles. Some machines have a notch at each end of the bed to hold yarns not in use, while others provide little clips to hold the yarn. If you have to, tuck the yarn under the bed and catch it at the back. The main thing is that the two yarns should not cross and tangle while you knit. Also, make sure you correctly thread the yarn feeder each time you re-thread the carriage and pull up any slack before knitting the first row of a new color to avoid dropping stitches.

Regardless of what kind of machine you use, always allow at least one plain stitch at each edge to simplify seaming and to produce an even edge. On punch card and electronic machines you can usually set edge pins or isolation cams to do this; on manual machines just don't select the edge stitches.

If you want to isolate stripes at the edge or within the body of a fabric, you need to prevent specific needles from patterning (i.e. knitting slip or tuck stitches) so that they can only knit stockinet. Because the color changes every two rows, that area will be striped. The example at (5) shows a collar detail of a cardigan sweater that was knitted on a standard gauge electronic machine. I used an isolation cam to prevent the acrobat pattern from knitting right up to the front edge of the fabric, moving the cam every 4 or 6 rows (for example) to create a widening band of stockinet stripes for the roll collar.

5 Moving the point cams to isolate the pattern resulted in a striped collar, knitted as the fronts of the cardigan were worked.

This can be done on manual machines as well simply by not selecting pattern needles within a specific area.

Most mosaic patterns look best when you begin by knitting two rows of the dark color and then continue alternating light and dark, but there are some patterns that look fine even if you begin with the light color (6) and (7). Sometimes, the color order will slightly shift the placement of a motif, while other times it can make the design less distinct because the background effect dominates. Keep this in mind as you begin knitting individual garment pieces and make sure they all begin with the same color so the pieces match.

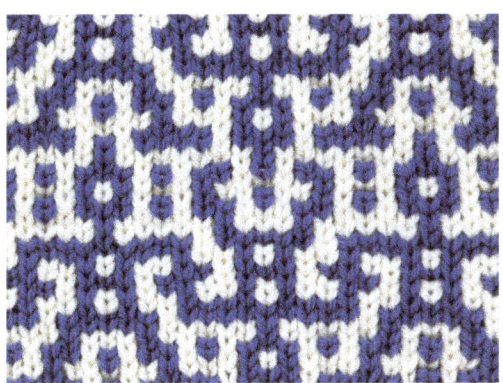

6 The acrobats stand out more clearly in this example which was knitted with 2 rows of blue to start.

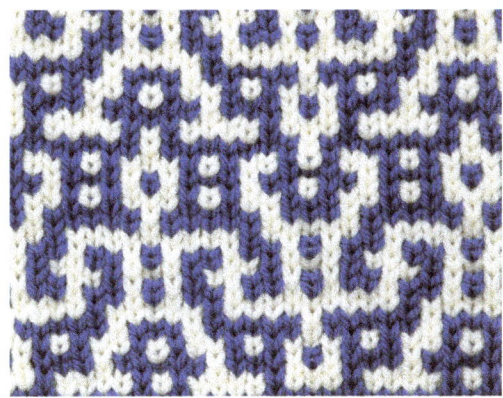

7 These acrobats began with 2 rows of white and while the pattern is still evident, it is not as strong as the example above.

Manually Selecting Mosaic Stitch

Even if you have a simple plastic machine (like the Silver Reed LK150), you can knit mosaic patterns by making use of the holding feature on your carriage. The charts at (8) –(13) are easy charts for a beginner to follow and the patterns they produce are interesting as borders or all-over designs. These patterns progress in fairly regular, simple ways that enable you to work without even consulting the chart once you establish the first row of pattern on the bed.

Begin by centering the first repeat on the bed at "0" and then make each subsequent selection relative to the previous one. I keep the chart right next to me and usually find myself reading the new row in relation to the last one, thinking, "one to the right" or "skip the next 5 needles", etc.

To minimize counting and to avoid mistakes, I sometimes use a grease pencil or china marker on the needle bed to indicate where each repeat begins and ends. The marks wipe off later with a dry tissue or paper towel.

For patterns like (8) and (9) which continually select every 4th needle (in different locations), I like using the 1 x 3 needle pusher that comes with most machines. (You can also purchase a handy adjustable needle selector from www.knittinganyway.com.) For pattern (13), you can use the 1 x 1 needle pusher that came with your machine. Otherwise, you don't need any special equipment to hand select these patterns.

Cast on with waste yarn, hang some claw weights, knit two rows with white and then re-thread the carriage with black. Set the carriage to hold needles in holding position (HP). Read the first row of your chart and push to HP any needles indicated by the tuck symbol. Knit two rows and then change colors.

(8) and (8a) This zig-zag pattern uses the 1 x 3 needles pusher, progressively selecting needles in one direction and then reversing.

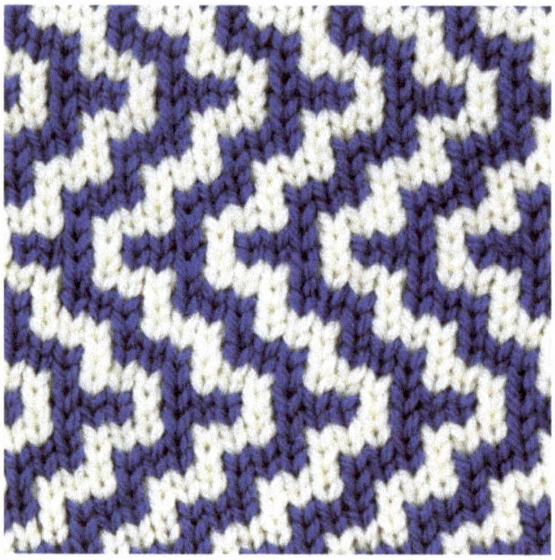

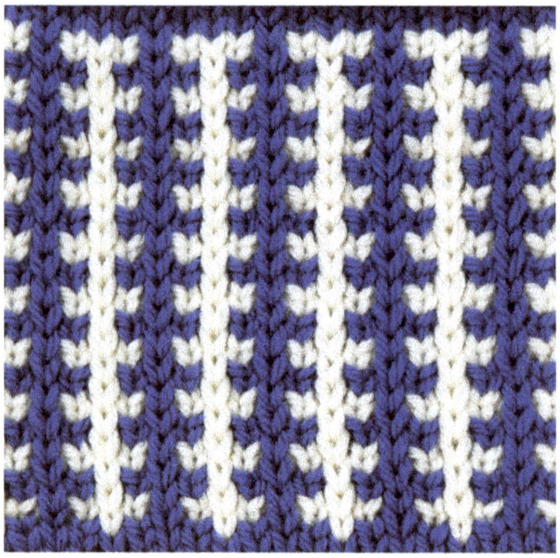

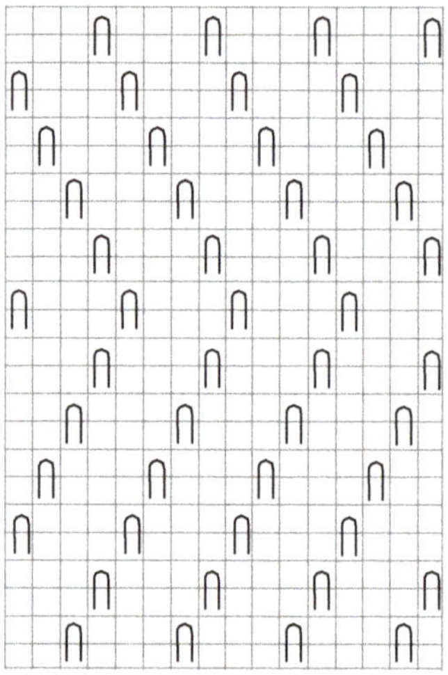

(9) and (9a) This simple design is easy to select using the 1 x 3 needle selector that comes with most machines.

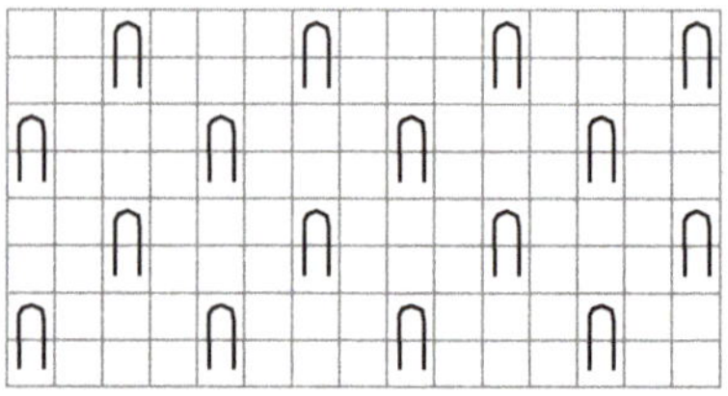

(10) and (10a) Needles are selected in a simple diamond progression. The pattern at the bottom began with 2 blue rows; the top fabric began with 2 white rows.

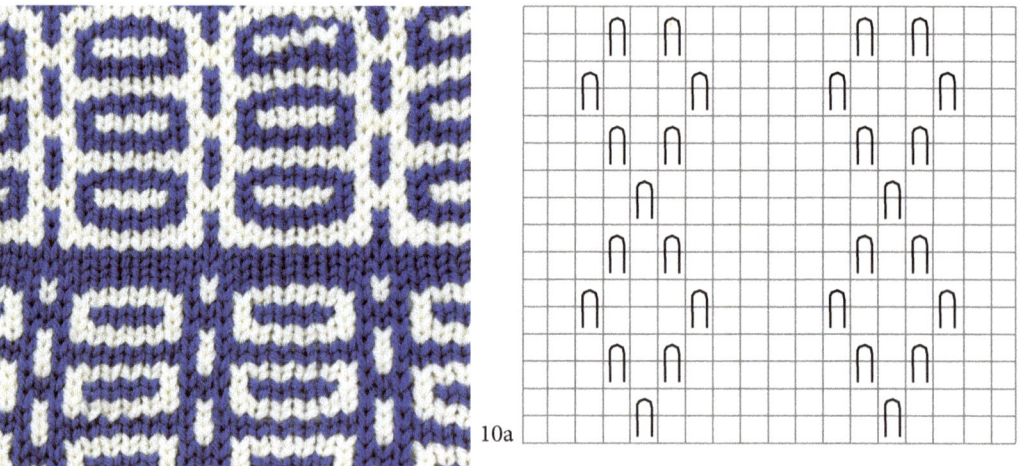

Mosaic Knitting 129

(11) and (11a) There are large, un-selected areas in this pattern. The alignment of the 2-row stripes that knit in those areas is skewed in response to the placement of the selected stitches. Note that, in spite of the pronounced diamonds in the chart, the knitted pattern does not contain any diamond motifs.

(12) and (12a) This simple chevron design looks much more complex when the pattern is selected in reverse at the end of an 8-row repeat.

(13) and (13a) As simple as this pattern looks, it can be quite tricky to knit because half the needles will be placed in UWP while the remaining needles are in HP. There are no needles left in WP when you make the pattern selections. This pattern knits a somewhat denser fabric than the other patterns, but it does give a fairly close approximation of vertically striped rib.

*Nudge the needles that are in HP back to upper-work position (UWP) so they can resume knitting in the next row but first, following the chart for the next row, push the pattern needles to HP. Knit two rows.** Repeat from * to ** .

Note that you cannot rely on the carriage levers to automatically knit the needles back from HP because, while some needles are returning to work after having just knitted two rows, other needles need to be placed in hold before knitting the next two rows. Also, as I said earlier, never select the edge needle at either side because their stitches are apt to drop or cause problems while you are knitting and the finished garment will not seam as neatly.

Although mosaic patterns always alternate two rows dark with two rows light, some of these pattern charts produce interesting patterns if you knit four rows of a color while re-selecting pattern every two rows as before or working four rows of each selection. Knitted as two-color tuck or slip, none of these fabrics resembles their chart, which they will if you knit them as Fair Isle.

Hand selecting these patterns as slip mosaic is much more work because the carriage must be set to slip all needles in working position and to knit all needles back from holding position. This means that only a few needles (those indicated by the tuck symbol on my charts) would remain in working position where they slip; all the other needles (the white spaces, the plain purl stitches, on the charts) must be pushed to HP so that the carriage can knit them back. Not only does this method require you to hand-select far more needles, you need to do it every row instead of every two rows. For this reason, slip mosaic is really only practical on punch card or electronic machines unless you absolutely *have* to have it.

Knitting Mosaic Patterns with Automatic Needle Selection

Punch Cards and Electronics

On machines with automatic needle selection, knitting patterns as slip mosaic is not a problem because although the carriage lever is set to slip, the punch card or electronic design card (or computer connection) tells the carriage which needles to *knit*. Specifically, when its cam lever is set to slip or to tuck, all knitting machine carriages want to slip or tuck *every* needle on the bed unless told to do otherwise by a design or punch card. The knit stitches are, in fact, the selected stitches that over-ride the slip or tuck cam lever settings.

When punching cards, this means that you need to punch holes for all the *background* stitches so the carriage knows they are the exception to the cam lever and are supposed to knit. Electronic machines, on the other hand, all have what is called a color reverser. It enables you to change pattern and background colors with the press of a button when knitting Fair Isle, but it also allows you to indicate the placement of the slip or tuck stitches when you draw your cards (or input your design electronically). Much faster than having to indicate all the background stitches, you simply input the design as shown on the chart and then press the color reverser button. The machine will take it from there. (This feature was one of the most exciting things about electronic machines when they first came on the market!)

Also, punch card and electronic machines all have an elongation feature that holds the card so that each row is read twice. This means that when you punch/draw your own designs, you only need to show each row once. Some punch cards, like card #10 in the usual Japanese–machine assortments, already have each row punched twice. In that case, you would not use the elongation button.

Taking Control of the Pattern

Designing your own or adapting hand knit designs to the machine

Rather than being surprised by what the stock punch/electronic design cards produce (the so-called "happy accident school of design"), you might want to adapt hand knit mosaic patterns to the machine or to design original patterns of your own.

In addition to Barbara Walker's books, there are several excellent collections of Chinese lattice designs available from Dover Publications (check Amazon.com) and while these designs are not charted for knitting, they will provide you with endless inspiration for creating your own patterns from scratch.

Whatever your source of inspiration, be aware that all mosaic designs must contain an even number of rows (before they are doubled) so that the pattern repeats connect properly. That is, the last row of each repeat should be two rows of the light colored yarn so that the next repeat begins with two rows of the dark color.

Charts for hand knit mosaic cannot be used just as they are and must be adapted for machine knitting. The acrobats and the large labyrinth designs I have used for the examples that follow are both from the Barbara Walker Mosaic Book and are used with the kind permission of Schoolhouse Press.

When you utilize hand knit patterns or begin to design your own, you will find that some designs do not work well in tuck mode and can only be knitted as slip mosaic. You can correct most problems by inserting a knit stitch between blocks of three or more stitches that are supposed to tuck - but probably won't. Both of these patterns were intended for hand knit (slip) mosaic. The final charts required fine-tuning to avoid problems with several adjacent stitches having to tuck.

First, draw your pattern on graph paper, showing two repeats horizontally and vertically to be sure the edges of the design connect properly in repeat. For a punch card

The Acrobats

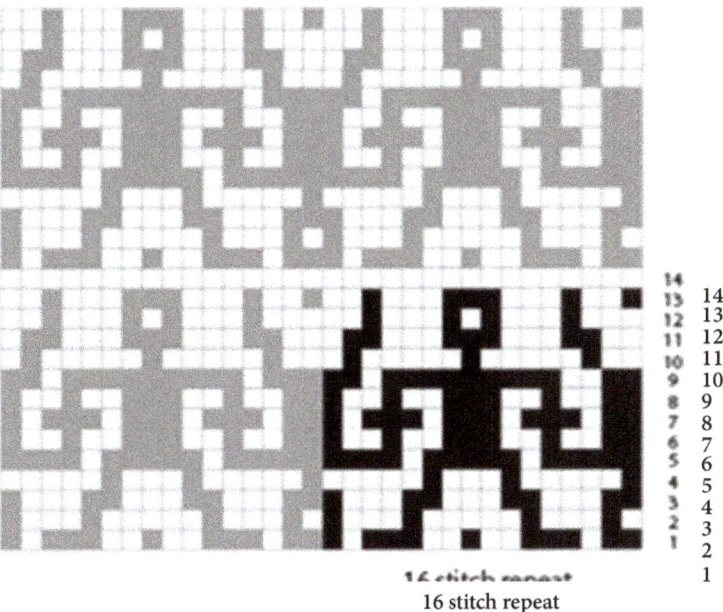

16 stitch repeat

14 This chart shows two horizontal and two vertical repeats of the 16 stitch/14 row acrobats exactly as shown in the Walker book. Each row of the chart is only shown once even though it will need to be knitted twice.

machine you will need to satisfy a specific number of holes on the card (usually 12, 24 or 40); electronic machines and computer design programs (like DAK) do not have this restraint and can accommodate any number of stitches per repeat.

Next, make a new chart to *record the white spaces only for row #1 and all of the odd numbered rows* in one repeat of your design (15).

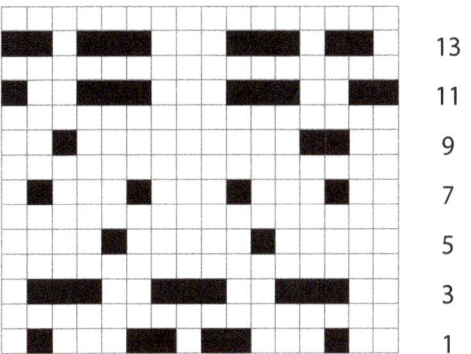

15 This chart *only* shows the position of the white squares in all the odd numbered rows.

Then make another chart to *record the position of all the black squares in row #2 and all of the even numbered rows* in your design (16).

Finally, combine these two breakdown charts into a third chart that alternates the odd and even rows. Once you understand how these charts are developed, you can probably work on a single chart right from the start, first coding all the odd rows and then all of the even rows, but I find it less confusing to produce the separate charts and then combine them as I have done here (17).

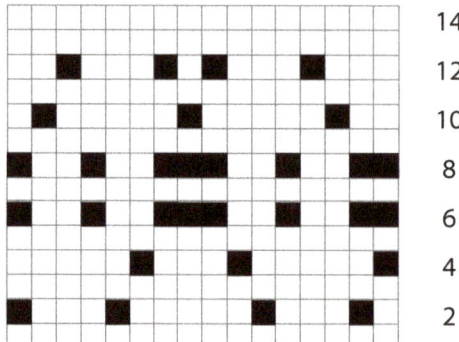

16 This chart *only* shows the position of the dark squares in the 2nd and all the even numbered rows of the original chart.

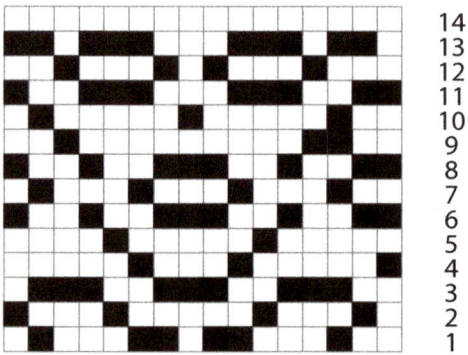

17 This chart is a combination of the two previous charts. Rows 1, 3, 6, 8, 11 and 13 need to be adjusted because there are two or three adjacent squares filled in, which would indicate two or three adjacent tuck stitches.

The final acrobat pattern

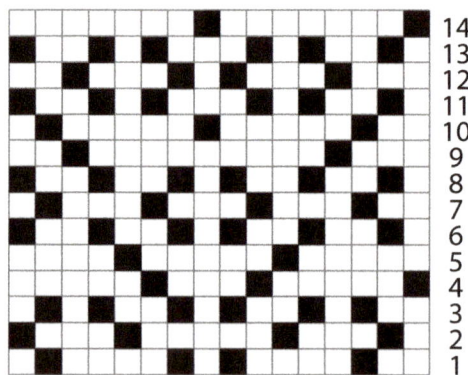

18 Working back from the composite chart at (17), this revised design chart shows where stitches have been removed or added to eliminate any possible problems from tucking adjacent stitches.

• stitch added   X stitch removed

19 This is the final chart for the acrobats, suitable for hand-selected or automatic patterning. Even though there is no sign of acrobats on the chart, they will miraculously appear in your fabric!

Mosaic Knitting   133

The Labyrinth Pattern

Just to provide a little extra practice, I have also included the step-by-step conversion for the labyrinth pattern. By the time you've worked your way through both of these examples, you should be able to convert any of the mosaic patterns you find in hand knit pattern books or to begin designing your own.

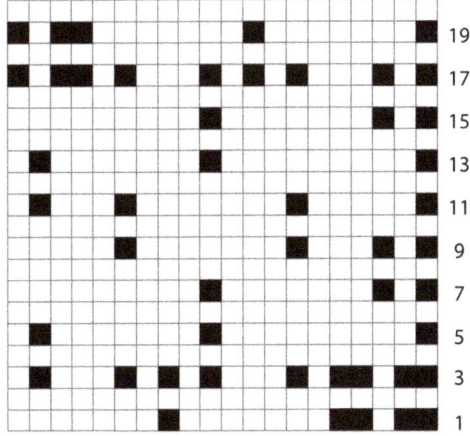

21 All of the white spaces in the odd numbered rows are represented in this chart.

20 This 20 stitch/20 row pattern includes a plain row (and a plain stitch) between repeats, exactly as shown in the Walker Mosaic book.

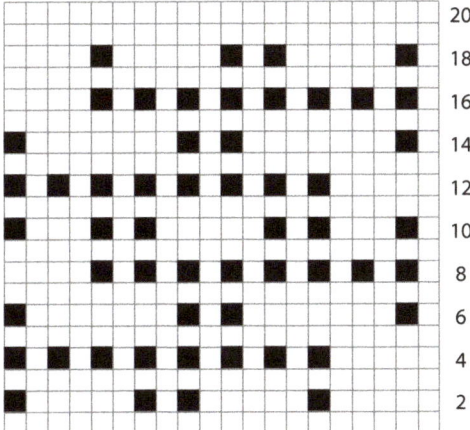

22 This chart records all the black squares in the even numbered rows.

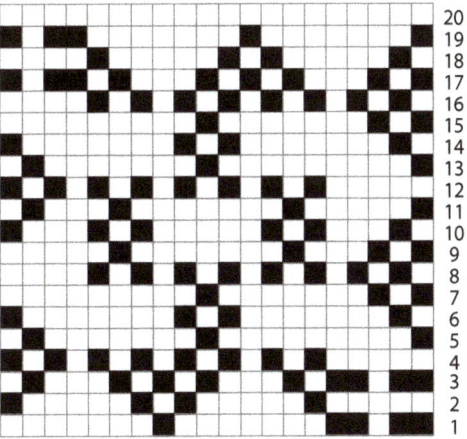

23 This third chart is a combination of the first 2 charts, but contains a couple of problem areas in rows 1, 3, 17 and 19.

● stitch added   X stitch removed

24 Stitches have been both added and removed to make sure the pattern knits tuck mosaic without problems.

To work from these new machine–friendly charts, remember that each row must be repeated twice. For punch card and electronic machines you can use the elongation feature and just show each row once on the card. If you create a chart for a manual machine, the filled squares represent needles pulled to holding position for two rows as in the previous examples.

Also, when you prepare a punch card, you need to punch the *background* stitches –not the pattern stitches– and you need to punch enough complete lengthwise repeats of the pattern for the ends of the card to overlap and fasten together correctly. That is, the pattern should read continuously without missing or repeating any rows of the pattern.

For electronic machines, you only need to show a single repeat lengthwise and width wise and mark the card and/or set the machine so that it knows how wide the repeat is and where the first and last rows are. Your manual can provide more detailed information on how to do this.

The final labyrinth pattern

25 Note that the final chart for the labyrinth includes a plain row at the end of each repeat and that the chart doesn't resemble the final fabric at all.

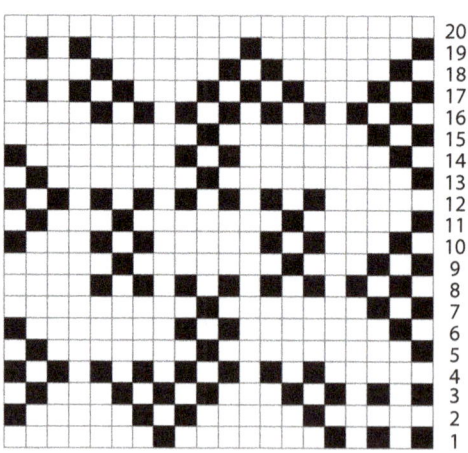

Entrelac

en·tre·lac [en-truh-lak]

noun: a decorative border of interlaced garlands and leaves; a knitting technique used to create a textured pattern that resembles basket weave.

origin: From the French entrelacer, to interlace.

Many knitters are intimidated by entrelac because it looks so complex. The truth, however, is that once you get started (by hand or by machine) entrelac knitting breaks down into a series of very straight-forward steps. Blocks of color appear to inter-weave while the stitches lie perpendicular to each other, creating colorful and sometimes 3-dimensional fabrics.

I started playing with entrelac the way most machine knitters do: scrapping off and re-hanging stitches. However, after a very short time I decided that since hand knitters could knit without stitch holders or scrap knitting, there must be a way to do it on the machine as well. Bridging, or the use of Holding Position to knit extra rows on specific needles, allows you to knit entrelac with absolutely no scrapping off. You will still need to pick up edge stitches while you work, which is exactly what you would do by hand.

When I wrote *Hand-Manipulated Stitches for Machine Knitters,* it originally included my bridged method for working entrelac, instead of the scrap and re-hang method, but the book started getting longer and longer; this was some of the material that we were forced to cut. It has been languishing in my file cabinet ever since.

I gave lots of examples of other bridged stitches in HMS and I devoted my entire second book, *More Hand-Manipulated Stitches for Machine Knitters* to the subject of bridging. If you own either of those books, you are probably somewhat familiar with bridging. If not, have no fear because the following directions and photos will break entrelac down, step-by-step, and will guide you through the entire process.

My directions are for knitting basic, stockinet entrelac. Once you are comfortable with this method, you might want to consider adding some hand-manipulated stitches to the rectangles: lace patterns, cables, twisted stitches, reformed stitches. You can also turn the work over to work rows in reverse stockinet. Unfortunately, garter stitch just isn't a realistic option when working entrelac on a machine because the method relies on having needles in both holding and working position at all times and those needle positions shift as the work progresses.

Entrelac is knitted using four distinct kinds of rows: First, the fabric always begins with one row of base triangles. This is followed by a row of right leaning rectangles with edge triangles that then continues alternating with rows of left leaning rectangles for the entire length of the fabric. Remember that left and right are being used here to refer to the way we see the stitches on the machine; it would be reversed for a hand knitter looking at the knit, rather than the purl, side of the fabric. Finally, when the fabric has reached the desired length, it is capped off with a row of inverted triangles across the top.

In the photos that accompany my directions, I have removed most of the color from the photos except for the areas that correspond to the text that describes each photo. So, when you see bright blue or creamy white in those photos, do not assume I have changed color, but do pay special attention to that portion of the photo.

Yarns that relax or "bloom" a bit when washed and finished give the neatest look, with the perpendicular stitches cleanly divided. There is almost always apt to be some "grin through" where an edge has been picked up and knitted with a lighter or darker yarn. This effect is most noticeable with strongly contrasting yarns (like my blue and white); when entrelac is worked in a single yarn (like the photo at the beginning of this chapter) the pick-ups are usually invisible.

You can knit entrelac fabrics in a single color or you can change color after every row or after individual rectangles if you want to. Initially, I think the color changes at the end of each row make it easier to understand what is happening in the fabric. Self-striping, tweed and space dyed yarns look great and whatever texture your machine can handle will be fine as well. Yarn ends should be woven in as you knit to minimize some of the finishing (see page 63).

Notice the "grin through" where the blue stitches have been picked up to knit the following white rectangles. This effect is diminished when entrelac is knitted with less–contrasting yarns or with textured yarns. Obviously, when entrelac is knitted in a single color, this is a non–issue.

The stitches are worked in groups and you can use any number of stitches as your multiple, but all groups should have the same number of stitches. My examples were worked with groups of 5 stitches because I have a 5-prong tool to move entire groups of stitches when needed and because I like the way entrelac looks on a somewhat smaller scale.

Throughout the process, you will transfer one stitch at a time from a Holding Position (HP) needle to an adjacent (or nearby) Working Position (WP) needle and will only need a single prong transfer tool to do this. However, after I have made 2-3 transfers, I find that I need to move the remaining HP stitches closer to the working needles to avoid straining them. I usually do this with a 3-prong transfer tool, making the transfer and the move all in one motion.

If your stitch groups are larger than 5 or 6, you will need either a multi-prong transfer tool or the ability to handle two transfer tools together in one hand. Alternatively, you can move the stitches in several steps. Having the right tool makes it faster, easier and less frustrating to knit entrelac.

As I said, the groups of stitches can be as large as you want, but be aware that when you need to decrease stitches by transferring them from HP to the adjacent working needle, after two or three decreases, the stitches will have to stretch too far to make the move and you will need to move the stitches over, returning them to HP once you do so. It isn't difficult, but it does add an extra step to every repeat. I'll explain this in more detail – and photos – in the example that follows, but just know that it is a consideration when deciding how large your groups should be. The larger your groups of stitches, the more often you will have to move stitches over to avoid straining the decreases.

Garment shaping can be an issue with entrelac, but I offer this basic caveat: always try to decrease or increase by a full repeat so that you don't have to figure out what to do with half enough stitches for a rectangle. Better yet, look for garments that require little or no shaping. A square or drop shoulder is easier to reckon with than a raglan or a set-in sleeve. Entrelac fabrics have so much personality to begin with that simpler shapes are more appropriate anyhow. Obviously, entrelac is great for pillows, purses and afghans because they usually require no shaping and the back (purl) side of the fabric is often quite attractive.

I always start knitting with some rows of waste knitting so I can establish the stitches cleanly on the machine and to hang my weights before I start knitting with the main yarn. You can start the entrelac sequences after e-wrapping or knitting one row above the waste. If you choose to knit a row, you need to finish that edge later to secure the open stitches. You can also begin with several rows of stockinet or another stitch for a base or just use entrelac as an insertion in any fabric.

The bridging process requires you to retain some needles in HP while others are in WP so set your carriage to hold needles that are placed in HP and leave it set that way. Any stitches that return to WP will do so either by manually placing needles in Upper-Working Position (UWP) or by transferring the stitches with a transfer tool. In the latter case, the empty needles will be placed in Non-Working Position (NWP).

Whenever the directions instruct you to pick up stitches, it will be from the finished (selvage) edge of the section below. Use a single or double transfer tool to pick up 5 full stitches, evenly spaced along the edge (see page 58). You can pick up half stitches, but I find that the fabric doesn't hold its shape as well.

You will find it easiest to pick up stitches later if, when you knit each section, you use a claw weight to keep the stitches from tightening along the edges. You should continually move any weights as the work progresses so they are always underneath working needles.

While entrelac is not difficult to master, it goes without saying that you need to be familiar with your machine and comfortable with the transfer tools before trying to knit a stitch with so many very specific steps. Entrelac would be a poor choice for a beginning knitter–by hand or machine.

Knitting the First Row

Base Triangles

With waste yarn, cast on a multiple of 5 stitches. Knit some rows and end with the carriage on right end of the bed (COR). For a closed edge, e-wrap cast on with the main yarn over the same needles. Knit 2 rows, ending COR.

Set the carriage to hold needles in HP and place all needles in HP.

*Move the first 2 needles on the carriage side to UWP and knit 1 row. COL. Return the needle closest to the carriage to HP and knit 1 row. COR. ** (The needle returned to HP makes an automatic wrap).

Entrelac 139

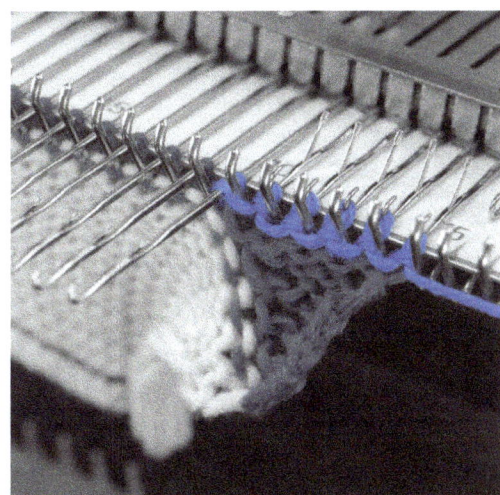

1 The first base triangle is complete and the next pass of the carriage will bridge to begin the second base triangle.

Continue repeating from * to ** until 5 needles at right are in WP and COR as shown in the photo at the top of the next page. (1)

[Move the next 2 needles from HP to UWP and knit 1 row to the left. There are 7 needles in WP. Return the needle closest to the carriage to HP for the wrap *and* move to HP the previous group of 5 needles at right. 1 needle remains in WP. Knit 1 row. COR]

Repeat * to ** until next group of 5 needles is in WP (2) and then knit 1 row to right. Repeat [to] to bridge to the next group and then repeat [* to **] to work those 5 needles. Continue alternating these two sequences across the bed, ending last group at left * to ** and COL. Put last 5 needles at left in HP. (3)

3 All of the needles have been returned to WP for photo purposes only. Each of the 5-needle sections has knitted a base triangle and the yarn has bridged continuously from one group of stitches to the next. They don't look much like triangles when they are still on the machine, but they will take their shape as the next sect is worked.

2 The second group of 5 needles has been worked. After knitting 1 row to the right, the next 2 needles at left will be moved to UWP to bridge to the third group as described [to].

Knitting the Second Row: Right Leaning Rectangles and Side Triangles

Left Edge Triangle

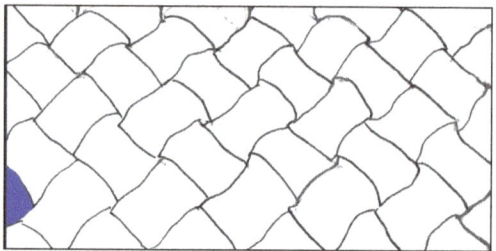

First, you need to knit a single triangle at the left edge of the fabric as follows:

Begin COL and all needles in HP. Move the first stitch from HP to the next needle at left and place the empty needle in NWP. Knit 2 rows. (4) Make an increase at the left edge by lifting the purl bar of the WP stitch onto the next empty needle at left and then move the stitch from the next needle in HP onto the right–most WP needle. (5) Leave the empty needle in NWP and knit 2 rows. (5a)

Continue, * increasing 1 stitch at the left edge and *at the same time* making a decrease by transferring the next stitch from HP to the nearest working needle. Leave the empty needle in NWP. Knit 2 rows.**

All increases are made by picking up the purl bar of the left edge stitch and placing it on the

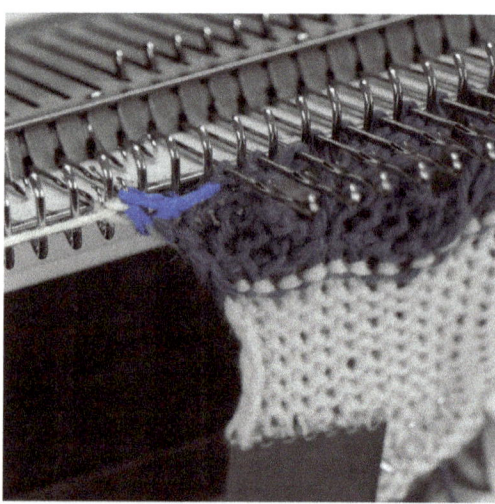

5 Second increase and transfer have been made.

4 Edge stitch has been moved, first transfer made and 2 rows knitted.

5a The next 2 rows have been knitted.

next empty needle. The stitches transferred from HP are always placed on the same needle at the right of the WP group.

Repeat * to ** until there are 5 needles in WP and 5 empty needles between them and the needles that remain in HP.

In photos (5) and (5a) there are 2 empty needles between the needles that remained in HP and the WP needles. In photo (6) you can see that I have moved the remaining 3 stitches in this group to the left while making the next decrease.

I use a 3-prong transfer tool to make these moves, placing the left-most stitch of the group on the right hand needle of the WP group to make the decrease and moving the stitches closer all in one motion. With larger groups of stitches, you would have to move more stitches over at this point or do it several times as the gaps widen again.

Moving all of the stitches over like this will prevent the stitches from stretching or breaking and it is a motion you will repeat throughout the fabric.

Whether you use multi-prong tools or make these moves several times, make sure that the left-most stitch is placed on the right edge needle of the WP group and that all of the other stitches you move are returned to HP before you knit the next 2 rows.

After the last decrease has been made and 2 rows knitted, there will be 5 empty needles between the WP needles and the needles in HP. The left edge triangle is complete. (8)

7 Make the next increase and decrease so that only 1 needle remains in HP. Knit 2 rows and then make the last increase/decrease.

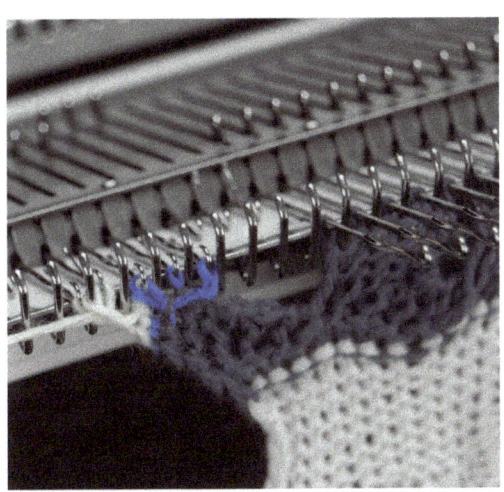

6 The next 3 stitches in HP have moved 2 needles to the left. Return 2 needles to HP and then knit 2 rows.

8 The left edge triangle is complete and there are 5 empty needles between it and the needles in HP.

9 Pick up the edge of the base triangle below and hang it on the 5 empty needles to the right of the edge triangle you just completed.

Right-Leaning Rectangles

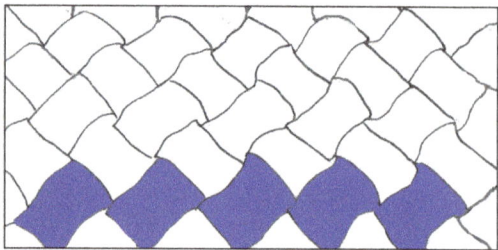

Next you will work an entire row of right leaning rectangles.

Begin COL. Pick up 5 stitches from the short selvage edge of the base triangle below and hang them on the 5 empty needles. Take care to pick up whole stitches. (9) Knit 1 row to the right on all 10 needles. (10) COR. Then move the first group of 5 needles to HP . (11)

Next, knit 1 row to the left on the remaining 5 needles. (12)

10 Knit 1 row to the right over all 10 needles. This is the bridging step.

12 1 row knitted to the left. Now you can begin shaping the rectangle.

11 At left, hold the 5 needles you used to work the edge triangle. The first rectangle will be worked on the 5 needles now in WP.

*Decrease by transferring the stitch from the next HP needle at right to the adjacent WP needle. (13) Empty needle to NWP. Then knit 2 rows. (14) COL.** Repeat * to ** until there are 5 empty needles to work the next group.

Periodically, you will have to move the last 2 or 3 needles in each HP group closer to the working needles to avoid stretching the stitches. The larger your groups of stitches, the more often you will need to do this. Be sure to return to HP any needles that you are not yet ready to decrease.

13 The first stitch has been transferred from HP to the adjacent WP needle.

15 The 2nd stitch has been transferred from HP to the working needle; next, 2 rows will be knitted.

14 2 rows have been knitted following the first decrease.

16 The 3 HP stitches at the right have been moved to the left (as a group) to close the enlarging gap between the WP and HP needles.

17 The last 2 needles have been returned to HP before knitting the next 2 rows.

18 The 4th stitch has been transferred to make the next decrease and the empty needle pushed to NWP. Knit 2 rows.

19 The 5th and last stitch in this group has been transferred to the WP needle. Once the next 2 rows have been knitted, the first rectangle will be complete.

20 The edge of the second base triangle has been picked up on the empty needles.

21 1 row has been knitted to the right to begin the next rectangle. The 5 needles used to knit the first rectangle will be placed in HP before continuing.

In the photos (16) and (17), HP stitches 3–5 have been moved to the left so that the 3rd stitch makes a decrease; the other 2 stitches are closer to the working needles and their needles have been returned to HP before knitting the next 2 rows.

Continue making decreases, followed by 2 rows until there are 5 empty needles at the right of the current group.

After making the last decrease, knit 2 rows, ending COL and then pick up the edge of the next base triangle as shown (20). Knit 1 row to the right (21) and then hold the five needles from the previous group at the left so that only 5 needles remain in WP to begin the next rectangle.

Repeat * to ** until there are 5 empty needles to work the next group. After each complete sequence, there should be 5 empty needles directly above the edge of the next base triangle.

Continue until the last 5 needles on the right edge of the fabric are in WP and then work one right edge triangle.

Move the last stitch to the 5th needle at the right so that there are four empty needles between it and the needles in HP as shown in photo (23). This completes the second row.

22 Every alternate row, when COL, make a simple edge decrease at the right edge until only 1 stitch remains.

Right Edge Triangle

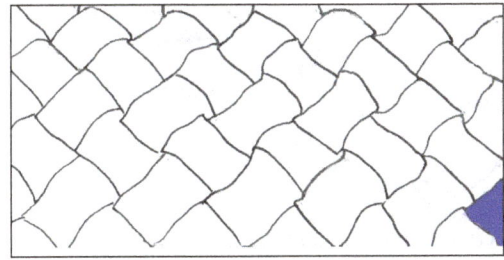

Begin COL. Pick up the edge of the last base triangle at right on the 5 empty needles above. Knit 1 row over all 10 needles. Hold all needles except last 5 at right. Knit 1 row. COL. Decrease 1 stitch at the right edge and knit 2 rows. (22)

Continue decreasing 1 stitch at the right edge every alternate row when COL until only 1 stitch remains. Knit 1 row.

23 Move the last stitch to the 5th needle from the edge of the fabric so that there are 4 empty needles between it and the HP needles at left.

Knitting the Third Row

Left leaning rectangles

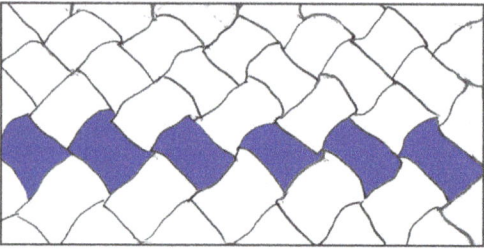

With COR, pick up the edge of the end triangle knitted in the previous sequence and hang it on the 4 empty needles. Knit 2 rows. (24)

[*Decrease by transferring the first stitch in HP to the adjacent WP needle. (25) Leave the empty in NWP. Knit 2 rows**.

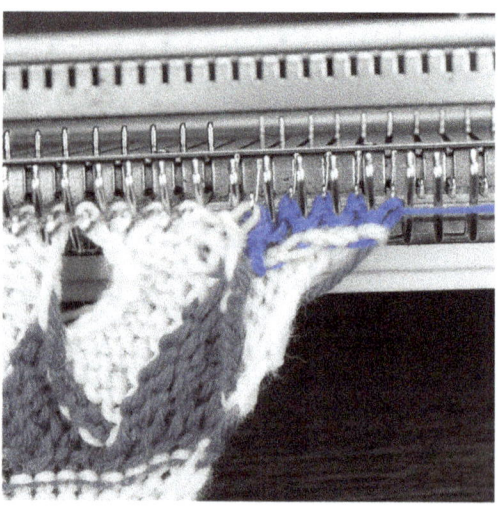

25 Transfer the first stitch from HP to the adjacent WP needle. Leave the empty needle in NWP and then knit 2 rows.

24 The selvage of the right edge triangle has been picked up on the 4 empty needles above. This pick-up was made on only 4 needles because there was already 1 needle holding a stitch from the previous step.

26 Continue transferring stitches from HP to the same WP needle, knitting 2 rows after each transfer, until there are 2 or 3 empty needles between the HP and WP needles. Move the stitches from the remaining 3 HP needles to the right, closing the gap and making one decrease at the same time as you did for earlier steps. Make sure you place the last 2 needles of the group in HP before knitting the 2 rows.

Entrelac 147

27 Move the remaining (3) HP stitches closer to the WP needles as you make the next transfer. 2 needles return to HP and 1 makes a decrease.

28 Once the 5th transfer has been made and 2 rows knitted, you will pick up the edge of the next white rectangle below and hang it on the 5 empty needles above.

Repeat * to ** until there are 5 empty needles in NWP. Close the gap that widens between the WP and HP needles by shifting the stitches from the last 3 HP needles to the right as a group (26) and (27). Move COR.

After the 5th stitch has been transferred from HP to the WP needle, pick up the edge of the next rectangle below and hang it on the 5 empty needles just as you did when knitting the right leaning rectangles. Knit 1 row across all 10 needles and then put the first group of 5 needles into HP. Knit 1 row to right.] Repeat [to] across the bed, ending COL.

29 After knitting 1 row across all 10 needles, the 5 needles at right are placed in HP to work the second rectangle on the remaining 5 needles.

Continue to alternately repeat the second and third rows for the desired length of the fabric. There will *always* be triangles at each end of the second row; the third row is just rectangles.

30 Cut the yarn at the end of the third row.

Binding Off

Ending Triangles

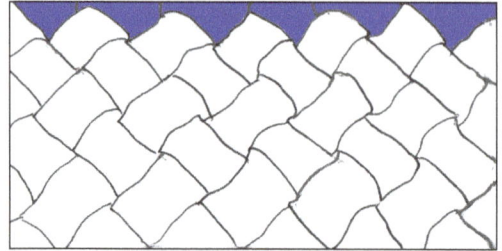

31 Begin COR with all needles in HP after having completed a row of *right leaning rectangles*. Move the remaining stitch to the 6th needle at right.

33 Transfer the first stitch from HP to the adjacent needle and make an edge decrease at the right edge. Then knit 2 rows.

32 Pick up the edge below and hang it on the 5 empty needles between those in HP and the single stitch on the 6th needle. Knit 2 rows.

34 *Then, continue making 2 decreases every-other row, decreasing 1 stitch at the right edge and at the same time transfer the stitch from the next HP needle to the adjacent WP needle as before. Knit 2 rows.** Repeat * to ** until 1 stitch remains.

35 The second set of decreases have been made.

36 To make the last couple of decreases, you will need to move the work over as you did when knitting the body of the fabric to avoid stretching the stitches.

37 The last decreases have been made. Knit 2 rows and then move this single stitch to the 6th needle at right to begin the next section. At the end of the last section, cut the yarn and pull the tail through the last stitch.

150   Chapter 9

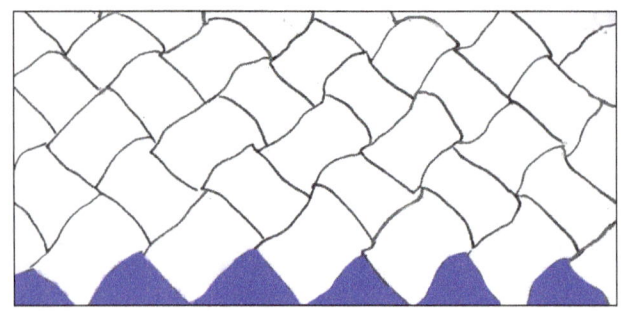

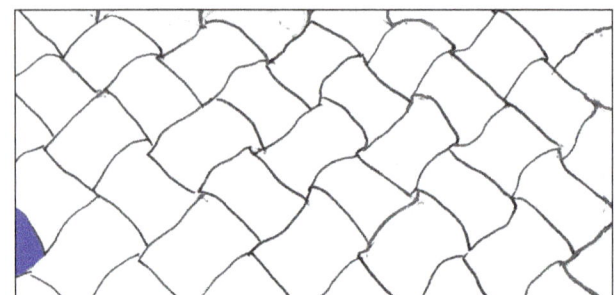

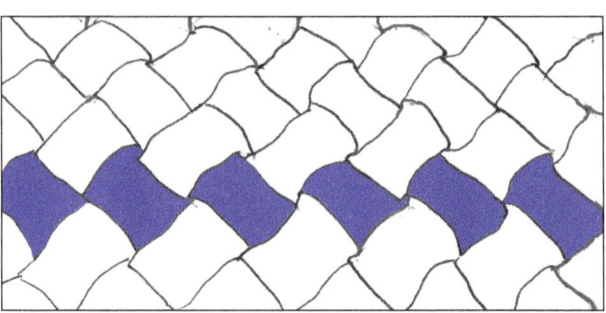

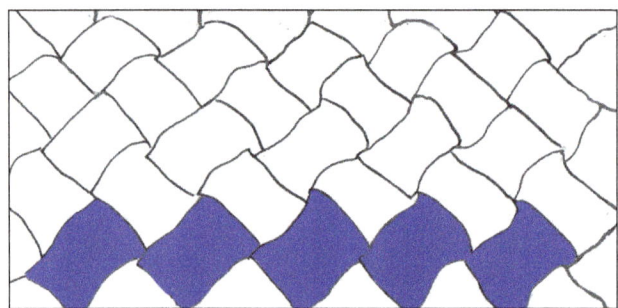

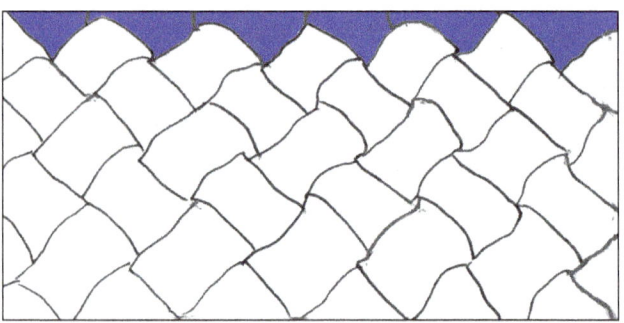

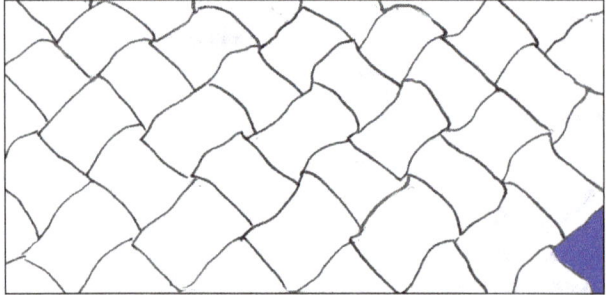

Modular Knitting

mod-u-lar

mäjeler

adjective

1. Employing or involving a module or modules as the basis of design or construction.

Modular knitting is a method of working where individual sections are knitted by picking up selvage edges or live stitches from a previous section to begin working the next. Most often knitted in squares, it is also possible to work modular knits with other geometric shapes.

By hand, most modular knitting is done in garter stitch because it is fast, produces a fabric with lots of body and it usually has a fairly balanced gauge. That is, the stitch and row gauges are the same (or nearly the same), which makes it easier to knit perfect squares by repeatedly decreasing 2 stitches every alternate row (for example).

Garter stitch is not a practical option for machine knit modular pieces because the garter bar accessory that is used to remove the work from the machine, turn it over and replace it on the needles, complicates the process with free passes. It slows things *way* down and introduces the possibility of splitting or dropping stitches with every turn. It isn't impossible, but I would say that it is definitely beyond the reach of novice knitters and probably has very limited appeal even to knitters with substantial garter bar experience.

It might, however, be practical to include just a couple of garter rows at the very beginning (or end) of a square for textural accent. You can also turn a completed square over and pick up from the knit side to begin the next square to introduce some reverse stockinet effects. Your joins might not be as even, but with a textured yarn it probably won't show very much anyhow.

Knitters who own an automated garter carriage for their standard gauge machine can work in garter stitch, but it is very slow and require lots of time just sitting in front of the machine, waiting to make the decreases.

I chose to work all of my samples in a worsted weight yarn that knits at 5 stitches and 7 rows per inch, but you can work in any gauge suitable for your machine or your patience. Modular knitting is a great way to use up odds and ends of yarn from your stash because it generally includes lots of color changes. And, although I have limited my samples to smooth yarns so that the details show clearly in photographs, you can certainly introduce textured yarns when you begin to plan your own projects and work your way through that yarn stash. Just be aware that very varied yarns will probably knit at different gauges, which may or may not pose problems in a full project.

Before you begin to explore modular knitting, please be sure that you know how to pick up stitches (Chapter 5) and to weave in yarn ends while you work (page 63). Both of these skills are essential to your success here. Also, although not absolutely required, multi-prong transfer tools will make the work smoother and faster and I encourage you to purchase them for your machines (page 184).

All of the diagrams that follow depict the way the fabric looks as it hangs on the machine with the purl side facing you. Therefore, the photographs of the actual swatches will be reversed as they are seen from the knit side. Some of the charts use the basic knitting symbols shown on page 22 and you should familiarize yourself with these symbols before you begin.

In addition to the basic symbols, I have included others that show the ending yarn tails, indicate e-wrapped and picked-up edges and the direction in which individual sections are knitted and decreased. The sections are also numbered in the order in which they are knitted.

⎔	ending yarn tail
﹏﹏﹏	e-wrapped edge or scrapped off edge
﹏﹏﹏	picked up edge
◩	completed square

Join-As-You-Knit Strips

The simplest modular pieces are knitted as strips that are joined one to the next while you knit. Machine knitters call this method "join-as-you-go" or "join-as-you-knit" and use it for decorative as well as structural purposes. Although I'll only discuss it here in decorative terms, it is often used to join garment sections together or to join bands onto garment edges. The sample shown below was worked with cable, fair isle, lace and stockinet strips; there is even an I-cord that was joined between the lace and the stockinet section at one edge.

You can, of course, knit a traditional fabric that changes from one pattern or texture to another every so many rows, but those bands of color or texture will form *horizontal stripes across the width of your garment*. If you knit a cuff to cuff, sideways sweater, the differing bands of color or pattern will be vertical, but the stitches themselves will then be horizontal.

The advantage to the join-as-you-go method is that the stitches still run vertically in the garment so that cables, for example, run from shoulder to hem as do vertical stripes of different yarns, textures, colors or patterns. Also, by joining additional sections to a piece in progress, the width of a sweater of afghan is totally unlimited.

On the downside, if you discover a mistake later on, you may have to rip out some perfectly good work to go back and correct it.

Even with a variety of yarns, minor differences in gauge can probably be blocked out of a finished piece. However, some stitches, like tuck, are apt to have very compressed row gauges and you will need to knit a separate gauge swatch so that you can adjust accordingly. The larger your project, the more you need to compensate for differing gauges (especially row gauge) if you are using a variety of different stitches or different weight yarns. If you want the beginning and ending edges to be even, you will need to do a swatch for any and all variation you plan to include. Because the work cannot be measured in progress (as it would when hand knitting) you must rely on the row counter to ensure that each section knits to the proper length and that requires accurate swatching to begin with.

The knitting method is quite simple. Cast on the required number of stitches for the first strip, either with waste yarn (for an open edge to be dealt with later) or with a closed cast on of your choice. Knit to the end and bind off or scrap off.

Then, cast on for the second strip. Knit 2 rows, ending COR. Hold the first strip with the wrong side facing you and use a single-prong transfer tool to pick up the edge stitch from the second row of the fabric and hang it on the left-most needle of the second strip. Pulling the needle to HP as you deposit the stitch will ensure that the two stitches knit cleanly with the next pass of the carriage. *Knit 2 rows. Then pick up another stitch from the first strip, skipping a row in between pick-ups.** Repeat from * to ** until all of the stitches from the first strip have been picked up and the same number of rows knitted.

From left to right, this fabric was worked with stockinet, I-cord, lace, cables, stockinet, Fair Isle, cables and stockinet.

The opening in the second strip from the right could easily become a pocket placement.

If you need to make gauge adjustments, you may periodically have to skip fewer or more rows along the edge of the first strip to compensate for the gauge difference. This is something you should work out on your swatch, before you begin a project.

In addition to using a variety of pattern and texture stitches, you can also reverse the face of a strip for reversed stockinet, join the edge of an I-cord, knit striped strips or vary the width of each strip a little or a lot. If you knit different length strips, you can leave openings or slits in the fabric for pocket openings or other design features. In short, you can let your creativity and imagination go wild!

Log Cabin

Most quilters are familiar with a pattern called "Log Cabin" where strips are built around each other until they form a large square. In the knitted version, you work the same way, joining the squares into strips that are then joined to form a larger fabric. The size of the squares themselves is limited only by the number of needles on the bed of your machine.

The sample at left (opposite page) was worked by simply picking up both selvage and live stitches and re-hanging them on the needles to knit each section. It is fast and easy, but produces a jog at the end of each section because the selvage edge sits lower and tighter on the needles than the live stitches do. The sample at right however, used the crochet hook method (page 60) to pick up the selvage edges so that the jog is eliminated.

Depending on the yarns you choose, those uneven edges at the ends of rows might not bother you and if so, you can just pick up the selvage edges and hang them on the needles and you can work an even number of rows instead of the odd number I specify in my directions. I felt that the sections didn't look smooth or even and chose, instead, to use the crochet hook pick up method. While it requires a little more effort (not much, really) I think it makes a huge difference.

For both of my examples, I cast on 5 stitches with waste yarn, changed to the main yarn and knitted 7 rows. Then I scrapped off the stitches. All of the following sections were knitted for 7 rows, but the number of stitches keeps increasing as the work progresses. Each sections is knitted for 7 rows (1") so when you make your future pick ups, you need to pick up 5 stitches from any selvage edges (regardless of how wide each strip is) because the stitch gauge is 5 per inch.

If you choose to use the crochet hook pick-up method, it is important to end each section COL so that, as the work is turned, the yarn tail will be available later to pick up stitches from right to left. (This makes the assumption you are right handed. If not, you will probably prefer ending COR.) Also–as with any modular knitting–weave in the ends as you work (to minimize the finishing later) but only *after* you have used the yarn tails to pick up the selvage stitches with the crochet hook. I generally remove the scrap and clip the woven–in tails after I have knitted and checked each section, but you can wait until the end if you prefer and don't mind all the ends hanging down as you work.

The easiest way to pick up the selvage edges with the crochet hook is to do so before anything is rehung on the machine so you can manipulate the work to see both sides. When you need to pick up stitches at both ends of a scrapped off section, pick up the right–most group on the crochet hook first, then pass the hook behind the stitches held on scrap to pick up the other selvage edge. Once you have transferred the first group of 5 stitches to the machine, the scrapped off stitches will no longer be all scrunched up and you will be able to hang them before hanging the last selvage group from the crochet hook. Because you can hold the work in your lap to do this, you can easily follow a single column of stitches to make sure the pick up is straight. Make sure you use a crochet hook suitable for the size of your yarn so that the picked up stitches are not overly large or small.

If your square is very large or the sections knitted for many rows, you might want to use an afghan hook instead of a regular crochet hook to pick up stitches. Afghan hooks look like a circular knitting needle with a hook at one end. The long cable attached to it will allow you to pick up and store lots of stitches. I only knitted 7 rows for each of my sections, but the more rows you knit, the more selvage stitches you will need to pick up later when re–hanging that edge; and the wider each section is, the more stitches you will have to scrunch up and pass the hook behind.

The sample at left was picked up in the conventional way. There are slight jogs along all of the lines that divide the sections. The sample at right was picked up using a crochet hook so that all of the picked up edges are even and regular.

First square to start: With waste yarn, cast on 5 stitches, knit some rows, ending COR. Change to the main yarn, leave a 12" long tail and knit 7 rows, ending COL. Cut the main yarn and scrap off.

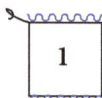

Turn the work 90° clock-wise. Use a crochet hook and, working from the right side of the fabric, pick up 5 stitches along the selvage edge of #1 using the attached yarn tail to form the stitches. Use a transfer tool to move the stitches from the crochet hook to the needles. Knit 7 rows CC, ending COL. Cut the CC yarn, leaving a 12" tail. Scrap off.

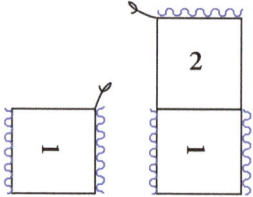

Turn the work 90° clock-wise and use a crochet hook, working from the right side of the fabric, to pick up 5 stitches along the selvage edge of section #2, using its yarn tail to form the stitches. Then pick up the 5 live stitches from the scrap on section #1. With CC, knit 7 rows, ending COL. Cut the yarn, leaving a 12" tail. Scrap off.

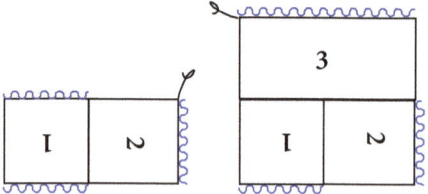

Turn the work 90° clock-wise and pick up 5 stitches across the selvage edges of sections both #3 and #1 and then knit 7 rows with CC. Cut the yarn, leaving a 12" tail. Scrap off.

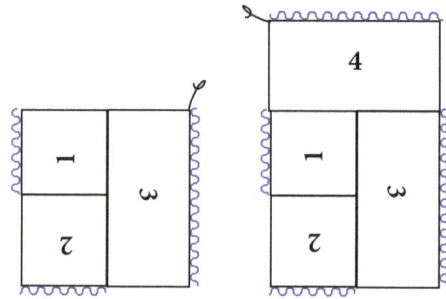

Once again, Turn the work 90° clock-wise and use the attached yarn tails to pick up and make stitches along the selvage edges of sections #4 and #2. Pick up the live stitches from the scrap on section #1. Then knit 7 rows CC, ending COL. Cut the yarn, leaving a 12" tail. Scrap off.

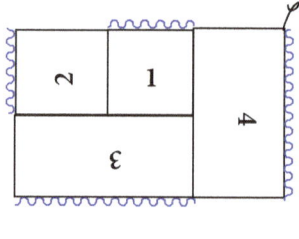

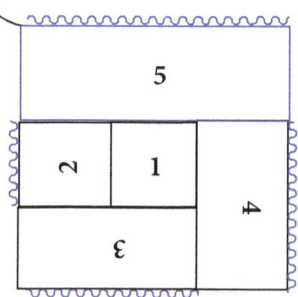

Continue in this way, rotating the finished rectangle 90° and picking up stitches from scrap and selvage edges until the piece is square with the same number of sections beyond the center on all sides. You can bind off the final stitches or leave them live (on scrap) to join to subsequent squares.

Modular Squares

Also known as Domino Knitting, modular squares are quite easy to work by machine. Like all modular knitting, these squares are interesting in solid colors, but when knitted with hand dyed yarns or well placed color changes, they appear even more colorful and complex.

By hand, you cast on an odd number of stitches and make a double decrease on the center stitch, every other row, working in garter stitch. Rather than narrowing the piece to form a triangle, the decreases pull the sides up in such a way that once you have decreased down to the last stitch, the work forms a square (or a perfect diamond if you turn it).

Garter stitch, however, is not an option for machine knitters so the squares are usually knitted in stockinet instead. Now, rather than garter ridges dominating the texture, the stitches appear sharply perpendicular to each other and the stitch direction becomes an important design element.

If you were to follow the directions for most hand knit modular squares, working in stockinet rather than garter stitch, you would end up producing a diamond shape similar to the one shown above left because, due to the different stitch and row gauges, alternate row decreasing requires too many rows when applied to stockinet. These diamonds can be an interesting shape to work with (as you will see later in this chapter) but one I will address after we have dealt with some of the basics.

Because stockinet gauge is never square, you need to adjust the rate of decreasing if you want to produce a square instead of a diamond. As I said earlier, for all of my samples I worked with a worsted weight yarn that produced a stockinet gauge of 5 stitches and 7 rows per inch. Also, my samples were all worked with 21 stitches that (usually) decreased down to a single stitch, but you can use any *odd* number of stitches you like.

According to my gauge information, a 2" square should result from knitting 10 stitches (2" x 5 stitches per inch) and 14 rows (2" x 7

When decreases are made every alternate row, the finished piece is an elongated diamond like the one at left. If the decreases are distributed according to the gauge, it produces a perfect square like the one at right.

rows per inch). 10 stitches accounts for half of the stitches (minus the single center stitch) and determines the width of the square.

For a larger square or a finer gauge, you would need to refigure the rate of decreasing accordingly. Just keep in mind that half the number of stitches you cast on (minus 1) determines the size of the square when divided by your stitch gauge. So, in my case, 21 stitches, minus the 1 center stitch, halved to account for the double decreases = 10 stitches. At 5 stitches/inch this will produce a 2" square. The single stitch that remains is used to start the next square.

Reducing 21 stitches down to a single stitch by making double decreases at the center will require 10 decrease rows, but not on alternate rows. Working the decreases on alternate rows would require 20 rows, rather than the 14 that the gauge dictated.

You can use the "magic formula" (see page 94) to help you figure out how often to decrease or you can just wing it. Unless you are working on a really large squares or with a fine gauge that calls for lots of stitches, you should be able to distribute the decreases over the allotted number of rows without too much difficulty.

For the examples that follow, I needed to make 10 double decreases over 14 rows. When I consulted the magic formula, it suggested that I make 1 decrease (each side of center) every row, 7 times and then 1 decrease every alternate row 3 times. With such a small square, I probably could have done all the every-row decreases first and then the alternate row decreases, but I wanted to produce as smooth and regular a square as possible so, instead, I shuffled the two orders and made my decreases after knitting the following rows:

1, 2, 4, 5, 6, 8, 9, 10, 12, 13

All of the diagrams that follow show how the squares look on the purl side, as they face you while you sit at the machine. Remember that the lines formed by the double decreases will slant in the opposite direction on the knit face of the fabric. Also, the decrease line always slants from the inside corner to the outside corner where the square has been reduced to a single stitch.

I begin all of my pieces with waste yarn so I can hang a weight before I start working with the main yarn. You can use an e-wrap cast on over the waste or you can just start knitting to preserve open stitches if you prefer to deal with them later.

Please review the information in Chapter 5 for picking up stitches. Because you usually pick up the longer edge stitch when picking up half stitches, you will find that there may not be enough places to pick up along an edge if you opt for the half stitch method. Therefore, I usually pick up whole stitches along the selvage edges when knitting and joining squares.

Once again, you will cut the finishing time later on if you weave in the yarn tails as you work.

Whenever possible, I usually try to work on the same group of (21) needles to simplify counting and keeping track. Its not always possible, but the repetition helps minimize mistakes. Sometimes, depending on where the next square will be cast on, you might need to move the last stitch of a square to a specific needle (at the edge or center of the group) before beginning the next square.

You need to rotate the completed squares before each new pick up, depending on the direction the next square will be worked. My diagrams and directions will specify this and tell you if/when you need to cut the yarn (if working in a single color) to start the next square. The diagrams also indicate when/where to pick up the selvage edge of the fabric or to cast on additional stitches with the e-wrap method.

All of the double decreases are worked like large full-fashioned decreases. I find it very helpful having multi-prong tools to do this. Otherwise, you need to make your decreases in several steps or learn to hold a pair of tools in your hands at the same time. The more stitches you start with, the larger the initial moves will need to be in order to move all the stitches over by one needle towards the center. As I make the second decrease towards the center needle, I pull those needles to HP and let the carriage knit them back on the next pass to ensure that the central needle holding three stitches knits easily and cleanly.

Knitting the first square

With waste yarn, cast-on 21 stitches and knit some rows, ending with the COR and set to knit needles back from HP. Bring all needles to HP and with the main yarn, e-wrap the shafts of the needles and then knit 1 row. Make a double decrease on the center needle as follows:

Move the 10 stitches at the right of zero one needle to the left and then move the 10 stitches at the left of zero one needle to the right. The center needle holds three stitches, one from each side and there are now only 19 needles working. Make sure the empty needle at each edge is in NWP.

Continue knitting and making double decreases *after* knitting rows 1, 2, 4, 5, 6, 8, 9, 10, 12 and 13 as shown in the chart below. At row 14, only 1 stitch remains. If you are working all of your squares in a single color, you do not need to cut the yarn.

This rate of decreasing is used for all of the *square* samples that follow.

The order in which the individual squares are joined and the place you cast on or pick up stitches for the next square will determine the direction that the decrease lines slant. That slant, in turn, contributes to the all– over pattern effect that results as the fabric builds. The following examples were knitted in a single color to ensure that the slanting lines (rather than color) dominate so you can see the differences clearly. Obviously, changing color from one square to the next will affect the pattern.

Unless the directions tell you to cut the yarn, you do not need to bother. Therefore, if the directions tell you to e-wrap needles, you should do so with the yarn that is coming from the last, single stitch of the previous square and then thread the carriage. And, as I said earlier, if you want to continue working on the exact same needles (which I do because it reduces the counting and possibility for mistakes) you might occasionally need to move that single stitch to a new starting needle. Choose the 21 needles to the right or left of zero to easily keep track of what you are doing.

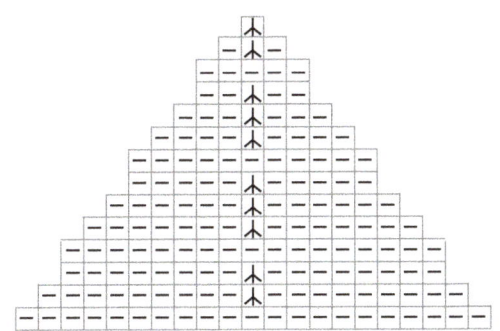

All of the squares in the examples that follow were worked according to this chart. Double decreases are made *after* knitting rows 1, 2, 4, 5, 6, 8, 9, 10, 12 and 13.

Left Slanting Squares

Do not cut the yarn after completing any of the squares unless you are changing colors. Remember that the last stitch from the previous square is counted in the next.

Knit the first square.

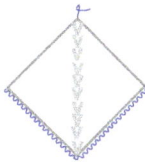

COL. Turn the first square 90° counter–clockwise and pick up 10 stitches along the edge of the first square. Knit 1 row across these 10 stitches and then e-wrap 10 needles at right. Knit the 2nd square.

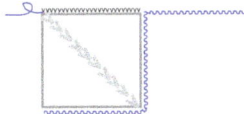

Begin the 3rd square COL. Pick up 10 stitches across the edge of the 2nd square, knit 1 row to the right and then e-wrap 10 needles just as you did for the previous square. Knit the 3rd square.

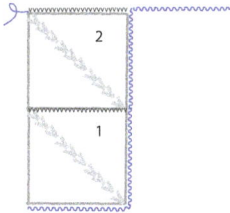

Continue in this manner for the 4th square in this strip (and for as many squares as you want for your own project). The strip can be the length of your garment or project. Cut the yarn after the last square and pull the end through the loop.

160   Chapter 10

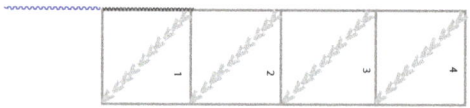

The 5th square in this sample is actually the first in the next strip. With COL, Pick up 10 stitches across the side edge of the 1st square then e-wrap 11 needles to the left of those stitches and thread the carriage. Knit the 5th square.

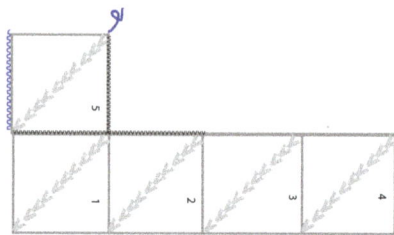

For the 6th square begin COL, place the single stitch on the far left needle. Pick up 10 stitches from the 5th square and 10 stitches along the edge of the 2nd square. Knit the 6th square. Complete all the remaining squares in this strip in the same way.

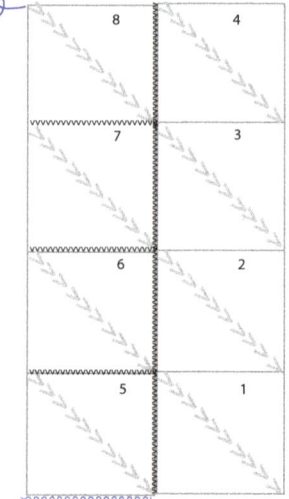

You should notice that when working the first strip, you picked up stitches and e-wrapped each time you started another square; but for the second strip, only the very first square needed to be e-wrapped. All of the others were worked from picked up edges.

Right Slanting Squares

Knit the first square and do not cut the yarn. Move the single stitch to the far right hand needle.

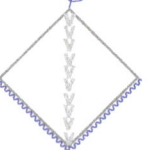

If all of the squares will slant the same way, it really doesn't matter whether you knit them as right or left slanting because you can turn the fabric top to bottom to reverse the direction. However, if you want both right and left slanting squares in the same piece of knitting, you need to be able to control that right from the start.

Turn the square 90° clockwise. With COR, pick up 10 stitches to the left of the single stitch, knit 1 row to the left and then e-wrap 10 more needles so there are now 21 needles working to knit the 2nd square.

Pick up, knit and e-wrap in the same manner to continue building squares above each other. Cut the yarn after completing the last square in the strip and pull the end through the loop.

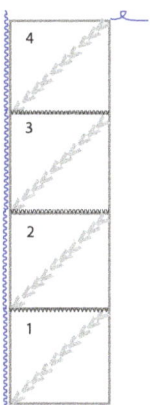

To begin the 5th square and a parallel column of squares that slant in the same direction, begin with COR and e-wrap 11. Turn the finished strip as shown and pick up 10 stitches along the edge of the 1st square at the left of the e-wrapped needles. Knit the 5th square.

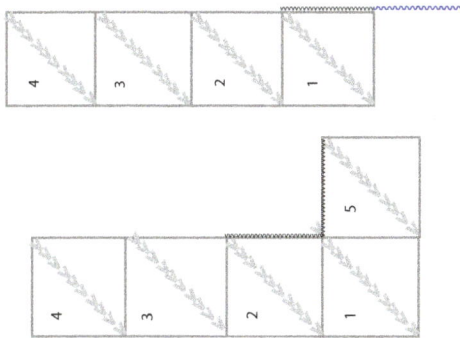

For the 6th square, pick up 10 stitches along the edge of the 5th square, and 10 stitches along the edge of the 2nd square. Continue in this manner for the 7th and 8th squares in this strip.

As in the previous example, the first strip was worked with both picked up stitches and e-wrapping, but for the second strip, only the very first square needed to be e-wrapped. All of the others were worked from picked up edges.

The chart at left on the next page illustrates where you would pick up stitches and where you would e-wrap to knit parallel strips of zig-zags. The 6th and 8th squares are interesting because they begin with a picked up edge and an e-wrapped edge, but you also need to pick up and hang a stitch from square #2 and #4 as often as you make the decreases so that the new square is joined at bottom and left edges– even though the decreases slant to the left.

In addition to the directional slant of each square, color placement can create large-scale patterns with the pieces presenting as either squares or diamonds.

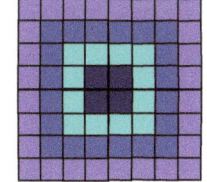

The chart below illustrates the pick-ups and e-wrapping to produce two opposing strips of zig-zags. You could also work this kind of a design by producing squares or strips that are sewn together later (either by hand or by re-hanging on the machine) or joined with crochet.

Cast on with scrap to knit the first square; change to the main yarn and begin knitting and decreasing as before. Do not e-wrap because you need live stitches to finish the larger square after knitting the 4th section. Do not cut the yarn.

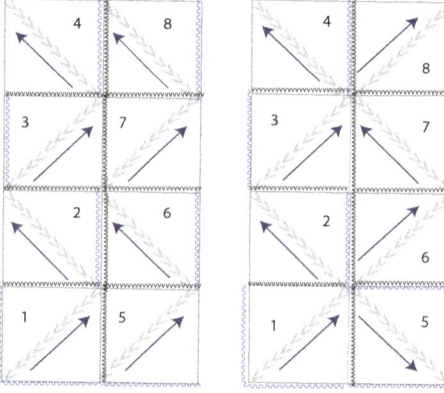

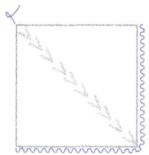

Begin COL for 2nd square. Pick up 10 stitches along the top edge of the first square to the right of the single stitch and then e-wrap 10 stitches to the left of them and thread the carriage. Knit the second square. Do not cut the yarn.

Diamond Squares

Four smaller squares are joined to create a larger square with a central diamond motif that results from the direction of the decrease slants. These larger squares can be joined to other squares or strips on the machine or later by hand.

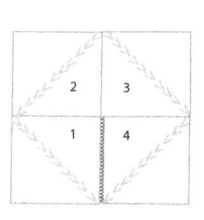

Turn the work 90° counter-clockwise to knit the 3rd square. Begin COL. Pick up 10 stitches along the side of the 2nd square and e-wrap 10 needles to the left of them and then thread the carriage and knit the 3rd square.

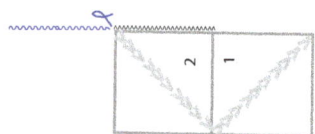

To knit the 4th square, once again turn the work 90° counterclockwise, pick up 10 stitches along the edge of the 3rd square to the right of the single stitch and e-wrap 10 needles to the left of them. Thread the carriage and knit the 4th square at the same time picking up 1 stitch from the scrap on the edge of the 1st square every decrease row and hanging that stitch on the right edge needle to close and complete the square.

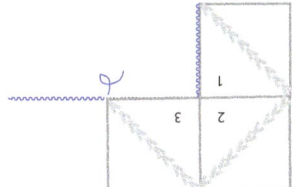

Square within a Square

Once again, the positioning of four small squares produces a larger, patterned square. In this case, three of the squares appear to be connected and the fourth stands out because the stitches are perpendicular to the others. If you knit the first square in a different color from the others, it stands out even more and suggests other patterning possibilities. The yarn is cut after each of the small squares is worked. Be sure to weave the ends in on the first row of the next square.

When picking up stitches from e-wrapped edges, I found that I got the cleanest pick-ups by using the crochet hook pick-up method described on page 60. Just make sure that you work towards the carriage so that when you are done picking up the stitches you can just thread the carriage and begin knitting.

Knit the first square (and cut the yarn only if you want to isolate a single color in the corner square).

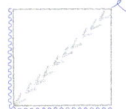

To knit the 2nd square, begin COR. Pick up 10 stitches across the edge of the 1st square and e-wrap 11 needles to the right of those stitches. Knit the 2nd square and then cut the yarn.

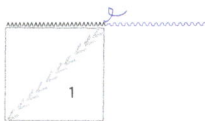

For the 3rd square, rotate the work 90° counter-clockwise. With COR, pick up 10 stitches along the edge of the 2nd square and e-wrap 11 stitches to the right of them. Thread the carriage and knit the 3rd square. Cut the yarn.

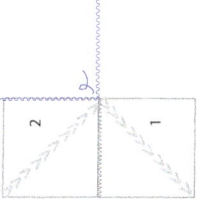

For the 4th square, rotate the work 90° counter-clockwise. With COL, pick up 10 stitches from the edge of the 1st square, 1 stitch in the corner and 10 stitches from the edge of the 3rd square. Knit this last square and then cut the yarn.

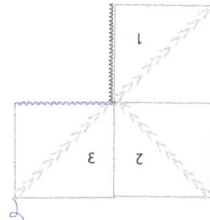

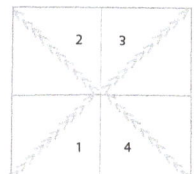

Diamonds

The square samples all required irregular spacing of the decrease rows in order to produce a square. If you make the double decreases every alternate row instead, the resulting shape is an elongated diamond. The following three examples utilize very different methods of working a fabric by joining diamonds to each other.

All of the diamonds in these examples are knitted by casting on 21 stitches and making double decreases every other row until only 1 stitch remains. Remember that each diamond will require 22 rows, rather than the 14 that created the squares, to produce the elongated shape. Make sure you remove some of your weight as the stitches are reduced.

The first and second samples use the diamonds on point and feature half–diamonds at each end of alternate rows. The 3–D Diamonds on page 166 will introduce you to the possibility of adding texture to a diamond as well as working a short row fill at the top of the swatch. So, even if you don't think you have use for fabrics like these, there are several good techniques to be learned from trying each of them.

The third sample, Tumbling Diamonds, joins the diamonds in an off–center way that creates little "wings" at the edges. These wings allow the resulting strips to be joined together to create a fabric that has much more movement. The edges of this fabric will be irregular, but you can smooth them out to create garment shapes that can be joined in the usual ways, by simply adapting the short row technique described for the 3–D Diamonds to those spaces.

Simple Diamonds on Point

The photo and chart on the next page indicate the order in which to join diamonds for a fabric that is stacked on point. That is, the pieces are joined to the edges of two previous sections so that the decrease line is vertical, rather than diagonal as it was in the squares that were stacked in the previous examples.

Knitting the First Tier (sections 1-3)

This sample is 3 full diamonds wide (though you can make yours as large as you want to) and I began by knitting 3 separate diamonds over 21 needles.

Knitting the 2nd Tier (Sections 5 & 6)

Each of these sections is knitted by picking up a total of *21* stitches; 10 stitches from the long edge of diamond #1 and 11 from diamond #2. Make double decreases every alternate row until 1 stitch remains. Cut the yarn and pull it through the last stitch to secure. Repeat for diamond #6.

The second tier also includes a half–diamond (#4 and #7) at each edge. These half–diamonds are knitted last, after all the full diamonds in the tier.

Rehang 11 stitches from the long edge of diamond #1. Set the carriage to hold needles in HP and with the COR, bring all needles to HP except the first needle on the right. Knit, wrap and knit back. *Return the next needle from HP to UWP and KWK**. Repeat * to ** until 1 needle remains in HP at left. Bind off all 11 stitches.

At the left end of this tier, knit the half–diamond (#7) with reverse shaping by picking up

Make the first double decrease after knitting 2 rows. Then decrease A/R until 1 stitch remains.

11 stitches along the left edge of diamond #3 and beginning COL. Bind off 11 stitches.

Knitting the 3rd Tier (sections 8–10)

The diamonds in the third tier are each knitted in the usual way by picking up 21 stitches from the long selvage edges of the two diamonds below. So, diamond #8 is worked directly above diamonds #4 & 5. Diamond #9 is worked directly above diamonds #5 & 6, etc.

The fourth tier is exactly like the second. Continue alternating the directions for the second and third tiers for the length of the fabric.

3-D Diamonds

Diamonds can be stacked in even, neat rows or you can include a couple of surprises as I did in the sample on the next page. This is really a fairly straight forward fabric with all four of the diamonds in the first tier knitted individually, cutting the yarn after each is complete. The second and fourth tiers, however, are knitted a little differently and add a 3-dimensional effect to the fabric.

As always, weave in the yarn tails when ever you can to avoid finishing later and make sure you keep your claw weights under working needles where they will do the most good.

Simple diamonds on point

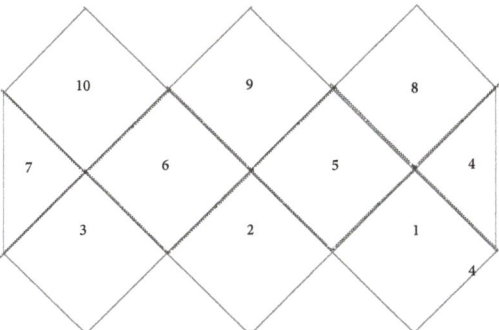

Begin by knitting three separate diamonds, cutting the yarn at the end of each. For section #4 (#7) P/U 11 stitches along edge of #1 (#3). For all other sections, P/U 21 stitches from the edges below.

Knitting the First Tier (sections 1-4)

My sample is 4 full diamonds wide as shown in the chart on 166 (though you can make yours as large as you want to) and I began by knitting 4 separate diamonds over 21 needles.

Knitting the 2nd Tier (Sections 6-8)

Each of these sections is knitted and then re-hung, folded and bound off to create the 3-D texture.

Change color and *pick up a total of *29* stitches; 14 stitches from the long edge of diamond #1 and 15 from diamond #2 . Knit 2 rows over all 29 needles and then begin making double decreases every alternate row, 5 times. Scrap off the remaining 19 stitches.

With the right side of the work facing you, fold the scrap knitting down and rehang 10 stitches of the knitting just completed. Then fold the work so that the wrong side faces you, fold down the scrap and pick up the remaining 9 stitches, skipping the last needle at left. Pull the needles forward slightly as you hang the second set of stitches so that the first group of stitches lie behind the open latches and the second set of stitches is in the hooks. Push the needle butts back so that the first set of stitches slides over the second and

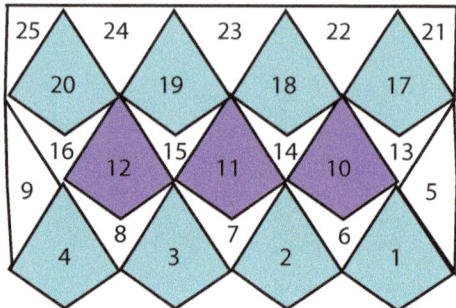

then bind off. Be careful *not* to push the 10th needle at left to HP because it will not receive a second stitch in the hook and would drop if you pushed it back empty. Just leave it in WP when you hang the stitches on the other 9 needles.** This is exactly the way that shoulders are joined on the machine (page 49), but in this case the method is used to form a large dart or tuck in the fabric.

Repeat from * to ** for the width of your work.

Half–Diamonds at the Edges (sections 5 & 9)

The second tier includes a half–diamond at each edge, knitted after all the full diamonds in this tier.

Rehang 11 stitches from the long edge of diamond #1. Set the carriage to hold needles in HP and with the COR, bring all needles to HP except the first needle on the right. Knit, wrap and knit back. *Return the next needle from HP to UWP and KWK**. Repeat * to ** until 1 needle remains in HP at left. Bind off all 11 stitches. At the left end of this tier, knit the half-diamond (#9) with reverse shaping by picking up 11 stitches along the left edge of diamond #4 and beginning COL. Bind off all 11 stitches.

Knitting the 3rd Tier (sections 10-12)

The full diamonds in the third tier are each knitted in the usual way by picking up 21 stitches from the long selvage edges of the 3–D diamonds below. So, diamond #10 is worked directly above 3–D diamond #6 and the next two above 3–D diamonds # 7 and 8.

Knitting the 4th Tier (sections 13-16)

To begin 3-D diamond #13, pick up 14 stitches from the 11 stitch edge of the half-diamond at the edge, a single stitch from the tip of diamond #1 and 14 stitches from the right edge of diamond #10. Knit 2 rows and then begin making double decreases at center until 19 stitches remain. Scrap off and complete this 3-D diamond as for those in the second tier.

Repeat for #14 - 16 in the same way.

Knitting the 5th Tier (sections 17-20)

Pick up 21 stitches across the tops of the 3-D diamonds below them and complete each as for regular diamonds, reducing down to a single stitch.

Knitting the 6th Tier (sections 21-25)

This part of the fabric is actually a short rowed fill. All of the shaping is done by placing needles in/out of HP. Do not cut the yarn after each section because the work is bridged from one section to the next so that the yarn travels continuously. Also, note that needles are only returned to UWP on the side opposite the carriage and that you should manually wrap on the carriage side (page 45).

Narrow Inverted Triangle at Right Edge (section 21)

Begin COR at right end of the bed. Pick up 11 stitches from the right edge of diamond #17. Set the carriage to hold needles in HP and place all needles except the first needle on the carriage side into HP. Knit 1 row and KWK. *Return 1 needle to UWP opposite the carriage and KWK**. Repeat * to ** until 1 needle remains in HP at left and COR.

Large Inverted Triangles (sections 22-24)

[Pick up 21 stitches for the next section; 10 from the edge of #17 and 10 from the edge of #18. Also pick up 1 stitch at the center from the tip of #10. Push the one remaining needle from the last section to UWP and hold the last 10 needles at left. Knit 1 row to the left and then hold all the needles from the section 21 *and* the first 9 of section 22 so that only 2 needles remain in WP. Wrap at left and knit 1 row to the right. *Wrap the next HP needle on carriage side and return 1 needle at opposite side to UWP. Knit 1 row.** Repeat * to ** until only 1 needle remains in HP at left.]

Repeat [to] for each of the other triangles (sections 23 and 24). The completed triangles remain in HP as the following triangles are knitted and the yarn bridges continuously from one to the next.

Narrow Inverted Triangle at Left Edge (section 25)

Pick up 11 stitches from the long edge of diamond #20 and knit 1 row to the left. Hold all needles except 1 needle at left. KWK. Return 1 needle opposite carriage to UWP and KWK until all 11 needles are in working position.

Knit 1 row across all needles and then bind off. You could also continue knitting above this short rowed fill if you decide to use the modular portion as a border.

Tumbling Diamonds

Because of the off-center way that these diamonds are joined as you knit, this method produces a fabric with an irregular edge that might be most suitable for an afghan or scarf. With careful placement of half diamonds or other shapes, the edges of the fabric could be refined though I suspect a perfectly rectangular shape is beyond the scope of this method. I will leave that for you to explore!

Some of the stitches are picked up from selvage edges and in that case, just re-hang the edge of the fabric on the needles, picking up the entire edge stitch. When a stitch is picked up and hung on an edge needle in order to join two diamonds while you knit, only pick up a half stitch.

When the instructions tell you to pick up an e-wrapped edge, use the crochet hook pick-up method described on page 60. If you leave the yarn ends uncut as I explain in the directions that follow, you will have a length of yarn available to do the crochet hook pick-up right where you need it.

There is a lot of picking up and re-hanging in a fabric like this and you have the advantage of working in small sections that can be checked on the right side after each one is complete. If you see an incorrect pick-up, rip out that section and do it again, paying special attention to consistency. The corners can be tricky so pay special attention to those stitches. I usually try to include the last stitch along the decrease line as one of the 15 picked up stitches. The bottom edge of each diamond will actually flatten out to form a curve as the fabric grows.

As with all modular knitting, weave in the ends whenever you possibly can to cut down on finishing later. You will notice that these directions only instruct you when *not* to cut the yarn tails or not to weave them in. So, unless the directions dictate otherwise, assume that you should weave in the yarn ends and clip them as you complete each section. The yarn tails that you leave will provide the yarn for the crochet hook pick-ups on the e-wrapped edges.

Whenever you are required to e-wrap 6 stitches next to 15 picked-up stitches, catch the end of the yarn used for e-wrapping over the adjacent needle and let it hang down (I usually hang a clothespin on the end to keep it weighted). This will act like a wrap and

Diamond 1-1 is the multi-colored diamond at lower left. Note that the chart on page 170 shows the purl side of the fabric as it faces you on the machine.

prevent a gap or hole between the re-hung and e-wrapped stitches.

This yarn end hangs down between the 6 e-wrapped stitches and the 15 re-hung stitches; the other end of the yarn is used to thread the carriage.

Begin the first diamond in each strip by casting on with waste yarn and then e-wrapping the same needles with the main yarn. The diagram on page 170 shows the relationship of three completed strips to each other and should give you an idea how they fit together as you join them on the machine. You will find it much easier to keep track of which diamond is which if you label and number the back of each one with a piece of masking tape until you really understand the construction. Once you have worked through a couple of strips, it will be a lot clearer, but initially there seem to be an awful lot of unattached edges to deal with. My diagram is numbered to coordinate with the directions. I have numbered each diamond by the strip and its location on it. So, for example, 1-3 is the third diamond on the first strip.

Knitting the First Strip

Diamond 1-1
Knit the first diamond, cut the yarn.

Diamond 1-2
With COL, e-wrap 6 needles from right to left and then re-hang the long left edge of the first diamond over 15 needles to the right of them. Knit 2 rows and then begin making the double decreases. Complete the second diamond, cut the yarn and pull it through the last stitch to secure.

Diamond 1-3
Begin COR. At the right edge, e-wrap 6 needles from left to right, leaving a tail about 10" long. DO not weave in this tail. Re-hang the long right edge of diamond 1-2 over the next 15 needles to the left. Knit 2 rows and then begin making double decreases every alternate row until 1 stitch remains. Cut the yarn and fasten off the last stitch as before.

Diamond 1-4
With COL, e-wrap 6 needles from right to left and pick up the long left edge of 1-3 on the next 15 needles. Complete diamond 1-4.

For the entire length of this strip, the diamonds alternately begin with COL when picking up the left edge of the previous diamond; COR when picking up the right edge of the previous diamond.

Knitting the Second Strip

When you begin joining the first and second strips, turn the first strip upside down so that you will be working from the 6th to the 1st diamond. Hold the first strip at the left of the new work, purl side facing you.

Each completed strip is turned upside down to join it to the next. The diagram at right shows the purl side of the work. Note the direction that each strip is worked.

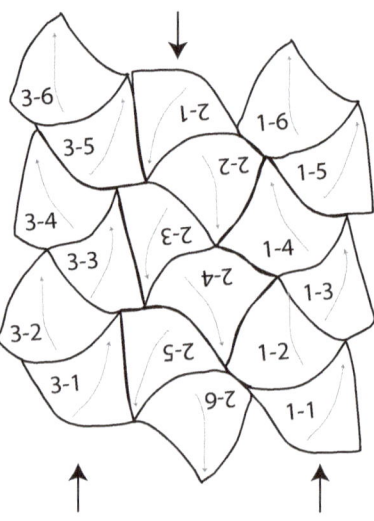

Diamond 2-4
COL. At left, use crochet hook to pick up 6 stitches from the e-wrapped "wing" of 1-4 and then pick up 15 stitches along the long left edge of 2-3 to right of them. Knit 2 rows. Begin making double decreases on alternate rows and at the same time, pick up an edge stitch from 1-2 at left. I find this easiest to do on the side opposite the carriage so I often end up making decreases when COL and picking up stitches when COR. Sometimes you can manage both at the same time–it is really just a matter of what you find simplest to do.

Diamond 2-2

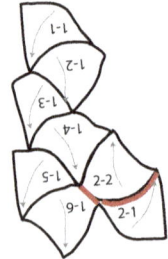

Diamond 2-1
Knit a single diamond, fasten off the last stitch.

Diamond 2-2
Begin COR. Pick up the long left edge of diamond 2-1 and hang on 15 needles. Turn the first strip top to bottom and hang the 6 e-wrapped stitches that formed the "wing" of 1-6 to the left of them so there are 21 stitches. *Knit 2 rows. Make the double decreases and then pick up an edge stitch (half stitch) from 1-4 and hang it on the left edge needle.** Repeat * to ** to complete this diamond. Cut the yarn and fasten the last stitch. Remember to use the crochet hook pick-up method for hanging all e-wrapped edges, using the yarn end from the e-wrapped edge. Once the crochet hook pick-up has been completed, the tail can we woven in and clipped.

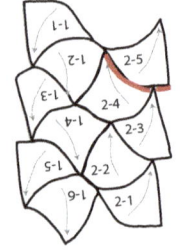

Diamond 2-5

Diamond 2-5
Begin COR and work this diamond by picking up 15 stitches from 2-5 and e-wrapping 6 needles to the right of them. Like 2-3, there are no additional stitches picked up to knit this diamond.

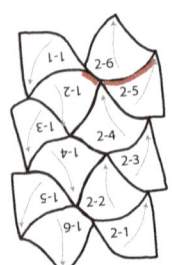

Diamond 2-6

Diamond 2-3

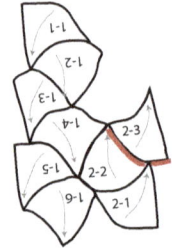

Diamond 2-3
Begin COR. At the right edge, e-wrap 6 needles and thread the carriage. Pick up the long right edge of 2-2 and hang on the next 15 needles. Knit 2 rows and then begin making alternate row decreases as before. There are no additional stitches picked up when working this diamond.

Diamond 2-6
This diamond is worked the same as 2-2 and 2-4. Begin COL. At left, pick up the 6 e-wrapped stitches from the "wing" of 1-2 and then pick up 15 stitches from the long left edge of 2-5 to the right of them. Because this is the last diamond in this strip, it is worked without picking up any adjacent stitches. However, for a longer strip you would need to pick up stitches from an adjacent diamond as you did for 2-4.

Diamond 2-4

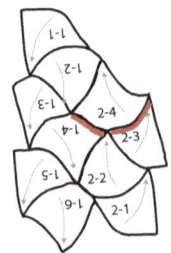

Knitting the Third Strip

Turn the work upside down so that 2–6 is on the bottom, purl side facing you. This strip is worked to the left of the second strip.

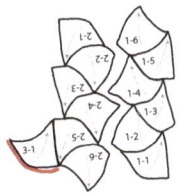

Diamond 3–1

Diamond 3–1
Begin COL. Cast on 21 stitches. Knit 2 rows. Work this diamond as before, making double decreases and at the same time picking up an edge stitch from 2–5 (starting at the point) and working down) every alternate row and hanging it on the right edge needle when COL.

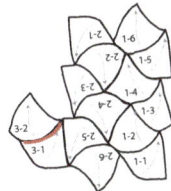

Diamond 3–2

Diamond 3–2
COL. At the left edge, e–wrap 6 needles and then thread the carriage. Pick up 15 stitches from the left edge of 3–1 to the right of them. Knit 2 rows and then begin working double decreases every alternate row. There are no edge stitches picked up when knitting this diamond.

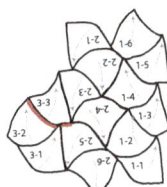

Diamond 3–3

Diamond 3–3
COR. Pick up 15 stitches along the right edge of 3–2 at left and 6 stitches from the e–wrapped "wing" of 2–5 at right. Work the decreases and at the same time, whenever COL, pick up the edge stitch of 2–3 and hang it on the right edge needle.

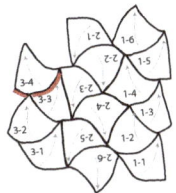

Diamond 3–4

Diamond 3–4
COL. Pick up 15 stitches from the long right edge of 3–3 at right e–wrap 6 needles at left. Work this diamond with no further pick–ups.

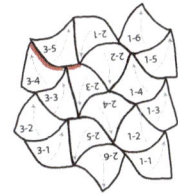

Diamond 3–5

Diamond 3–5
COR. Pick up 6 stitches from the "wing" of 2–3 at the right and 15 stitches from the edge of 3–4 to the left of them. Knit 2 rows and then begin double decreases as before and at the same time picking up an edge stitch from 2–1.

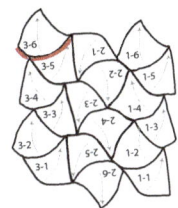

Diamond 3–6

Diamond 3–6
COL. At left, e–wrap 6 needles and then pick up 15 stitches from the edge of 3–5 to the right of them. Because this is the last diamond on the strip, there are no further pick–ups. If the strips were longer, you would also be making pick–ups to join 3–6 to a diamond on the second strip.

Continue adding strips in the same manner, turning the work top-to-bottom each time so that the shapes nest into each other. Additional strips will be worked alternately at the left and right of the growing fabric.

Half Diamonds

When diamonds are stopped short after just 5 decreases, the side edges are pulled upwards towards a narrowing top. This creates an interesting shape that can be repeated in strips that interlock with each other. After each strip is completed, the work is turned upside down so that the last section of the previous strip is joined to the first section of the next strip.

If you examine the chart on the opposite page, you will see that each section begins with 21 stitches and reduces down to just 11. In order to begin the next section (in the same or a different color) you must e-wrap 5 additional stitches at each side; first at right and then at left. These e-wrapped edges form little "wings" that notch into each other as you join the strips. Weave in all yarn tails as you work.

When picking up edge stitches, half stitches will show less than full stitches.

Knitting the First Strip (Sections 1-4)

Following the chart on the next page, cast on 21 stitches and knit 2 rows. Make a double decrease at the center every alternate row, five times. Cut the yarn after knitting the last row.

*With COR and threaded with a contrast color (or not) e–wrap 5 additional needles at right. Knit 1 row to the left and e–wrap 5 needles at left so there are 21 needles working again. Knit 1 row and then begin decreases and work through this section.** Repeat * to ** for the length of the strip and B/O. Note that only this first strip calls for e-wrapping at both the right and left edges; the following strips will only require e-wrapping at one side or the other as the "wings" from previous sections will be rehung instead.

Knitting the 2nd Strip (Sections 5–8)

The sections have been numbered (see diagram below) to show how they join together; arrows indicate that the strips should be turned top to bottom as they join.

Begin and end these sections COR. Cast on 21 stitches and knit 2 rows. Turn the first strip upside down and hold at left of new strip. EOR (when COR) make a double decrease at center and *at the same time* pick up a half stitch from the bottom right edge of section #4 (at the B/O edge) and hang it on the left edge needle of #5 to join the two. Make the decreases before you hang the edge stitch. *At the end of section #5, cut the yarn. With COR, pick up the "wing" of section #4 and hang it on the 5 needles at the left of section #5, e-wrap 5 needles at right and thread the carriage with the new color. Knit 2 rows and then begin making double decreases as before and hanging a stitch from the edge of section #3. At the end of this section, repeat from the * for following sections.

Knitting the 3rd and Following Strips (Sections 9–12)

Turn the completed work upside down. Begin all sections of the third strip COL, making pick ups and hanging "wings" at right edge as explained above. The fourth strip will begin all sections COR with pick-ups at left.

Whenever picking up the left edge of the previous strip to hang on the right of the next, begin COL; when picking up the right edge of a previous strip to hang on the left of the

If you have trouble visualizing how the strips connect, photocopy this stitch chart 3 times, cut each one out and use the cut outs as a guide.

This chart shows the purl side of the work as it faces you on the machine. It is extremely helpful to number each section and strip (use masking tape) as I have done to keep track of things while you work.

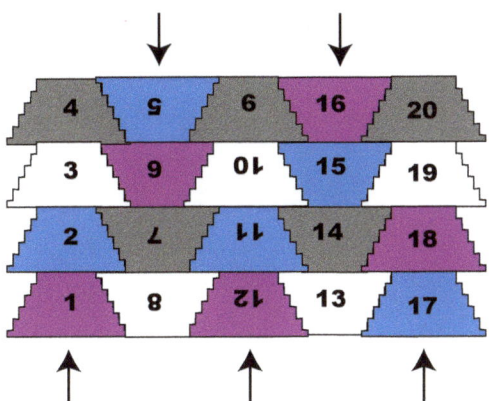

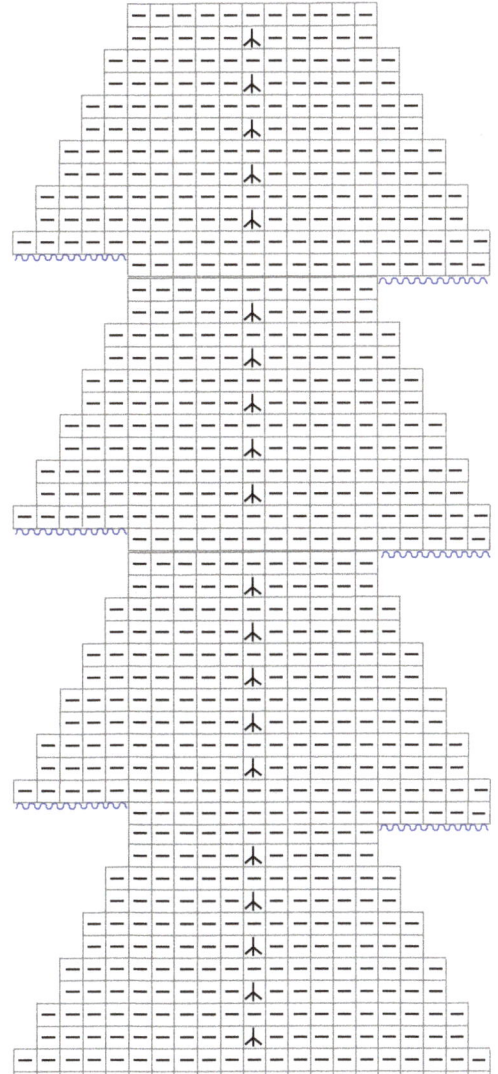

Note that you need to e-wrap at the right edge after the 11th row and at left after the 12th row.

next, begin COR. This will ensure that the carriage is always on the correct side to make the 5 e-wraps and that the yarn doesn't get caught up in the pick-up at the edge. Knowing this rule enables you to work on either side of the fabric to add strips left or right.

Modular Strips with Off-Center Decreases

The sample below is a further exploration of ways to join diamonds; this time, off-center. I think the irregular edges at top and bottom could add nice detail to a neckline or hem. To work the side edges into garment seams, you would either need to be sure that the front and back pieces notch into each other or be prepared to work some short row fills.

Begin and end all strips on waste to simplify adding a continuous edging or to bind off the final, finished piece all at once.

Unlike the previous modular designs, these sections do not reduce down to a single stitch and the decreases are made *off-center,* which gives each strip a distinct, meandering shape.

Because these decreases are worked closer to one side than the other, I worked the decreases in a way that does not require moving all of the stitches to make the double decreases. Instead, only the double decrease and the stitches on that side of the fabric are moved in to fill the empty needles. The larger group of stitches stays put.

I find a multi-prong tool essential for this fabric, but you can hold two transfer tools together or make the moves in several steps.

I worked each strip in a single color, but you can change colors for each section if you prefer. You could also add lace transfers, cables or popcorns on the side of the section without decreases.

The strips are joined-as-you-knit by picking up the edge stitch of the previously knitted strip, every alternate row. Also, each strip is

turned top to bottom when joined to the next so that they notch together perfectly.

It is easiest to keep track of the joining if you use masking tape to mark each section for the strip and section (i.e. 1-1, 1-2, etc).

You will need to e-wrap 10 additional stitches at one side or the other after knitting each section of the first strip. This e-wrapped edge forms a little "wing" that later notches perfectly into the next strip. When joining strips, you will alternately pick up the edge of an e-wrapped wing after one repeat and e-wrap 10 new stitches after the next repeat.

As you continue knitting new strips, remember that they will alternately be picked up on the left and right edges of the new work. Always pick up stitches on the side opposite the carriage. All odd numbered strips should begin and end with right edge decreases; all even numbered strips with left side decreases. You can work strips any length you want to as long as you alternate left and right side placement for the decreases You can work as many strips as you want to as long as you alternately join them at left and right so that they notch into each other correctly.

Knitting the First Strip

The decreases in the first (and last) sections are made on the right:

CO 21 sts and knit 2 rows, ending COR. Transfer the 8th stitch from the right onto the 7th needle. Then transfer the 6th stitch onto the same needle and then move all 3 stitches back to the 8th needle. There are 2 empty needles in NWP and then 5 WP needles with stitches. (In practice, I do it all in a connected motion by removing the 8th stitch and placing it on the 6th needle and immediately moving those two to the 7th needle and then shifting it all over by 1 needle so the triple stitch is on needle #8). Now move the 5 stitches at the edge 2 needles towards the center to close the gap. Knit 2 rows.* (I have a 5-prong tool to make this faster).

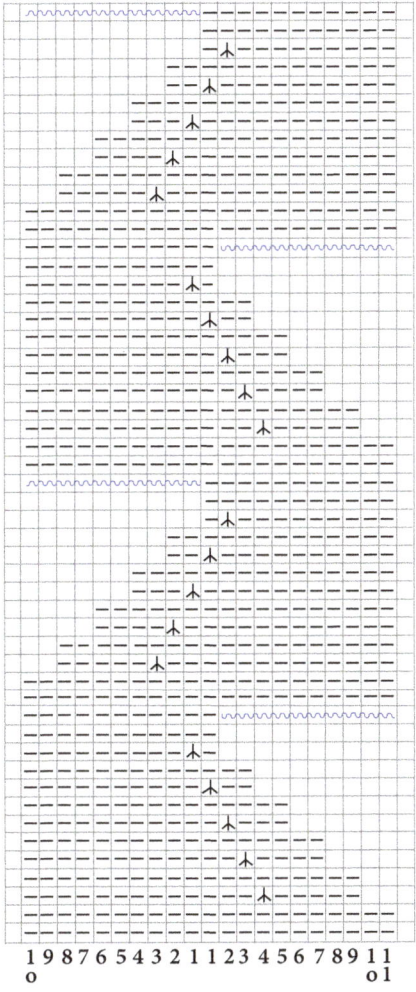

19 8 7 6 5 4 3 2 1 1 2 3 4 5 6 7 8 9 11
0   0 1

Next move the 7th and 5th stitches to the 6th needle and move everything over, knit 2 rows.
6th and 4th to 5th…knit 2rows
5th and 3rd to 4th….knit 2 rows
4th and 2nd to 3rd…. (1 ndl remains at edge)
Knit 2 rows

Once 5 double decreases have been made and only 11 needles remain working and COR, knit 2 rows and e-wrap 10 needles at right (21 needles again) and knit 1 row to the left.

Work the next section (1-2) in the same way. Begin COL, knitting 2 rows and making the decreases at the *left* side of the knitting. Knit 2 rows after the fifth decrease, e-wrap 10 needles at left and knit 1 row. COR.

Once again, these are incomplete diamonds that do not knit enough rows to reduce down to a single stitch. In addition, the decreases are alternately made to the left and right of center. Before knitting the next sections, you need to e-wrap additional stitches at one edge or the other.

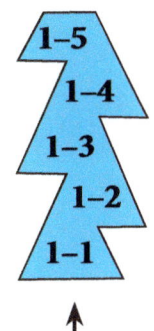

For my sample, each of the strips is knitted in 5 sections. These colored illustrations show how the sections notch together.

Begin the third section (1–3) by knitting 2 rows and working decreases at the right. The left and right side placement of the decreases alternates from one section to the next, but all strips should end as they begin, which means working an odd number of sections. So, work as many repeats as desired, ending the first strip with a right side decrease section. At the end of the last section, scrap off the remaining 11 stitches. For my sample, I worked 5 sections in each strip.

Knitting the 2nd Strip

CO and work the second strip as for the first, but beginning and ending the strip with left side decrease sections and *at the same time*, picking up and joining the right edge of the first strip to the left edge of the second strip as follows:

Turn the first strip top to bottom (scrapped off edge of (5–1) even with CO edge of 2nd strip) at the left of the new strip with purl side facing you.

Knit section (2–1). Every time COR, in addition to making the double decreases at the left, you will pick up every alternate stitch from the right edge of the first strip (1–5) and hang it on the left edge needle of the second strip (2–1) then knit the requisite 2 rows.

You will be able to work one section (2–1) before the first strip runs out of stitches to pick up at the edge. Make the last double decrease and then knit 2 rows. COR.

At the left edge, rather than e-wrapping the 10 empty needles, pick up the 10 e-wrapped stitches that were cast on to increase the width of the first strip after section (1–4) and hang them on the 10 empty needles at left of the second strip. 21 needles in WP again.

Knit 2 rows and work section (2–2) with right decreases, picking up the edge of (1–4). After the fifth decrease, when 11 stitches remain, knit 2 rows and e-wrap 10 needles at the right edge.

Work section (2–3) with left side decreases and picking up the edge of (1–3). At the end

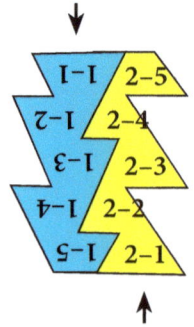

Joining the 2nd strip to the first

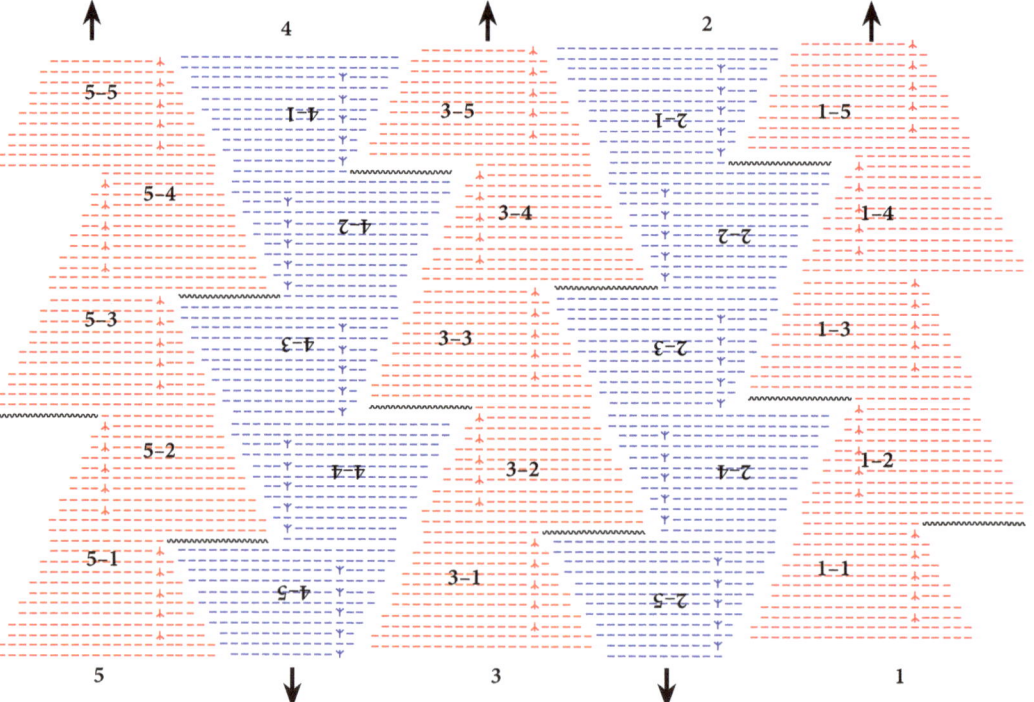

Each strip is turned top to bottom for joining to the next strip so that the "wings" notch into each other. This chart shows the purl side of the completed fabric.

of this section, pick up the e-wrapped wing of section (1–3).

Work section (2–4) with right decreases and picking up the edge of (1–2). At the end of (2–4) e-wrap 10 needles at right. Knit section (2–5) with left decreases, picking up the edge of (1–1).

End this strip with a left decrease section, scrapping off the 11 remaining stitches.

Knitting the 3rd Strip

Begin and end this strip with right decrease sections. Turn completed fabric (strips 1 and 2) upside down so that the scrapped off edge of the second strip (2–5) is at the bottom. Hold the completed work to the **right** of the new strip. Hang the left edge stitch from the second strip (2–5) onto the right edge needle of the third strip (1–3) on alternate rows when COL.

At the end of section (3–1), with COL, Pick up the wing from section (2–5), knit 2 rows and then begin working section (3–2) with left decreases and picking up the edge of (2–4).

At the end of (3–2) with COL, e-wrap 10 needles at left. Work (3–3) with right decreases, picking up the edge of (2–3).

Pick up the wing of (2–3) to begin working section (3–4) with left decreases, picking up the edge of (2–2). End section (3–4) COL. e-wrap 10 needles at left to work section (3–5) with right decreases and picking up the edge of (2–1).

Knitting the 4th and 5th Strips

Begin and end the 4th strip with left decrease sections. Turn the completed work upside down and hold it at the *left* of the new strip. Hang the right edge of the third strip (3–5) on the left edge needle every alternate row on the right edge needle of 4–1 you did when starting the 2nd strip.

The fifth strip starts and ends with a right decrease section. Turn the work upside down and hold at the right of the new strip. Join the left edge of the fourth strip (4–5) to the right edge of the fifth strip (5–1) in progress.

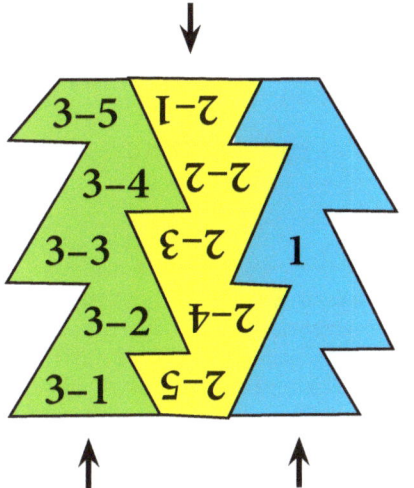

The first 2 strips are turned to join to the 3rd strip. The arrows indicate the direction in which each strip is knitted.

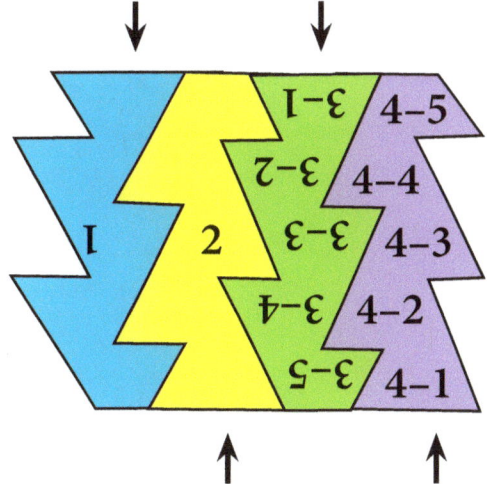

The fourth strip is worked exactly like the second strip was worked.

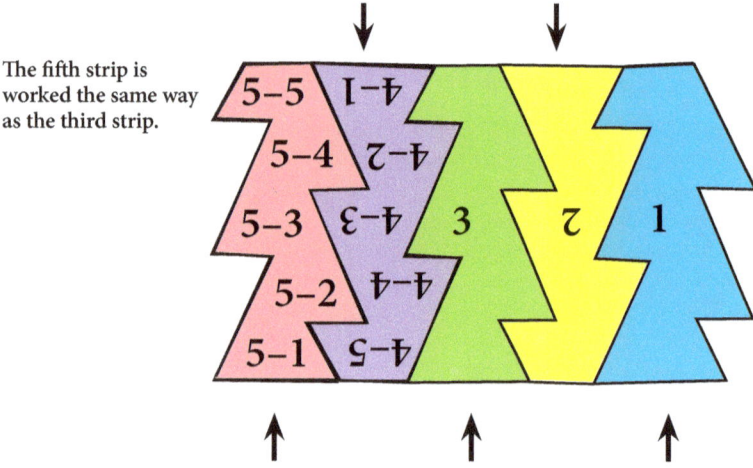

The fifth strip is worked the same way as the third strip.

Pentagonal Stars

This last example is very different from all the others I've included in this chapter because the shapes do not interlock to form a complete fabric. Instead, there are gaps and open spaces between the stars.

The first two complete pentagons that I knitted went together beautifully, but then there was no way to add additional pieces that would continue fitting and forming a complete fabric. I tried everything I could think of and after many wasted hours I consulted my library shelf where Norah Gaughan, in her brilliant book, *Knitting Nature,* says definitively that pentagons will not connect endlessly to form a closed fabric.

I'll admit that given the open spaces, this fabric is somewhat limited in application beyond shawls, scarves, table runners or floral appliqués, but with a little creativity you can use a strip of these flowers as part of another project, creating a yoke for a sweater like the one Norah shows in her book or using short row fills to even up edges.

A complete star is made up of 5 sections that each begins with 11 stitches. You can use any odd number of stitches you want, but, keep in mind that the larger the sections, the more transfers you need to make to complete the double decreases at center. The work is then decreased down to a single stitch by making double decreases at the center stitch every alternate row, forming small diamonds. Cut the yarn to tie off the last stitch.

You can begin each section on scrap and then e-wrap with the main yarn, but I found it much faster to just e-wrap with the main yarn and bring the needles to HP before the first 2 rows to make sure the stitches knitted cleanly. If you hang a claw weight, you should remove it before working the last few stitches to avoid stretching them.

Each of the following three sections is knitted by picking up an edge stitch from the previous shape every-other-row and hanging it on the edge needle of the section in progress. The

The dark green section was began and ended with left decreases; the multi-colored strip with right decreases (as worked on the purl side).

final, 5th, section is worked a little differently to close and complete the shape.

Knitting the Fifth Section

Cast on, knit 2 rows and make the first pair of decreases. Hold the four joined sections behind the work on the machine with the right side facing you. Turn the work back slightly so that you can see the edge stitch and with a single-prong transfer tool, pick up a stitch from the lower side edge of section #1 and hang it on the right needle. Then pick up a stitch from the lower side edge of section #4 and hang it on the left needle. Insert the transfer tool from the wrong side to the right side, starting at the bottom edge of the sections you are picking up.

Knit two rows and repeat * to ** until there is only 1 needle working and both edges of the completed piece #1–4 have been hung. Cut the yarn and pull it through the last stitch to secure. The shape should be closed, forming a little star. The series of photographs on the next page details the fifth section.

Even if you weave in all the beginning yarn ends, there will still be five tails to deal with at the center of each star. You can work them into the back of the fabric or think about knotting them on the right side and clipping them close for a fringed accent in the center. It would add a little interest and reduce the finishing and visibility of ends on the back for a shawl or scarf.

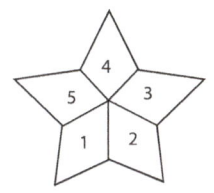

1 The first four sections are complete.

2 With the purl side facing you, pick up the outer-most stitch from each edge.

3 Continue picking up stitches along the open edges.

4 Continue picking up stitches EOR.

5 Cut the yarn and pull it through the last stitch to secure it.

6 Pull all of the yarn ends through to the back to finish them.

You can create larger stars by working sections off the inverted "V's" of a completed star by picking up stitches from the side of each point and one stitch at the center to make a larger star. You can also use a short row fill to square off the edges and form a more regular pentagon; a rectangle will still require more creative pick-ups and additions.

In the example below, I knitted the innermost star by casting on 11 stitches for each section. For the following sections I picked up 11, 13 and finally 21 stitches for each section. I used the crochet hook pick-up method because I wanted to be certain that the decrease lines of each section matched and continued as smoothly as possible from the smallest star right through the largest.

If you pick up too few stitches to begin the next tier of sections, it will cause the fabric to pucker. While this definitely won't work for a scarf or other flat project, it might act as the springboard for a hat, bag, pillow or other project that needs to create volume.

Joining Stars for a Fabric

As I said earlier, it just isn't possible to notch one star into another to create a closed fabric. There will be open spaces unless you are very creative and diligent about filling them with short rows or different modular shapes.

I spent a long time manipulating five-pointed stars with Illustrator computer software and came up with some arrangements that I thought would work quite well for fabrics, but all of them incorporated open spaces. If you do not have software that will allow you to manipulate shapes, I suggest cutting out half a dozen five-pointed stars to manipulate and play with.

I found that the easiest way to join the stars on the machine was to pick up the entire side of one point from the first star while knitting the next. That said, in a couple of instances I also picked up just the very point of a section to help control the size and structure of an open space. At all times, it is easiest to make the double decreases before picking up stitches to join sections.

Acknowledgements

This book originally started out as one chapter for a totally different book and quickly grew and took on a life of its own. Any project of this scope requires lots of help and I want to thank a number of people for being interested in what I do and so willing to share their expertise.

First and foremost, I want to thank Nancy Roberts for knitting through so many of the techniques that I tried to put into words and photos. Right now, she is probably the country's foremost expert on Entrelac and Modular techniques, having worked through all of my directions and raising the kinds of questions that keep an author on her toes – and makes the directions as clear as they can be.

I am fortunate to have known knitters like Gini Woodward and Charlene Shafer so that I could call upon them to ask "Does that sound right to you?" when I found myself stuck or traipsing through somewhat foreign territory. Their editing was invaluable to me.

Thank you to Anne Morrison for her eagle eye copy editing. She prevented me from making the usual typing-too-fast mistakes I am prone to.

Some of the yarn companies and magazines have been especially supportive of machine knitting over the years. Cascade Yarns has always provided me with yarn for my books – their 220 ranks as my favorite wool – and I am so appreciative of that continuous support.

Both Rowan Yarns and Berroco have always been generous with yarn for various books and projects, and this time they were willing to share the photographs I needed to illustrate specific stitches.

Trisha Malcolm, editor of Vogue Knitting didn't hesitate when I asked for permission to use some photos from past issues of Vogue Knitting. These photos added so much life to the pages and relevance to the book as a whole. Thank you.

Kris Basta, owner of Kris Krafter supplied me with one of the brand new 6.5 mm garter bars. I like it so well that I will never go back to the old style GB!

Thanks to Meg Swanson at Schoolhouse Press for permission to use some of Barbara Walker's wonderful stitch charts for Mosaic Knitting.

My love and thanks to Arthur who makes it so easy for me to be me and shares the joy and trials through every project.

Last, but certainly not least, thanks to my dear friend, Jeanne Criscola for laying out the grid for this book and guiding me through the layout process and providing endless answers to my questions about CS6 software.

Thank you all!

Supplies and Sources

Cascade Yarns	http://www.cascadeyarn.com
Berroco Yarns	http://www.berroco.com
Rowan Yarns	www.knitrowan.com
Vogue Knitting Magazine	www.vogueknitting.com
Scholhouse Press	www.schoolhousepress.com
Kriskrafter	www.kriskrafter.com
	New Garter Bars
Machine Knitting to Dye For	www.machineknittingtodyefor.com
Knitting Any Way	www.knittinganyway.com
	Adjustable needle selectors
Machine Knitting Monthly Magazine	www.machineknittingmonthly.net
Jaggerspun Yarn	www.jaggeryarn.co
Silk City Yarn	www.silkcityfibers.com
Designaknit	http://www.knitcraft.com
Stitch Painter & Garment Designer	http://www.cochenille.com
DAK and hand knitting CDs for mosaic and other pattern knitting	http://www.allpointsyarn.com

And, of course, www.guagliumi.com for free Tips & Techniques and other downloads, books and specialty tools

Index

Abbreviations 21

Binding off 47–56
    Hand sewn bind off 51
    I-cord bind off 54
    Picot bind off 50
    Popcorn bind off 50
    Scrapping off 51
    Sinker post bind off 48
    Three needle bind off 49

Beaded knitting 73

Cables 88
    Cabled Edging 89

Casting on 23–32
    Cable cast on 27
    Crochet cast on 25
    Double bed casting on 32
    Figure 8 cast on 30
    Knitted on cast on 25
    Long tail cast on 29
    Open cast on 25
    Picot cast on 28
    Rolled stockinet cast on 31

Computer aided design 20
    DAK 20
    Stitch Painter 20

Decreases 38–46
    Decreasing across a row 44
    Double decreases 42
        Double vertical decrease 42
        Left slanting double decrease 43
        Right slanting double decrease 43
    K2tog 39
    Left slanting decrease 38
    Right slanting decrease 39
    S1K1Psso 38, 39
    Short row decreasing 45
    SKP 38
    SSK 38

Entrelac 135–150
    Base triangles 138
    Ending triangles 148
    Left edge triangle 140
    Left leaning rectangle 146
    Right edge triangle 145
    Right leaning rectangle 142

Fair Isle 17

Floats 18

Garter stitch 9, 67

Garter bar 66–72
    Garter stitch 67
    Increasing and Decreasing 71
    Needle stabilizer 66

Hand knit patterns 92
    Matching gauge 92
    Schematics 93

Hats 81

Increasing 34–38
    Edge increases 34
    Eyelet increase 35
    Full-fashioned increases 35
    Hanging a chain 38
    Hanging a rag 37
    Increasing across row 38
    Increasing multiple stitches 37
    Knitting front & back of stitch 37
    Ladder increase 37
    Lifted increase 36
    Make 1 increase 35
    Short row increasing 45

Intarsia 10

Knitting machines 2
    Comparison of gauges 2
    Electronic machines 7

Index

Manual machines 7
Punch card machines 7

Ladders 37

Lace knitting 99–122
Hand-manipulated lace 103
Converting hand knit charts 111
Simple lace 112
Fashion lace 113
Normal lace 113
Lace leaf trim 120

Lace carriages 108
Silver Reed 109
Brother 110

Magic formula 94

Mittens 80

Modular knitting 151–188
Join-as-you-knit strips 153
Log cabin 154
Modular Squares 159
Modular diamonds 164
3-D Diamonds 165
Diamonds on point 164
Tumbling diamonds 163
Half-diamonds 172
Off-center decreases 174
Pentagonal stars 178

Mosaic knitting 123–134
Converting charts 131
Electronic mosaic 130
Manually selected mosaic 127
Punch card mosaic 130

Needle Stabilizer 66

Picking up stitches 57–64
Combination pick-ups 62
Crochet hook pick-ups 60
Hanging hand knit ribbing 63
Live stitches 58
Picking up surface stitches 60
Selvage edges 58

Plaiting 20

Popcorns and bobbles 86

Ravel cord 6

Ribbing 14
Latching up ribs 15
Ribbers 14

Sandwich bands 83

Scarves and shawls 81

Scrap yarn 5

Slip stitch 17

Socks 76
Turning a heel 78

Speed ripping 66

Stockinet 8
Rolled edge 31

Symbols 22

Tuck stitch 16

Twisted stitches 90

Waste yarn 5

Weaving in ends 63

Yarns 3, 5

Yarn tensioning 4